English Teaching in the Secondary School

A Handbook for Students and Teachers

Michael Fleming
and
David Stevens

David Fulton Publishers
London

David Fulton Publishers Ltd
Ormond House, 26–27 Boswell Street, London WC1N 3JD

First published in Great Britain by David Fulton Publishers 1998

Note: The right of Michael Fleming and David Stevens to be identified as the authors of this work has been asserted by them in accordance with the Copyright, Designs and Patents Act 1988.

Copyright © Michael Fleming and David Stevens 1998

British Library Cataloguing in Publication Data
A catalogue record for this book is available from the British Library

ISBN 1–85346–531–3

Typeset by Textype Typesetters Ltd, Cambridge
Printed in Great Britain by The Cromwell Press Ltd, Trowbridge,Wiltshire

Contents

Acknowledgements

We owe a considerable debt to the teachers and student teachers with whom we have been fortunate to work. Don Salter read an early draft of the book and made encouraging and helpful suggestions. Kath Herring, Maggie Wilson, Helen Simpson, Louise Horwood and Katie Rowland provided ideas for particular chapters. We are grateful to Marianne Fleming who helped to prepare the manuscript.

Introduction

Language is a labyrinth of paths.
You approach from one side and know your way about;
you approach the same place from another side
and no longer know your way about.

Ludwig Wittgenstein, *Philosophical Investigations*

The central aim of English teaching is at one level very straightforward and uncontroversial. At its simplest, the purpose of English as a subject is 'to develop pupils' abilities to use language effectively'. However, below the surface of that apparently incontestable and transparent statement lie all sorts of conflicting opinions, ideologies, methodologies and philosophies. What precisely is meant by the various terms within the statement? For example, it is only relatively recently that English has included speaking and listening as an important aspect of what counts as 'using language'. The inclusion of reading has been less controversial but there has been no similar agreement over what should be read, or indeed what exactly is involved in the process of reading. Presumably the idea of 'responding to language' is implicit in the word 'use'. Does 'using language effectively' mean using language 'accurately' or should the emphasis be on 'appropriateness' to specific purposes and contexts? In order to use language effectively how much knowledge about language is necessary and what form should it take? The word 'develop' as opposed to 'teach' does not make clear what the primary role of the teacher should be in the whole enterprise: as instructor, creator of contexts, facilitator or adviser. Implicit in these concepts are contrasting theories of the way language is acquired and develops.

As with English teaching, the central purpose of this book – to help readers to become more effective teachers of English – has hidden complexities. The word 'effective' is not neutral but can be interpreted differently according to individual values and beliefs. Most people would agree that a balance between theory and practice is necessary in writing about English teaching but it is much less clear what that balance should look like. A comprehensive, practical, no-nonsense guide has an obvious appeal but may run the risk of fostering the idea that learning to implement 'a practice defined by others' is more important than independent, critical thinking (Goodson 1997). Good theoretical writing often has significant implications for practice but it is not always possible for newcomers to teaching to see those connections or make them relevant.

In attempting to fulfil the main aim of this book we have tried to offer many practical suggestions and examples within a broad framework of discussion. Our intention is to seek to promote in the reader a critical distance from some of the prevailing current assumptions about English teaching and indeed from some of the practical and theoretical ideas in this book. 'Critical distance' does not necessarily always mean disagreement but it does suggest a stepping back from the more pragmatic and functional preoccupations one inevitably has as a teacher in order to think about issues of value and purpose. The suggestions for lessons and schemes of work and the lists of approaches to topics are intended to serve not as practical imperatives but as invitations to thought.

Paradoxically, teachers of English need to 'keep their distance' in order to be able to engage fully with the whole enterprise of teaching. The curriculum both for English teaching and for the training of English teachers has become increasingly controlled and centralised in recent years. There is an obvious danger that as a result teachers will experience a loss of individuality and ownership as mere followers of external directives. We do not however believe that this is a necessary consequence of such developments. A framework can be enabling rather than constraining if approached with the right attitude. A National Curriculum for English neither guarantees nor prevents good teaching.

The aims of the book, then, can be summarised as follows:

- to provide students, newly qualified and experienced teachers with a comprehensive practical guide to the teaching of English in secondary schools;
- to show that it is possible to preserve best practice in English within the framework of the National Curriculum;
- to provide specific practical ideas in a framework of discussion which stimulates critical reflection related to relevant theory;
- to provide a guide to the major issues and available literature on the teaching of English.

These aims are closely related. It is only possible to provide a comprehensive guide to the teaching of English in a book of this length by including detailed further reading sections which point the reader towards more specialist authors within each topic. It was not our aim to offer a 'grand theory' of the teaching of English but nor was it our intention to offer simply a bland and 'balanced' guide to the field. The book is written from a particular set of beliefs and convictions about what English as a subject should be and what good teaching entails. Indeed the objective of seeking to stimulate critical thinking would hardly be possible if there was no sense of unifying perspective.

Our conviction that it is possible to preserve best practice in English within the framework of the National Curriculum carries an implicit assumption that best practice is in fact in danger of being threatened. As suggested above, good teaching does not happen simply through the imposition of external structures nor is it prevented by their existence. However, the need to fulfil external requirements may result in mechanical and reductive practices which lose sight of the fact that teaching is above all a human enterprise. That view does not imply any dogmatism over particular methods. Along with most teachers we would see a place in the contemporary English classroom for a wide variety of approaches to the subject, such as whole-class teaching, group work, knowledge about grammar, dramatic presentations, poetry writing, punctuation exercises. Too often, debates about the teaching of English in the past have centred on whether particular activities are appropriate or desirable instead of examining broader questions about the whole enterprise: whether for example pupils have a sense of purpose and engagement in their learning.

Part of the process of preserving critical distance is not taking matters too much for granted, including the nature of English itself. There are various ways of 'coming to know' English as a subject: reflecting on how one was taught English, observing lessons, reading about practical and theoretical approaches. There is also no single correct way of acquiring a theoretical perspective. It should be explored from different angles and by taking different journeys, sometimes traversing the same place from different directions. Few writers can avoid reference to the analysis of English teaching given in the Cox Report and the categories listed there will be examined in Chapter 1. Other common ways of gaining a perspective on English are through examining its history and the evolution of different schools of thought or by focusing on developing ideas in relation to language and learning, knowledge about language and critical theory.

It is beyond the scope of this Introduction to provide a detailed history of English as a subject but some familiarity with its development helps to provide a perspective on current assumptions and policies. It is sometimes easy to forget that the National Curriculum for English is only nine years old: there have been several different versions (two of which have been implemented) and it is due for another change. It is also salutary to discover that many 'progressive' ideas about the subject date back further than one might imagine. English had to struggle at the turn of the nineteenth century to replace classics as the main literary discipline although it had existed as a low status subject (mainly for girls) since the late sixteenth century. Two major landmarks in the teaching of English were the Newbolt Report (HMSO 1921) and *English for the English* written by George Sampson, one of the members of the Newbolt Committee. Both publications were in many ways very forward looking, arguing for the importance of a humane education which would be a preparation for 'life' not 'livelihood'. They can be seen as belonging to a tradition which owes much to the writing of Matthew Arnold with English standing as a bulwark against the dehumanising effects of the industrial revolution.

Educational thinkers who influenced English teaching at this time were reacting against the excesses of restrictive Victorian methods. Holmes in 1911 argued that in contrast to 'the path of mechanical obedience' which prevailed in schools, teachers should follow 'the path of self-realisation'; rote learning and mechanical drills should give way to the development of creativity and imagination. The emphasis on individuality and self-expression owed much to the thinking of Rousseau and concepts of natural growth. Writers such as Caldwell Cook (who employed play and drama extensively in his teaching) and Hourd (*The Education of the Poetic Spirit*) while differing in emphasis in their thinking belonged to what can be seen as a broadly humane and liberal approach to the teaching of English.

Even a brief examination of the history of English teaching puts paid to the popular notion that progressive ideas took hold in the mid to late 1960s. Neither is it possible to make too many assumptions about the way ideas developed. Sampson, who questioned excessive attention to grammar and emphasised active approaches to the teaching of reading and writing, was nevertheless uncompromising about the need to teach standard English even at the risk of sacrificing differences in language: 'Even if the school tends to extinguish a local idiosyncrasy of speech, it is not necessarily doing evil'. The Newbolt Report referred to the 'evil habits of speech' acquired in the home and the need for pupils' language to be 'cleansed and purified'. In the work of the early writers on the subject can be found both romantic ideas about creative imagination and a lack of tolerance of diversification in language.

Historical accounts often tend to distort reality if they assume that a neat progression took place from one set of ideas to another. That is why thinking in terms of 'schools of thought' can provide a helpful way of representing the teaching of English because different strands of that thinking can be seen to persist through the decades. Abbs, writing in 1982, distinguished between three traditions in the subject and tried to identify strengths and weaknesses in each. The progressive school (identified with authors like Holmes and Cook) recognised the importance of emotion and subjectivity in learning but erred in its view of art as undisciplined self expression. What Abbs termed the Cambridge school (associated with names like Sampson, and especially Leavis) while identifying the importance of tradition, criticism and the public element which was ignored by the progressives, in their turn ignored the importance of subjectivity and creativity. The third tradition, which was described as the contemporary socio-linguistic school, had the virtue of recognising the importance of the active use of language and of allowing pupils to formulate their own responses but tended to reduce English to linguistics or social studies.

Abbs' analysis of English is helpful because one can associate the particular schools with characteristic descriptions of classroom practice: the free, creative writing lesson of the progressives; the practical criticism of the Cambridge school and the discussion of issues of the socio-linguistic approach. It is important to note that this way of dissecting the subject is not necessarily 'correct'. Watson for example writing in 1981 distinguished between approaches to English which centred on 'literature', 'experience', 'language' and 'skills'. No analysis tells the whole story and all attempts are necessarily reductive in some way. For example, the descriptions of English as a subject offered in the early 1980s tended to take the concept of 'literature' for granted.

If 'literature' was taken for granted this was not true of language; different views of its role and development had a major influence on the teaching of English. The Bullock Report (DES 1975) is rightly seen as another major landmark and embodied much of the theory which had been coming to the fore in preceding years related to the role of language not just in communication but in thinking and making sense of the world. Writers like Britton and Barnes had been emphasising the importance of the relationship between language and learning which was a significant theme in the Report. An example of what this meant in practical terms was that more stress was to be placed on genuine exploratory talk in order to allow the expression and development of concepts. Attention was to be paid to the various functions of language instead of concentrating purely on form. A central idea which had a significant effect on English teaching was that language develops by its active use in meaningful contexts rather than by narrow instruction in skills.

An extreme 'language in use' view was one of two opposing positions described in the Kingman Report (DES 1988). The traditional error in teaching English was to concentrate on grammar exercises and skills at the expense of meaning; the progressive mistake was to concentrate exclusively on the *use* of language without taking opportunities to focus adequately on language itself. The important word here is 'adequately'. There is no evidence that writers or teachers advocated a complete neglect of language; it is difficult to imagine what that would look like in practice. The question was rather how much and what kind of attention it should receive. The Kingman view was to accept that the way we acquire language is to use it in all its forms but that in addition pupils should acquire specific knowledge *about* language. This issue will be explored in more depth in Chapter 9 but it is important to note here that the Report was not only concerned with knowledge of language forms. Also important was knowledge about the ways in which language is used in society, how language is affected by social contexts, appreciation of the value of dialect, knowledge that language changes and factors affecting communication other than words spoken. Much of the debate at the time focused on whether knowledge about language is necessary for its effective use. This preoccupation sometimes obscured the fact that the change of emphasis was much wider and had to do with what can be described as a new 'self-consciousness' about language.

Some of the more recent writing on the teaching of English can be described, at its simplest, as not taking previously accepted concepts like 'literature', 'reading' and 'writing' for granted. The influence of literary theory on the teaching of English is manifested in different approaches to reading; for example, in the way reader-response theories emphasise the importance of the contribution which the reader makes to the meaning of texts. Other aspects of critical theory promote an examination of text and categories of text in a wider cultural context, questioning the exclusive category of 'literature'. In the classroom this might mean exploring different meanings of texts, understanding how readers have to fill gaps in order to read and comparing different texts, such as a novel and a soap opera. These approaches go beyond traditional notions of character and theme when reading literature.

Ideas of this kind are sometimes presented as a radical alternative model for teaching English but we see them as sitting fairly comfortably in an approach to the subject which places emphasis on the importance of explicit knowledge and awareness – whether this be in relation to text, genre, punctuation, spelling or other conventions of language. The importance of the Kingman Report as a landmark in the teaching of English is sometimes underestimated because the Cox Report (DES 1989) and the National Curriculum were published so soon afterwards. It was the Kingman Report however which, despite the ambiguity of its tone and the lack of clear practical direction for teachers, presented the broad divisions between 'language in use' and 'knowledge about language' so clearly and so significantly for English teaching.

The mistake made by advocates of an extreme version of 'language in use' was to assume that language develops simply by being used in a variety of contexts. Using language is a necessary but not sufficient aspect of learning English (the mistake made by exponents of traditional models was not to see using language in meaningful contexts as being essential). The error partly arises from treating 'language' as a single category, of assuming that what is true of speaking can be applied equally to reading and writing. Pinker (1994:18) (after Chomsky) has argued very convincingly that the acquisition of spoken language is an instinct, a natural process:

> Language is not a cultural artefact that we learn the way we learn to tell time or how the federal government works. Instead it is a distinct piece of the biological makeup of our brains. Language is a complex, specialised skill, which develops in the child spontaneously, without conscious effort or formal instruction, is deployed without awareness of its underlying logic, is qualitatively the same in every individual, and is distinct from more general abilities to process information or behave intelligently.

Language here of course refers to spoken language and the same is not true of writing and reading, both of which developed relatively recently in the history of the human race and have to be taught more explicitly and systematically. It is deceptive to speak of 'language' as a generic ability because this disguises very important differences in the approach needed to the different language modes. The National Curriculum treats the three components of reading, writing, speaking and listening in exactly the same way with some unfortunate consequences which will be explored in Chapters 4 and 7.

That language can be deceptive is a theme we shall return to elsewhere in this book. The fact that 'literature' is not an easy category to demarcate or a straightforward concept to define should not come as a surprise because language does not operate with clear boundaries and is rarely transparent. To become effective users of language, in addition to acquiring specific skills, it is important to be able to see underlying meanings, connotations, subtleties, contradictions and 'colour'. Language does not lend itself to a constraining black and white, objectified logic or exactitude.

One of the themes which emerges in various chapters in this book is contrasting notions of 'subjectivity' and 'objectivity'. Such concepts are also not reducible to simple definitions. Traditional western philosophy has struggled with the question of how a human subject can come to know an objective world. The question formulated in that way assumes a dualism between an inner private self and external 'reality'. The problem arises from a particular conception of the way language works and is resolved by taking a different view. If language is seen not as a means of giving expression to inner thoughts and meanings which are somehow separate from it, but is itself the embodiment of meaning, the problem is dissolved. The 'private' (in the philosophical sense) inner subject disappears. Understanding and meaning through language need to be seen as taking place *between*, and not simply *within*, people.

The emphasis on collaboration in this book (both pupils' collaborative learning and that which takes place between teachers) is not simply a form of pragmatism. The process of sharing understanding and meaning is a *sine qua non* of a rich human existence. Nor is collaboration a denial of individuality. The writing of this book has been a collaborative venture but each author has taken the major responsibility for particular chapters. We have, therefore, in some places retained the first person singular and in others the more common plural form.

We have used the term 'subjectivity' in this book not in the philosophical sense of postulating an inner self nor in the more popular meaning referring to individual opinions or beliefs where its use so often becomes redundant. How can opinions be other than subjective? The term 'subjectivity' has been used to denote a level of individual engagement and involvement in learning and coming to know the world.

Education has become increasingly dominated by ideas which have an 'objective' ring, suggesting a world of neat logic and rationality, systems and structures, objectives and targets. The danger is however that this world has no place for human complexity: it presents an arid context devoid of culture and spirituality. For some readers the last two sentences will have immediate profound meaning and will strike a chord with their experiences; for others the words will sound like empty rhetoric. The book as a whole is intended to be an exemplification of what is meant by those statements.

The fact that words written in this Introduction will have a different impact on different readers is precisely the point about language which is central to our view of the teaching of English. Language has meaning not by any simple correspondence with reality or with ideas in someone's head but through shared, human contexts or 'forms of life'. It is in this sense that engaging 'subjectivity' is an essential element of good English teaching because without it pupils will merely be performing mechanical operations, with no sense of purpose or engagement. Once again it is worth emphasising that we refer here to a quality of participation rather than to the nature of specific tasks; it is possible to be disengaged when writing a dutiful poem or response to *Macbeth* just as it is possible to be really hooked by trying to get the use of speech marks right.

When using words like 'engagement' we do not wish to appear to underestimate the challenge facing teachers when trying to teach large classes with limited resources. We have taught in secondary schools for a combined total of thirty years and we have each worked as Head of English in two different secondary schools. A good deal of our professional lives is now spent visiting schools. Young people have in the last twenty years become increasingly independent, challenging and individualistic. The development of these 'qualities' could be seen as a laudable educational aim but they present more as problems when pupils come in groups of thirty or so at a time. Despite pressures on teachers to differentiate, identify and respond to individual needs, use innovative methods and a variety of teaching and learning styles, schools are still resourced as if Victorian, authoritarian methods prevail. Such comments are made in order to strike a note of realism rather than to be defeatist. This book is intended to be optimistic but written with an awareness of practical constraints and with the knowledge that teaching today is often about compromise.

Many writers on the subject have argued for the importance of English as an art, asserting for example that experience is comprehended not only through linear, abstract thinking but through feeling and intuition, that the arts as sensitive instruments for self awareness have importance in developing the emotional and imaginative energies of children. Abbs (1982:7) had a vision of schools being committed to the 'inner life of the student'. Staples (1992:9) identifies polarities between the 'cognitive' and 'affective' with aesthetic experience seeking to keep the polarities in unison. The problem with many approaches to English as an art is that emphasis is placed largely on the reading of literature and on expressive forms of language (with pupils' written poetry representing the pinnacle of achievement). Such arguments often do not speak to contemporary English teachers who are busy trying to fulfil the broad requirements of the National Curriculum. An alternative, more inclusive, view is that seeing English as an art is unavoidable if language is taken at all seriously.

Such a view becomes possible if the rigid boundaries which separate the 'aesthetic' from other forms of experience are seen to dissolve. Language is both 'intelligible and sensuous' (Bowie 1990:147). Even in its simplest form it is often subject to different interpretations; it invariably carries different levels of meaning. It allows us to engage with life but also to distance ourselves from experiences. There is much that we can learn about the way it works but its depths can never be fully explored and explained. It has meaning not simply by reference to something outside itself but by its occurrence in cultural contexts of human communities. Language itself has many of the characteristics which have been traditionally associated with art.

To summarise: the concept of 'subjectivity' as used in this book must not be seen in the traditional metaphysical sense as representing the private, inner world. Just as language only has meaning in public contexts, subjectivity only makes sense in a context of shared understandings. A defence of subjectivity is not an argument for individuality but is quite the opposite. Shared meanings which define the self are derived from collaboration and engagement in objective contexts.

The central aim of English teaching, 'to use language effectively', can be interpreted in different ways. It can imply that learning language is a logical, mechanical, individualistic, shallow process governed by rules. Or it can suggest that using language effectively is a rich, deep, communal activity bound by conventions which occur in cultural contexts. Only the latter view makes philosophical and human sense or can provide any proper rationale for the teaching of English.

FURTHER READING

Useful chapters on the history of English teaching can be found in Jeffcoate (1992) *Starting English Teaching* and Davison and Dowson (1998) *Learning to Teach English in the Secondary School.* More detailed histories are by Shayer (1972) *The Teaching of English in Schools 1900-1970* and Michael (1992) *The Teaching of English from the Sixteenth Century to 1870.* Mathieson (1975) has written very interestingly on the changing role of English in the last two centuries in *The Preachers of Culture.* Books which describe the influence of literary theory on English teaching include Griffiths (1987) *Literary Theory and English Teaching* and Burton (ed.) (1989) *Enjoying Texts: Using Literary Theory in the Classroom:* both have helpful further reading sections. Peim (1993) *Critical Theory and the English Teacher* has drawn on critical theory to argue for a fresh conception of English as a subject. Readers who would like to pursue some of the theoretical ideas about language outside the context of English teaching might turn to Finch (1995) *Wittgenstein,* Harland (1987) *Superstructuralism* and Norris (1991) *Deconstruction Theory and Practice.* Wittgenstein used the idea of 'forms of life' in the *Philosophical Investigations.*

1: The English Teacher and the National Curriculum

Bring out number, weight and measure in a year of dearth.
William Blake, *The Marriage of Heaven and Hell*

Over the past few years – although to many it may seem more like an eternity, and not in the liberating Blakean sense either – English teachers in secondary schools have become increasingly used to living with number, weight and measure. The National Curriculum, ushered in by the 1988 Education Act and, for English, substantially revised since, has been largely responsible for the obsession with measurement. Not that 1988 was a year of dearth as far as most secondary English teachers were concerned: new examination syllabuses at sixteen and eighteen, based largely on coursework, opened up exciting opportunities for effective and innovative teaching of both language and literature, increasingly integrated at all levels. At the same time pioneering work was going on in English departments in a range of other areas: speaking and listening; integration with drama; media education; active approaches to literature, including Shakespeare; awareness and knowledge of the workings of language; and collaboration with other curricular subjects. If there was dearth, it perhaps arrived as a result of and simultaneously with the fashion for 'objective' measurement, rather than pre-dating it, and this is of course precisely what I imagine Blake himself meant. As Knight (1996:22) has it,

> the desire for an unattainable objectivity is the key to many of the difficulties we have faced in formulating an adequate version of National Curriculum English. The quest for objectives and certainties where none is to be found produces paradoxical results: that matters in which we (teachers and pupils) should trust our intuitive understanding are made both more complex and more shallow when we do not.

This is quite an indictment. But what English teachers have to do, and in many cases are doing, is to convert this threat into an opportunity: not only to live with the National Curriculum, but actually to make it work for us. Fortunately the National Curriculum is not only about measurement but is also about establishing a framework for teaching through specification of programmes of study. It has more broadly served to focus attention on the nature of English teaching: why the subject has such a prominent place within the curriculum, and what to do with it once it is there. This is not some esoteric debate undertaken solely by those professionally involved in the teaching of English: for better or for worse, education has been opened up to an unprecedented degree to the wider public – New Labour's battlecry during the 1997 General Election, 'Education! Education! Education!', for example, clearly struck a chord with the electorate. Most people feel that they have something to contribute to the education debate; certainly most have an opinion to offer, based either on their own remembered education or on their children's continuing schooling, in a way unlikely to apply, say, to the processes and professions of law or medicine. The position of English is perhaps even more extreme, in that the English language is almost universally shared by the citizens of the UK and virtually everyone feels a degree of expertise. In a sense, of course, there is a great deal of truth in this – language is by its very nature owned by those who use it and the learning of spoken English is achieved without any formal teaching – but these same people would be less likely to pronounce upon the nature of art, geography or mathematics in education. The special position of English teachers in this context presents an opportunity both to influence opinion and to draw on existing views; but it is an elusive opportunity, all too easily missed.

In the reality of English teaching in a secondary school, one can expect huge diversity of opinions and expectations as expressed by parents, governing bodies, colleagues and many others, and it is part of the English teacher's function to integrate, discuss, deflect, confirm and argue the viewpoints as the case may be. In a world of flux, the National Curriculum must be seen as a reasonably broad church: it may appear – indeed it seeks to appear – as completely authoritative; in truth it offers a series of touchstones, and the real nature of the subject has to be discovered and invented ever anew by those most intensely involved.

This process requires a certain immersion in the subject, and at the same time an ability to see both wood and trees in formulating over-arching aims and values. It is all too easy, especially perhaps in the first year or two of teaching, to be drawn into thinking that mechanistic teaching of the National Curriculum is an end in itself, spawning its own self-justification. Following Rex Gibson (1986), we could term this position 'instrumental rationality': the dichotomous separation of fact from feeling, demanding an absence of thought about the consequences and context of one's actions in any profound sense. The process thus becomes its own legitimisation with its own particular – sometimes impenetrable – rationality. This, of course, is nothing new. The poet Thomas Traherne (*c.* 1665), for example, writing of his own Oxford education in the seventeenth century, having initially paid tribute to the breadth of learning possible there, went on to regret that

> Nevertheless some things were defective too. There was never a tutor that did expressly teach Felicity, though that be the mistress of all other sciences. Nor did any of us study those things but as aliena, which we ought to have studied as our enjoyments. We studied to inform our knowledge, but knew not for what end we so studied. And for lack of aiming at a certain end we erred in the manner.

So in Traherne's view of the curriculum, felicity, for him the full and visionary enjoyment of life's possibilities, becomes the central tenet, the 'mistress', of all else. What was lacking in the Oxford education of the mid seventeenth century is still perhaps avoided by the curriculum legislators of today. It is important to keep a broad sense of what is the purpose of education.

In the version of the National Curriculum for English based on the Report of the Cox Committee (DES, 1989), it was suggested that there were essentially five models of English teaching, and that most English teachers combined in their teaching several if not all of these. The types of English teaching posited by Cox were as follows:

- a personal growth view, which tends to emphasise the pupil as a creative and imaginative individual developing, in terms of the teaching and learning of English, primarily through an intensive engagement with literature and personal creative writing;
- a cross-curricular approach, stressing the distinctive nature of English as the language of learning for virtually all curriculum areas and implying a definition of service to these areas and to education in a generic sense;
- an adult needs emphasis, as essentially a preparation for the demands of life beyond school in terms of effective understanding of and communication through the English language in its many forms, including those vocationally based;
- a cultural heritage model, with the teaching based heavily on 'great' works of literature, generally drawn from the past;
- a cultural analysis view, leading pupils to a critical understanding of the social and cultural context of English, particularly the value systems which are inevitably embedded in the ways language is used.

In many ways, these characteristics also underlie the current (1995) National Curriculum – but do they suffice as a statement of principle? In particular, it is worth considering whether the five 'versions' of English are as comfortably compatible as Cox implies in his accompanying gloss: 'they are not sharply distinguishable, and they are certainly not mutually exclusive'. Is there not rather something of a struggle for ascendancy between some, if not all, of these views? In what sense is the second formulation a view of English as a distinctive subject at all? Certainly, the subject English has been something of a battleground for years – since its comparatively recent inception, in fact – and it is all the more important to take a principled position with regard to its teaching, eschewing the temptations of a superficial compromise; as Goodwyn (1997:39) puts it,

> English teachers do not. . .recognise the cross-curricular model as a model of English. . .They are quite clear that this model belongs to the whole school and should not be identified with English. . .The other four models are acknowledged as a normal part of English, but they do not have a comfortable or neutral relationship with each other; neither are they politically or historically innocent, they are not simply 'there'.

There is some value in differentiating between views, if only as an aid to reflection about one's own practice. It may be possible – in the best tradition of teenage magazines – to undertake a self-analysing quiz to ascertain where you stand: asked to devise a scheme of work for a Year 8 mixed ability group, is your first instinct to

(a)   plan alongside other departments in, for example, giving presentations and conducting library-based research, *or*
(b)   examine advertising as an introduction to media education, focusing on the manipulation of language and images to boost product sales, *or*
(c)   base the scheme on a celebration of character and plot in *Twelfth Night*, exploring also the development of English theatre during Shakespeare's period, *or*
(d)   block-book the IT facilities with a view to examining the ways in which IT skills could be used in a range of vocational areas, including journalism, advertising and the promotion of tourism, *or*

(e)   plan around the theme of the environment, aiming for the production of a series of colourful anthologies of creative writing celebrating personal relationships with aspects of the environment?

Clearly this is something of an artificial exercise, and the answer is not to be found on the back page, but it may well serve to illustrate how teachers of English will differ in the weight they give to different views of the subject. Before the National Curriculum an English teacher (depending on the degree of autonomy given by a department or school) was able to follow individual strengths and preferences. This had clear advantages. It meant however that pupils' experiences could be very narrow and unbalanced.

It is also interesting to consider the name of the subject English. Clearly, as it stands, it carries many connotations (as does the term National Curriculum) beyond its definition as one subject in the curriculum: some, perhaps, of nationality and exclusivity which may not be entirely desirable. What's in a name? you may ask, but thinking about alternative possible names will focus on what precisely the subject is all about and where the thrust of its teaching should be situated. Possibilities are:

- the language arts (favoured by Abbs (1976) amongst others);
- rhetorical studies (implied by Eagleton (1983));
- literacy studies (certainly in line with the present governments concern);
- cultural studies;
- communications;
- discourse awareness;
- language and literature studies.

Examining English from the perspective of different people in society – curriculum legislators, teachers concerned with the practicalities of planning lessons or simply, for example – thinking about the name of the subject illustrates a wide diversity of thinking. A principled position is necessary but it is of course practicable to remain reasonably eclectic in approach, keeping an open mind not only to different philosophies – which assuredly will develop and change with time – but to the different needs and ideas as discerned in and expressed by the pupils themselves. It is perfectly feasible, for example, to cover all five of the hypothetical schemes of work designed for the Year 8 class within one year; indeed, this may be a very effective way of ensuring breadth of entitlement. What we need to do, above all, is to reflect on our own preferences and predilections, compensating when appropriate for any personal shortcomings through a conscious effort to adapt to new ways and areas of English teaching. The subject provides an extremely fertile field for exploration and experimentation, for differing relationships between theory and practice. It may be instructive here to examine some of the tensions involved in this complex interrelationship, and I should like to use Stead's theories of poetic creativity to draw one or two parallels with the subject English, before re-appraising the National Curriculum in the light of the findings. Stead (1964:11) had this to say about poetry:

A poem may be said to exist in a triangle, the points of which are, first the poet, second, the audience, and, third, the areas of experience which we call variously 'Reality', 'Truth', or 'Nature'. Between these points run lines of tension, and depending on the time, the place, the poet, and the audience, these lines will lengthen or shorten. . .There are infinite variations, but. . .the finest poems are likely to be those which exist in an equilateral triangle, each point pulling equally in a moment of perfect tension.

It strikes me that there is a great deal of validity in this with reference to the whole process of writing, which will be explored in Chapter 3, and Stead develops his own argument through close textual analysis of the work of several poets; but in what sense might this taut or sagging triangle refer to the teaching of English?

A great deal depends on what goes into the triangle, and what exactly is represented by each of the three points. If we take the triangle to enclose and express the whole business of English teaching, which, like Stead's poem, is *created*, then it may follow that one point represents the English teacher; another, the audience of pupils (although this may not be the only possible audience); and the final point symbolises the context – the outer world, perhaps, which exerts so many often contradictory pressures on the processes of teaching. If we pursue the parallel further, we can see that effective teaching depends on the maintenance of a certain tension along the lines joining the points: if the points become too close to, or too distant from, either each other or the central project of teaching itself, there may well be a danger that the creative art of teaching could be damaged. This is in the end an argument for a dynamic combination of reflective distance and imaginative involvement – qualities which may seem like opposites, and perhaps they are; but to go back to Blake's *Marriage of Heaven and Hell*, 'Without contraries is no progression'.

To aim for such a dynamic combination is to inform the totality of the experience of teaching English, not only in relation to the considerations outlined above but, perhaps more importantly and certainly more immediately, as affecting classroom practice. The principle of reflective distance combining with imaginative involvement must be a principle encouraged in pupils' attitudes towards their own experience of the subject as well as being embedded as a pedagogical cornerstone. We need, paradoxically, to be rigorous in *creating* the objective circumstances to allow our pupils' own subjectivities to take root. In addition to ensuring appropriate coverage of the National Curriculum requirements, the teacher must also be prepared to give space, to keep a distance, to allow for genuine and autonomous development. I am reminded of the Zen koan that the way to control a flock of sheep is to give them a wide pasture to wander in. Harrison (1994:7), pursuing the apt metaphor of education as theatre, asks pertinently:

> Could the theatre of education. . .be trying too hard to 'deliver the goods' to its clients, the learners, and leaving no space for them to create their own vision? Are we providing enough space for learners to bring their own minds and cultures into taking part in learning? Have we lost sight of essential qualities such as play, curiosity and friendship in learning? Whose 'production' *is* it, anyway?

Whose indeed? The question demands an affirmative answer: ours, both teacher's and pupils'. It is not simply a matter of standing back, of showing more tolerance – although these are often underrated virtues, particularly when teaching adolescent boys – but of being able at times to live with a Keatsian negative capability, 'that is when man is capable of being in uncertainties, Mysteries, doubts without any irritable reaching after fact and reason'.

The teaching and learning of English needs adventurousness, but also must be accompanied by a positive effort to create the right conditions and provide the boundaries to ensure a sense of security for those involved: the shepherd of the Zen koan (and it is interesting how often the pastoral metaphor finds its way into education) would be less than wise if the ultimate boundary of the wide pasture was a cliff edge. One of the implications for practice is the need to create an appropriate environment for each other's learning, if possible as part of whole-school practice, and, more particularly for English, attending to such concerns as:

- the layout of the classroom;
- excellence and relevance of displays;
- provision of designated areas for reading, audio-visual work and other activities;
- class libraries;
- facilities for ICT and self-directed studies.

In many ways, secondary English teachers need to learn, indeed have learned already, from the best of primary school practice: it has often struck me that by Year 6 many youngsters have become significantly autonomous learners, only to take a step or two backwards on arrival in secondary school. We need to safeguard such principles of independence against the onslaught of insistence from some quarters for more and more didactic teaching as narrow preparation for equally narrow SATs.

Which brings us back to the National Curriculum. In the light of the considerations noted above, it may be helpful at this stage to take stock of the National Curriculum for English through conducting a Strengths/Weaknesses/Opportunities/Threats (SWOT) analysis. This is a convenient and widely used management tool effective in summarising ideas and potential conflicts about any topic; the idea is to convert the threats and weaknesses into opportunities and strengths – not always that easy! The eventual diagram may look something like Figure 1.1.

STRENGTHS	WEAKNESSES
Clear basis for planning	Inflexibility: lack of scope
Criteria for assessment	Overcrowding of curriculum
Progress and continuity	Summative not formative assessment
Reasonably full idea of English	Focus on 'traditional values'
Speaking/listening given status	Scant regard for special needs
OPPORTUNITIES	THREATS
Scope to develop beyond the stated curriculum	Temptation to 'teach to the SATs'
Minimum entitlement established	Teachers reduced to 'technicians'
Collaborative possibilities within and outside English departments	Undue pressure on scarce resources
	Cultural bias: marginalisation of ethnic groups

Figure 1.1

The particular strengths, weaknesses, opportunities and threats listed here are the result of PGCE students' reflections on fairly early acquaintance with the National Curriculum, and it is likely that no two groups would come up with the same list: what is important is achieving an appreciation both of balance and of conflict in order to make sense of the practicalities of actually teaching the English curriculum. The idea is to work collaboratively to convert the weaknesses into strengths, the threats into opportunities.

In order to illustrate the possibilities of working with the National Curriculum for English, consider the set of ideas based around an exploration of the world of traditional ballads for Year 7 through a broad range of activities shown in Figure 1.2.

EXPLORATION OF THE WORLD OF TRADITIONAL BALLADS

Resources might include recorded versions of the following:

- 'Little Musgrave' or the variant 'Matty Groves' (Nic Jones/Planxty/Fairport Convention)
- 'Rosie Anderson' (Dave Burland)
- 'The House of the Rising Sun' (The Animals/Joan Baez)
- 'Dark Streets of London' (The Pogues)
- 'The Dark Eyed Sailor' (June Tabor/Steeleye Span/Kate Risby)

Activities

- Drama: group interpretation of ballads for performance.
- Reading aloud, rehearsed, in pairs to the rest of the class.
- Arranging a coherent sequence from jumbled verse order as poetry.
- Discussion of and research into the importance of oral tradition, including modern equivalents of tales, urban myths, jokes, rhymes.
- Presentation through posters, book illustrations, comic strips, music.
- Writing a ballad version of a modern story based on press cuttings.
- Writing a modern prose version of a traditional ballad.
- Writing based on characters and plots in ballads.
- Newspaper account of ballad events.

Broader issues and extension work may include, through research, drama and discussion: study of dreams and the supernatural, the nature of the experiences often sensationally highlighted in ballads, the social and historical context of myths, the subsequent decline of the ballad form, and cross-curricular possibilities.

Figure 1.2

You can see at a glance the wide range of different activities possible through study of one particular genre, and of course this sort of list of diverse activities could be replicated or extended for an endless variety of themes, texts or genres. Using the National Curriculum for English booklet, it may be instructive at this point to 'map out' the above activities, or their equivalent, using the official framework. This process can also provide a useful means of giving more direction to the teaching. The table in Figure 1.3 shows how each activity links to the Programmes of Study and the teaching focus which may result.

This process will be further developed in Chapter 2, but it may already be evident that planning in this way, in this order, helps to keep the National Curriculum's demands in perspective: good English teaching starts from what is desirable and possible in the reality of classroom engagement, with a 'best possible fit' into the detail of the National Curriculum. If at the end of a specific period of study the English teacher – or, better still, the English department working collaboratively – finds that certain areas have not been sufficiently covered, then is the time to extend or adapt the scheme of study.

Pupil activities	Relationship to the National Curriculum	Possible teaching focus
Group interpretation of ballads.	*Analyse and engage with ideas, themes and language; analyse and discuss alternative interpretations; take notes from written and oral sources.*	Pupils take notes and compare each others' performances in discussion.
Reading aloud, rehearsed, in pairs to the rest of the class.	*Reading aloud, telling and enacting stories and poems; adapt their presentations.*	Teacher advises about intonation and expression.
Arranging a coherent sequence from jumbled verse order.	*Analyse and engage with the ideas, themes and language in poetry.*	Pupils asked to give reasons for their choices and decisions; pupils given guidance through language use, symbolism, conventions of the genre, poetic devices.
Discussion of and research into the importance of of oral tradition, including modern equivalents of tales, urban myths, jokes, rhymes.	*How usage, words and meaning change over time; current influences on spoken and written language; differences between speech and writing.*	Pupils present research findings in terms of specific aspects of language change.
Presentation through posters, book illustrations, comic strips, music.	*Analyse and evaluate the use of language in a variety of media; compare and synthesise information drawn from different texts.*	Pupils compare and analyse the different versions after completion with reference to the original.
Writing a ballad version of a modern story based on press cuttings.	*Write in a range of forms; read to select information.*	Teacher draws attention to form and style of ballads; pupils shown how to select and adapt information for composition.
Writing a modern prose version of a traditional ballad.	*Use knowledge of distinctive ways of organising and expressing ideas; examine discourse structure.*	Teacher draws attention to use of paragraphs in prose.
Writing based on characters and plots in ballads.	*Reflection on motivation and behaviour of characters, the development of plot and the overall impact of a text.*	Pupils underline words and phrases which give insight into character before attempting their own writing.
Newspaper account of ballad events.	*Use knowledge of the distinctive ways of organising and expressing ideas and information; evaluate how information is presented.*	Comparison of use of headline and exaggeration in modern newspapers; media study based on comparison between sensational journalism and ballads.

Figure 1.3

The example in Figure 1.3 is deliberately broad in its range, and clearly the English teacher should focus on specific needs and preferences in detail as appropriate. At other times, especially when addressing a particular 'gap' in pupils' coverage of the National Curriculum stipulations, the need for greater detail should inform planning from the start. The examples in Figures 1.4 and 1.5, both created by beginning teachers of English, are based on Janni Howker's short story 'Badger on the Barge' as taught to a Year 9 group; the first examines narrative structure and development; the second seeks a creative way to teach the skills of letter writing and appropriate register.

A. Introductory lesson on 'Badger on the Barge' with a Year 9 English group.

Resources: the story 'Badger on the Barge': one copy for each pupil;
  sets of ten cards, each containing the following words: badger, wheelchair, geriatric ward, motorbike helmet, truant, brandy, earthworms.
Development: arrange the class into five friendship groups. Given the cards, each group has to invent a storyline using all the depicted words within ten minutes. Each group then presents its skeleton story, with all pupils taking some part (possibly using some dramatic role-play).
  Whole-class discussion ensues on the nature of narrative development and the significance of key words, the teacher using the whiteboard to summarise. During a subsequent lesson, the class is introduced to the short story itself, and, as the reading progresses, compares the original to the groups' ideas. A further possibility is to examine in detail the use Janni Howker makes of the key words in the narrative development.

Figure 1.4

B. The skills of letter writing through study of 'Badger on the Barge'.

After reading the short story, pupils are given the choice of writing a letter from the following list, and the whole class discusses the appropriate register and vocabulary for each, making notes if necessary:

- Helen's mother to the school, explaining Helen's absence;
- An interfering neighbour to the school's headteacher, complaining about truancy;
- A nursing sister to the old lady's daughter;
- Helen to a friend, telling her side of the story;
- A passerby to the local newspaper complaining about the state of the barge.

The letters could then be shared amongst the class, with each pupil writing a reply to a letter in a contrasting register to that sent originally.

Figure 1.5

Again we can see how, with a little imagination, the requirements of the National Curriculum may be met through an organic rather than mechanistic approach. The National Curriculum can be viewed not just as a set of individual syllabus requirements but as providing a broad conception of the way English should be realised as a subject in schools. Attention has tended to focus on the more controversial aspects like the place of standard English (to be discussed in more detail in Chapters 7 and 9). However, the following selected quotations from the current (1995) National Curriculum indicate that it can be judged to require a dynamic and varied approach:

- Pupils' abilities should be developed within an integrated programme of speaking and listening, reading and writing.
- Pupils should be given opportunities to talk for a range of purposes.
- Pupils should be given opportunities to read a wide variety of literature. . . to read widely and independently solely for enjoyment.
- The main emphasis should be on the encouragement of wider reading in order to develop independent, responsive and enthusiastic readers.
- Pupils should be encouraged to extend their confidence in writing for a variety of purposes and to develop their own distinctive and original styles.
- Pupils should be given opportunities to write for specific readers, for a large unknown readership and for themselves.

We can add to this list two quotations from the early formulation of the English Order:

- Working on tasks which they have chosen and which they direct for themselves.
- Working with teachers who are themselves involved in the processes, with special expertise, as talkers, listeners, readers and writers.

A list of this kind can be used to evaluate how well the objectives are being achieved. Such aims are at best extremely difficult to achieve as a lone English teacher isolated in his or her classroom. This realisation opens the door for a spirit of collaboration, and the advent of the National Curriculum for English has ushered in a highly practical sense of working together – even at times sharpened by the sense of opposition to a common enemy in some of the more foolish aspects of this curriculum. Sometimes the only creative response to a threat is to fight back, as with the original SATs, and this can serve to highlight common ground and shared ideals amongst English teachers. The need for collaboration has been sharpened further by the increasing – and generally very healthy – diversity of new entrants' degree backgrounds. Even amongst those whose degree is in some sense 'English', there are bound to be areas of knowledge and expertise in which practitioners feel less secure than others. Correspondingly, the scope and breadth of the subject English have increased enormously in recent years. With these factors in mind, mutual support amongst English teachers in a department or some other kind of network (for example an LEA-inspired group of newly qualified teachers, or one convened through the National Association of Teachers of English, or a PGCE partnership) could be swiftly facilitated through completion and distribution of a simple form requesting information which can be shared (Figure 1.6).

This sort of questioning can indeed form a useful starting point, but the real work – and the real rewards – starts afterwards and must be sustained. In the sense that this is a vision-inspired process to be skilfully managed, all English teachers involved in it are both leaders, providing the vision, and managers, grappling with the means of attainment. This is in reality a process of professional development. It is a question of achieving some sort of balance between creative, individual autonomy (traditionally the hallmark of the English teacher) and the needs of the organisation in interpreting and teaching the National Curriculum. For Knight (1996:1) it is precisely this curriculum which is the problem:

> Traditionally there has often been a healthy tension between the individualism invited by the subject and the systems within which it was obliged to work. Until the coming of the National Curriculum it was possible for many teachers of 'English' to reconcile the two: to teach the subject according to their best conscience *and* to ensure that their pupils were not thereby disabled when it came to public certification of their achievements.

AREAS OF EXPERTISE IN ENGLISH TEACHING
Mutual support for aspects of English in the secondary school curriculum

Areas of particular interest or expertise:

Key English texts, used in schools, with which you are familiar:

Area(s) in which you'd welcome assistance:

Experience of cross-curricular possibilities:

Specific experience of such aspects as:

    drama
    media education
    GNVQ
    Special Educational Needs
    Teaching of grammar
    Post-16
    Mixed ability/setting

Figure 1.6

The fundamental issue at stake here is whether the National Curriculum and its attendant policing mechanisms need be seen entirely as a threat, as Knight maintains; is there, even, an opportunity lurking there? Perhaps we have already demonstrated that there is one, for the taking, and English teachers, resilient as ever, are not slow on the uptake. Characteristics of positive collaboration, in practical terms, may include:

- shared schemes of work, collaboratively formed;
- swapping of resources;
- regular meetings to share pedagogical ideas and practices;
- mutual observation of lessons;
- reaching out to other departments to examine cross-curricular potential;
- involvement in wider contexts such as NATE or PGCE partnerships;
- collaborative mentoring of new teachers;
- involvement of pupils in formulating and responding to practice;
- informal involvement in extra-curricular and social activities.

Collaboration without individual flair can be sterile, as Fullan and Hargreaves (1992:14) note: 'People can find themselves collaborating for the sake of collaboration. . .and, contrary to popular opinion, it can reduce innovation and imaginative solutions to individual situations, as susceptibility to the latest chosen innovation and "groupthink" carry the day.' English teachers seem particularly well equipped to avoid pitfalls like these, but it is a position that has been hard won and that will need to be defended with a watchful eye by those entering the profession. As we turn to look in more detail at the areas of experience involved in the teaching of English, whether stemming from the National Curriculum or bursting its boundaries, it is as well to keep this in mind. To conclude this chapter we could do worse than finish as we started with William Blake, who asserted through his character Los in *Jerusalem,*

> I must create a system or be enslaved by another man's.
> I will not reason or compare: my business is to create.

FURTHER READING

Two books by Cox: *Cox on Cox* (1991) and *Cox on the Battle for the English Curriculum* (1995) give fascinating insights into the emergence of the English Order. Of the official documents, the Report of the Kingman Committee (DES 1988) and that of the Cox Committee (DES 1989) are still worth reading. Books by Goodson and Medway (1990) *Bringing English to Order*, Protherough and King (eds) (1995) *The Challenge of English in the National Curriculum*, Davies (1996) *What is English Teaching?*, Knight (1996) *Valuing English: Reflections on the National Curriculum* and Goodwyn (ed.) (1995) *English and Ability* contain critiques of the English Order. Kress (1995) in *Writing the Future* looks forward to re-fashioning the English curriculum on more pertinent foundations, and *A Guide to the National Curriculum* (Moon, 1996) has a useful summary of the English situation as well as the rest of the curriculum.

RESOURCES

Many educational publishers have attempted to ease the English teacher's burden of planning and implementing the National Curriculum. Some of the most effective in combining imaginative and rigorous approaches are to be found in: *The English Pack* (Bates, Goddard, Norris, Turton), Framework Press, 1994 (photocopiable); *Key Stage 3 English Units* (ed. Broadbent), English and Media Centre (photocopiable, and including detailed planning sections); thematic resource booklets for Key Stage 3: *Myself, School Under Siege, The Island* and *The Unknown*, English and Media Centre.

2: Planning

The fact is, human reason may carry you a little too far –
over the hedge, in fact. It carried me a good way at one time;
but I saw it would not do. I pulled up; I pulled up in time.

Mr Brooke in George Eliot's *Middlemarch*

This chapter will examine practical approaches to planning individual lessons and schemes of work. It will also explore some of the tensions and difficulties involved in planning work in English. As described earlier, the teaching of the subject needs to be sufficiently centred on the National Curriculum to provide coverage, continuity and appropriate progression while at the same time sufficiently pupil-centred to ensure engagement in learning at a rich level.

The need to fulfil the competing demands of 'systematic coverage' and 'rich subjective engagement' can be translated in practical terms into different conceptions of the planning process. These can be more vividly described if presented as caricatures. If planning is seen as something akin to a military operation with very precise targets, rigid structures and exact timings, the secure semblance of order may conceal a lack of involvement and ownership by those involved. At the other extreme, a *laissez faire* 'happening' which may appear on the surface to be affording room for creativity and personal expression may amount to no more than an aimless and empty experience with no significant outcome. Finding an appropriate balance between these two extremes is the obvious but by no means straightforward task.

Newcomers to the teaching of English may be forgiven for being confused as they sometimes receive conflicting messages about the setting of *objectives* and how precisely and clearly these should be defined. The whole notion of objectives can seem very constraining and in direct opposition to the nature of English as an art, privileging logical modes of thought over the aesthetic. It is after all easier to be more specific about the teaching of punctuation skills than it is to describe precisely what is to be gained by reading a poem. In the standards for the award of qualified teacher status students are required to be able to identify clear objectives. It is also a criterion of teaching quality in the OFSTED framework for the assessment of schools that teachers have clear objectives for their lessons. Yet these official directives have to be reconciled with the apparently contradictory views expressed by experienced and influential writers on education that good English teachers 'often don't (quite) know what they are doing' (Creber, 1990:6) and 'When I was supervising teaching practice I told students to forget about aims and objectives and the prescribed paraphernalia. . .What I wanted to see in their files was a brief statement of intended content – a kind of *aide memoire* for themselves – plus an evaluation of the lesson afterwards.' (Jeffcoate, 1992:74).

When discussing the place and purpose of objectives in English teaching, much depends on what is meant by the term 'objectives' itself, whether it is being used in a general sense to describe the purpose of a lesson (small group discussions and feedback on. . .) or whether it refers more specifically to precise learning outcomes (pupils will be able to. . .). Frequently in the educational literature of the 1970s battle lines were drawn between those who adhered to a model of rational curriculum planning by behavioural objectives and those who felt that such an approach was too narrow and reductive. Much of the recent writing on the development of teaching skills reduces lesson planning to a simple, mechanical process (what headings to use, importance of timings, etc.). It will be argued here that in order to plan well it is necessary to have a deeper understanding of the tensions involved. In order to be able to make use of objectives in English teaching to further learning, it is necessary to have an insight into their limitations.

Most accounts of planning in the literature on teaching (whether concerned with generic teaching skills or specific subjects) distinguish between long-term planning of schemes of work and the planning of individual lessons. Frequently the advice is that a logical approach should be adopted whereby the teacher will decide on the learning objectives, choose the appropriate means which will be used to achieve those ends and devise a method for evaluating whether the objectives have been achieved.

The problem with this account is not so much that it is wrong but that it is not the whole story; the way people learn and consequently the way people plan for learning are both rather more complex than this model implies. The setting of clear outcomes even for individual chapters in books has become *de rigueur* in writing about education, particularly in books addressed to newly qualified teachers or students. The style will be familiar, 'By the end of reading this chapter you will be able to. . .' Imagine the same formula applied to a reading of *King Lear*:

By the end of reading Shakespeare's *King Lear* you should be able to

(a)   manage relationships with parents or children more productively;
(b)   understand the difference between 'man' and 'nature';
(c)   identify and use animal imagery effectively;
(d)   recognise fools by the way they speak.

The absurdity of the formula in this context is fairly self-evident. The type of learning which occurs through experience of great art is not easily expressed in discursive propositions. Of course, it may be thought that the argument is a false one, that there is a considerable difference between reading a training manual and reading a great work of art. However, much can be gained from drawing parallels with engagement in making and responding to art and learning in other contexts. At the very least, recognition of the inappropriateness of formulating objectives in this way in relation to the reading of a Shakespeare play will urge caution in applying the formula in an unthinking fashion to other contexts.

Reading a book or chapter of any kind is likely to work more effectively as a potential source of learning if it sets up associations, patterns of thought, lines of enquiry – if it engages the passions and attention of the reader in a very real, active, creative sense. The way humans learn in any rich sense is rather more messy and complex than the rational model implies. The setting of clear outcomes or objectives has an orderly, clinical appeal but the reality is rarely that simple.

It is not uncommon for newcomers to the teaching of English to find it more natural to specify *tasks* rather than learning objectives. For example, it is often easier to describe the purpose of a lesson as being the reading and study of a particular poem than to offer any more specific information about the intended learning outcomes. This arises not necessarily from lazy or imprecise thinking but from an intuitive recognition that in any teaching encounter several different levels of learning may be taking place at once. A lesson which has as its purpose the reading and understanding of a poem is likely to have a variety of *implicit* intended outcomes such as: expressing a personal response to the poem; recognising stylistic and poetic devices; describing the content or theme of the poem; learning the meaning of unfamiliar words. Identifying just one or two objectives may serve to exclude others in the teaching process: one can easily imagine a teacher trying to teach 'similes and metaphors' in a single-minded way which destroys any interest in language or poetry. The specification of precise learning outcomes (e.g. identifying different sonnet structures) may neglect important questions of value (developing a love of poetry). How one teaches (the means) is likely to have a very significant effect on what children learn.

This may be illustrated by a concrete example. Imagine the passage from *David Copperfield* on p.17 being used to teach a class to identify nouns or to vary sentence structure by the use of commas, colons and semi-colons. In both cases, the potential for engaging personally with a vivid and evocative piece of writing could easily be circumscribed by the narrowness of the focus. Being very precise about what one is trying to teach in an English lesson is not just a pedagogical question but relates to wider theoretical issues. How, for example, does one reconcile the narrow model with post-structuralist writing (including reader-response theory) which places emphasis on the active role of the reader in the creation of meaning? The argument can be extended to the very language used to describe objectives because there is an implicit assumption that the meaning will be clear and transparent, rather than ambiguous.

Very often the language used in the current National Curriculum to describe the purpose of an English lesson is couched in terms other than 'teaching' and 'learning'. Pupils are expected to 'explore', 'consider', 'understand', 'examine' rather than 'learn' and the teacher's role is often to 'introduce', 'encourage', and 'provide opportunities for' rather than 'teach'. This is true of the programmes of study at Key Stages 3 and 4, in which pupils should be given opportunities to:

- talk for a range of purposes;
- participate in a wide range of drama activities;
- consider significant features of their own and others' performance;
- read a wide variety of literature;
- talk and write about a range of reading;
- read factual and informative texts;
- write for specific readers;
- analyse their own writing;

and pupils should be encouraged to:

- listen attentively;
- structure their talk clearly;

- make contributions that clarify and synthesise others' ideas;
- read more demanding texts;
- respond, both imaginatively and intellectually, to what they read;
- be confident in the use of formal and informal standard English;
- consider apt and imaginative choices of vocabulary.

It would be a mistake to make too much of the choice of words here; the intention might have been simply to avoid too much repetition rather than to convey an underlying philosophy of English. It is significant however that what might be termed 'soft' objectives listed above embody a 'language in use' philosophy of English teaching (some writers would deny that many of them are objectives because they do not specify learning outcomes). There is a compelling argument that if language develops primarily by its active use in meaningful contexts, there is less call for specific teaching or instruction but more emphasis on providing appropriate tasks and contexts for language use. If, however, as argued in the introduction, a pure 'language in use' approach is not tenable, this does have implications for planning.

All teachers will be familiar with the fact that even when learning objectives are specified in advance of a lesson, outcomes are often different from those intended. Actively involving pupils in the lesson may serve to change its direction. Moreover, individual pupils may bring their own meanings and understanding to what is going on. Alternative outcomes may be the sign of effective rather than ineffective teaching. If we agree with Curtis (1993:33) that the teacher 'needs to encourage her students to play their full part in shaping the English curriculum' then a rigid objectives model is unlikely to allow that to happen. Many of the insights into pupils' learning in the last hundred years through the work of such writers as Dewey, Vygotsky and Bruner have stressed the importance of pupils' taking ownership, being actively engaged in the learning process and the formation of ideas. It is possible, then, to summarise why the setting of clear learning objectives in English can be problematic:

- learning outcomes sometimes differ for individual pupils;
- learning in English is not easily separated into discrete units;
- pupils must be actively involved in the creation of meaning;
- the learner is often involved in determining the learning outcome;
- setting predetermined learning outcomes may run the risk of setting unhelpful limitations;
- language is more ambiguous than an objectives model implies;
- the separation of means from ends is not always desirable.

The problems with objectives is that they are precisely that, 'objective', and may be employed in such a way that they do not acknowledge the importance of subjectivity in learning. However, an excessive reliance on subjectivity brings its own dangers and it is necessary to examine when and how objectives may be usefully employed in teaching English.

It was suggested above that it is not uncommon for newcomers to the teaching of English to find it more natural to specify tasks rather than learning objectives because the intended learning is implicit in the task. However, there may be a fine line between what is implicit and what is in fact non-existent. Unless objectives actually influence the way a lesson is structured and taught, they are of little value and often 'implicit' objectives are of that kind. Quite often lessons which are based simply on the specification of tasks lack sufficient direction and focus. This can be illustrated by reference to the following extract from *David Copperfield*.

> Looking back, as I was saying, into the blank of my infancy, the first objects I can remember as standing out by themselves from a confusion of things are my mother and Peggotty. What else do I remember? Let me see.
>
> There comes out of the cloud, our house – not new to me, but quite familiar, in its earliest remembrance. On the ground-floor is Peggoty's kitchen, opening into the back yard; with a pigeon-house on a pole, in the centre, without any pigeons in it; a great dog-kennel in a corner, without any dog; and a quantity of fowls that look terribly tall to me, walking about, in a menacing and ferocious manner. There is one cock who gets upon a post to crow, and seems to take particular notice of me as I look at him through the kitchen-window, who makes me shiver, he is so fierce. Of the geese outside the side-gate who come waddling after me with their long necks stretched out when I go that way, I dream at night: as a man environed by wild beasts might dream of lions.
>
> Here is a long passage – what an enormous perspective I make of it! – leading from Peggoty's kitchen to the front-door. A dark store-room opens out if it, and that is a place to be run past at night; for I don't know what may be among those tubs and jars and old tea-chests, when there is nobody in there with a dimly-burning light, letting a mouldy air come out at the door, in which there is the smell of soap, pickles, pepper, candles, and coffee, all at one whiff.

Imagine a simply structured lesson based on this text. Having read the extract, the teacher leads a whole-class discussion/question and answer session which ranges over the writer's feelings, the meanings of particular words, the clues which tell us that the scene is set in the past, the wider context of the story, and the interpretation of the information. The class are then given the task of writing about their own earliest memories. The problem here is that the oral work on the extract, whatever intrinsic value it may have had, has not been sufficiently linked with the writing task. An even more disjointed lesson might proceed as follows: reading of extract; pupils identify aspects of the content and style which tell us that this was written in the past; pupils asked to write about a time when they were afraid. In both cases the task was to read the extract and do some writing of their own but the lack of focus could be attributed to an absence of clear objectives.

Another approach after reading the extract might be to ask the class to recall their early memories of childhood so that they have ideas to use in their writing. Pupils tend to enjoy this kind of sharing of experience and again there is nothing intrinsically wrong with the task. However the Dickens extract has become somewhat redundant except as a very mild (and somewhat inappropriate) stimulus. For this particular activity, a contemporary extract or even just a brainstorm of ideas would serve the purpose better.

The choice of appropriate objectives would of course depend on the particular class and the overall context of the scheme of work. The extract could be used as a 'way in' to the novel (in which case speculation on who the characters are and what might happen would be appropriate), as a way of examining the way language is used to convey feeling and mood (analysis of the words which have negative connotations) or to explore style and sentence structure. As a preparation for pupils' own writing, analysis of the writer's techniques and in particular the way he uses size to evoke childhood memories of the past could be the focus. Specification of objectives will give focus to the lesson without necessarily narrowing the teaching approach and excluding the children's personal experiences. Depending on their age and experience, pupils might be asked to:

- recall and share their very earliest memories;
- think about the way early memories are often 'blank', hazy or distorted;
- underline all the phrases in the extract associated with size and then words or phrases which convey the writer's feelings;
- think of objects (possibly from personal experience) which might frighten a young child because of their perceived size;
- share any similar experiences;
- try a similar paragraph of their own in which size is a key ingredient using the original extract as a model.

Lessons sometimes lack sufficient focus when no objectives are specified. This also happens when too many are identified, partly as a result of trying to link the plan to the National Curriculum. Many English lessons contain some element of speaking and listening, reading and writing but it is far more helpful to identify the key focus of the lesson rather than to describe all the links with the National Curriculum in a 'scatter gun' fashion.

To summarise then: the fact that the specification of objectives in English is a complex process does not mean that they have no value at all. Without objectives, lessons may have insufficient focus and clarity; unless pupils know what the purpose of a lesson is the whole enterprise may be bewildering to them. Merely describing tasks may not give enough direction to the teaching. It is not uncommon for beginning teachers to feel uncertainty about what they are trying to achieve and for the lesson to lose direction or lack coherence. On the other hand not all lessons lend themselves to the specification of clear learning outcomes and flexibility needs to be adopted in the planning process. Learning objectives are more likely to be employed positively in English if the following considerations are kept in mind:

- all lessons must have a purpose which is clearly identified;
- lessons take different forms and have different purposes (introductory lessons, continuation lessons);
- some lessons require 'soft' objectives and others require more specific learning outcomes;
- the scheme of work will be a key element in giving a broad framework of aims and ensuring balance;
- the specification of precise objectives will not necessarily restrict the teaching and learning if the broader aims of the scheme of work are borne in mind;
- specification of too many objectives may prevent a sufficiently sharp focus;
- evaluation of outcomes to monitor coverage after the completion of lessons and schemes of work will preserve flexibility.

The National Curriculum does not dictate how the teaching of English should be organised and structured, nor does it specify, except implicitly, particular teaching methods. It may be something of a relief to teachers that the degree of centralisation does not extend to the specification of pedagogy except in as much as the National Curriculum for English requires that certain approaches in the classroom, such as the use of group work, cannot be avoided. Although the National Curriculum specifies skills and content, it could be argued that the truly significant aspects of education are determined by teaching methodology; means and ends are not contingent in the context of teaching. It is possible to fulfil the requirements of the National Curriculum and to produce an arid, uninspiring, disparate, course.

There are a number of broad approaches to the teaching of English, each of which has its disadvantages and dangers. These days departments are likely to plan their schemes of work using a mixture of the methods which will be described in this section rather than by focusing on one approach alone. It is however useful to consider the advantages and disadvantages of the different ways of organising the teaching in order to be aware of the dangers and drawbacks of each one. They can be very loosely identified with particular eras and ideologies but the degree to which a historical or theoretical interpretation can be imposed on the different models should not be exaggerated.

The traditional approach to teaching English dominant in most schools up to the mid 1960s was one which divided the subject into *discrete* lessons and activities: Mondays would be comprehension, Tuesday the class reader, Wednesday composition and so on. The approach had the advantage of offering a comforting predictability and a degree of flexibility which could allow an imaginative teacher to exploit serendipitous opportunities which presented themselves. This type of structure tended to coincide with a narrow approach to the subject, focusing on comprehensions, compositions and class debates rather than a wider range of reading, writing and oral activities. There is nothing endemic to this way of working which makes it narrow; a balanced curriculum is possible provided the range of activities is wide enough. Such an approach, however, fragmented the subject and offered few opportunities for integrating the language modes of speaking, reading, and writing.

This was precisely the advantage of a *thematic* approach which came to the fore in the late 1960s and early 1970s and is still prevalent. Pupils saw themselves not so much as developing skills in English as studying particular topics, like the family, life in the city or crime. Personal growth was a strong underpinning aim and a 'language in use' conception of language development tended to prevail. The approach has the laudable aim of giving unity and meaning to the pupils' experiences but runs the risk of circumscribing the meaning of literature by using it in the service of a theme. An exclusively thematic approach leaves little room for the teaching of specific language skills. On the surface this seems to be the most pupil-centred method of English teaching but in fact it runs the risk of robbing pupils of any opportunities for genuinely free and open responses to literature. It can offer a spurious kind of integration because the content of every lesson is related to a theme but that integration may not be at a very deep level.

Text-centred approaches to English meant that the central play or novel being studied became the focal point for all the related language as well as literature work. This way of teaching had been popular for some time but perhaps it gained ground with the advent of 16+ and GCSE which endorsed creative responses to literature as being suitable methods of assessment. There was a burgeoning of published support texts with ideas for 'things to do with literature'. At its worst English started to look like maths with pie charts, time lines, graphs of emotions. There were times when it felt as if pupils could not read a book without having to draw 'wanted' posters or write journals and diaries in role. The advantage of the approach was that the varied activities related to the text helped to ensure that pupils of all abilities in the class were able to understand and respond to its content and themes.

While thematic and text-centred approaches are commonly referred to in the literature on English teaching, the concept of a *project-based* approach is less well established but it is being used here to refer to specific work on language or other extended work which is not related to a single theme. After the publication of the Kingman Report there was an increased emphasis on broad knowledge about language which will be described in Chapter 9. This gave way to the development of more units of work specifically related to language, focusing on language change, accent, dialect, etc.

Few departments are likely to structure their English teaching around *skills* because one would simply not be fulfilling the programmes of study in the National Curriculum. However it does raise the question whether the teaching of specific skills should arise in context or be the subject of a systematic programme. Some course books are structured not around themes or literature extracts but according to the types of writing which are being taught and practised; for example, descriptive, factual, argumentative. Spelling, which would in a pure 'language in use' approach be taught entirely in context, is increasingly receiving particular attention in schools as a specific unit of work (see Chapter 10).

The different approaches are summarised in Figure 2.1. It should be emphasised that the disadvantages apply if any one approach is used exclusively. Possible related theoretical positions are suggested but they are not definitive and other connections could just as easily be described. As suggested, any department is likely to use a mixture of approaches but the advantages and disadvantages of each illustrates the tensions involved in broad planning. It is possible to guarantee coverage by planning in a highly systematic way but the engagement of subjectivity which is essential to rich learning is more likely to take place with a less rigid approach.

Schemes of work are often seen merely as organising devices, as collections of resources and ideas as opposed to lesson plans which deal with educational purposes and the structuring of learning experiences. This is unfortunate because thinking about the aims of a unit of work is important not only to give it direction, breadth and balance but to retain a sense of broad purpose and values which underpin every lesson plan. After all, learning in English is more likely to accrue over a period of time than in a single lesson. Much of the literature on planning stresses the need to give much thought to the shape and structure of a lesson without acknowledging that it is important to give the same level and type of attention to planning a scheme of work. The importance of structuring schemes of work will also be considered in Chapter 10 in the context of a discussion on differentiation.

We have reserved the term 'aims' for use with schemes of work and 'objectives' for specific lessons. This is an arbitrary decision. Trying to distinguish 'aims' from 'objectives' (a common pursuit of the rational planning literature of the 1970s) in some essentialist way is fairly pointless. The important issue is that schemes of work and lesson plans need to have specific purposes, whatever terms are used.

All English departments will have syllabuses for English, although these will vary in the degree of detail they contain and the amount of flexibility given to individual teachers to decide the content of lessons. They are likely to be structured around themes, texts or projects as described earlier and are likely to specify the type of

Approach	Advantages	Disadvantages	Related theoretical underpinning
Discrete	allows teaching to be spontaneous; flexibility;	offers fragmented experiences; language modes not integrated;	cultural heritage; new criticism;
Text at centre	active approaches to text and reading; ensures under-standing of texts; integrates language and literature;	may exclude specific work on language;	reader response;
Thematic	emphasis on meaning; integrates language modes;	concentration on extracts; meaning of literature circumscribed; distinct nature of English as a subject easily lost; focus may be on content rather than language;	personal growth; language in use;
Project-based	systematic; learning focus is clear;	context may lack meaning;	adult needs;
Skills-based	systematic; inclusive; objectives clear.	may exclude sufficient use of language in context.	adult needs;

Figure 2.1

speaking and listening, reading and writing activities which need to be set in order to ensure coverage and balance over a year. No matter how much detail is prescribed by a department syllabus, the individual teacher needs to translate the prescribed content into a scheme of work which has a structure, content, tasks and inbuilt flexibility appropriate to the class for which it is designed.

When planning schemes of work it is often easier to think initially at the level of resources and tasks rather than aims, despite the rhetoric of advocates of the rational planning model. Teachers are more likely to approach the initial stages of planning by choosing activities which will 'go down well' or which will 'work'. These terms can be seen as shorthand ways of recognising that the material and activities must engage the pupils and there is no reason to feel apologetic for thinking in those terms. The subsequent establishment of aims, assessment tasks, coverage of the National Curriculum, etc. serve to provide the necessary external structures and systems which are equally important. The following example will illustrate how the initial ideas need to be shaped and developed. A brainstorm on a topic entitled 'autobiographies' might generate the thoughts in Figure 2.2.

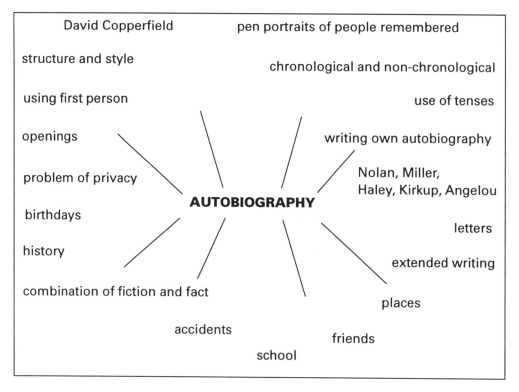

Figure 2.2

The brainstorm is presented here in a deliberately random fashion to illustrate the degree to which thinking about tasks and possible reading material may also be accompanied by anticipation of possible difficulties (pupils might see the writing of their own autobiography as an intrusion into their privacy), associated material/topics (autobiographies as insight into history), specific aspects of language (tenses, first person) and ways of deepening the topic (Dickens' view that autobiography is always a combination of fiction and fact). Attention is also given to ways of providing a central focus; for example, a piece of extended writing, a possible series of letters. The activities range from the very accessible (drawing on personal experience by remembering details of their own life) to the reading of fairly challenging material and grappling with demanding concepts. This suggests a structure which will move pupils from the subjective and personal to the objective, giving form and expression to personal thoughts, feelings and ideas through reading other examples.

It is easy to see how the scheme of work can be justified in relation to the National Curriculum but it is also possible to see how checking against the programmes of study might also inform and extend the type of work undertaken. The initial brainstorm has less emphasis on speaking and listening activities and, depending on the broad balance of the curriculum, the teacher might choose to include drama activities related to some of the reading.

If the extended task will be to write an autobiography (perhaps allowing the pupils to use an invented character as author if they choose) the preliminary work could aim to give pupils insight into the techniques writers use to structure and present personal experience. Another focus might be to understand the difference between fact and fiction and how these boundaries can sometimes be blurred. The scheme could start to take shape in the following sequence:

1. pupils make notes on early childhood memories (favourite toy, accidents, first day at school, arguments, special place);
2. creation of a time line presenting life as a journey;
3. reading of *David Copperfield* extracts, analysis and writing based on model;
4. sharing of childhood fears, times when felt excluded, times when adult world not understood;
5. reading a variety of extracts from published autobiographies which evoke these themes;
6. tableau and dramatic presentations designed to extend understanding of themes;
7. reading vivid portraits of people from the work of Dylan Thomas, James Kirkup, Laurie Lee, with analysis of stylistic devices;
8. remembering people from the past and capturing them in words;
9. reading of opening of Arthur Miller's *Timebends* (use of present tense, first person, child's perspective);
10. examination of other openings – analyse and list devices – use of third person, direct speech, flashback, child's viewpoint;
11. reading of extracts from autobiographies which give insight into socio-historical context;
12. drafting of own autobiography using devices studied.

The scheme of work can only be properly planned in the specific context in which it will be taught and will depend on such factors as the achievement/range of levels in the class, the likely interests of the group, previous work completed. Particular attention needs to be given to the way the topic or text will be introduced and a useful pattern for many schemes of work in English is to start with a fairly tight structure, allowing more flexibility and choice as the work progresses. The following questions will help bring structure to the planning of the scheme:

- what are the broad aims?
- how does the scheme relate to the pupils' prior learning?
- what is the range of attainment in the class?
- how much time is available – number and duration of lessons?
- what resources are available?
- what will be the major pupil tasks?
- what are the assessment opportunities and strategies?

The following suggested headings could be used to write up the final version of the scheme:

- Topic/title
- Aims
- Links with National Curriculum

- Resources
- Major pupil tasks
- Assessment
- Outline plan (introduction of topic, number of lessons, possible sequence which will be adapted as lessons are taught).

There are different preferred methods for setting out a *lesson plan*; the actual headings employed are less important than thinking about the dynamics of the teaching and learning context. It is clearly important to have a systematic approach to planning lessons simply to save time but it should be remembered that the written plan is not an end in itself and should support rather than distract from the teaching. The following headings are amongst those commonly recommended:

- Information about class, date, lesson time, etc.
  Apart from the need to keep plans organised, the information here may be a useful reminder to the beginning teacher, e.g. is the lesson the right one for a Friday afternoon?
- Purpose/main objective(s)
  This heading may seem somewhat clumsy but it is intended as a reminder that whereas some lessons require focused objectives (in the sense of learning outcomes), others do not.
- Resources
  It is a matter for individuals to decide whether a reminder of this kind is necessary but in the early days of planning it is easy to forget some vital item needed for the lesson.
- Special considerations
  A catch-all heading of this kind can be useful to make notes about special needs pupils, differentiation, room changes, reminders about homework, etc.
- Development of lesson
  In the early stages of teaching it is highly advisable to include rough estimates of timings for each stage of the lesson. Some writers like to distinguish between teacher and pupil activities. Whatever the approach taken, the stages of the lesson should be identified clearly.
- Evaluation
  Reflection on the degree to which the lesson has been successful or not is a useful way of improving practice. A systematic record of what has been achieved in the lesson is also a way of preserving flexibility and avoids the obsessive need to fulfil intentions every lesson which can make for poor teaching

Training courses and schools will have different policies and preferences as will individual teachers; there is no correct way of setting out a plan. In these days of accountability and external scrutiny lessons plans are not just aids to teaching but they are also ways of demonstrating competence and proving compliance with standards. Other headings (differentiation, assessment, homework, special needs) could also be included but it is wise not to make the plan too cluttered. The intention here is to stimulate thinking about the process rather than to argue for one particular approach.

This chapter will end with a critical discussion of two lesson plans (Figures 2.3 and 2.4) as a way of examining some of the general observations in more specific contexts.

LESSON A

Class: Year 9 mixed ability

Objectives: to read the short story 'The Mysteries of the Heart' by Nigel Hinton
to complete a written task in response to the story

Resources: copies of short story
rough paper for drafts
exercise books

Special considerations: John and Paul very poor readers.
Write extract on board before start of lesson.

Pupil Tasks: Class discussion
Letter in role from one character in the story to another

Lesson Development
Introduction: Extract from story written on the board to engage their interest:
Ask pupils to guess what is in box; what is the story likely to be about?
Pupils write a brief note in rough on their ideas, share with partner and then some sharing with the whole class. (10 mins)
Read story (15 mins)
Class discussion of central ideas and themes. (5 mins)
Pupil task: to chose a character from the story and write a letter in role as that character to someone else. Pupils may invent characters if they wish, e.g. a friend or relative. Rough drafts to be completed first. (15 mins)
Conclusion: Volunteers to read out letters or beginnings of letters. (5 mins)

Relationship to National Curriculum: ATs 1, 2 and 3.

Evaluation: The pupils seemed to enjoy the initial task of trying to guess what was going on in the extract and the activity did create interest in knowing what the story was about. I was disappointed with the class discussion which did not seem to get anywhere. They did say they liked the story which was encouraging and they settled down to the written work quite well.

Figure 2.3

The plan for Lesson A has a clear structure and the teacher has thought of a simple, controlled method of introducing the story and trying to capture the interest of the class. The use of approximate timings is a helpful guide. However, there are three related ways in which the plan could be given more focus: by defining objectives more clearly, by making the relationship to the National Curriculum more precise and by planning in more detail what is meant by 'class discussion'. The latter mistake is not uncommon amongst beginning teachers because to plan a discussion in advance can seem very mechanistic and inflexible. However, without some sense of purpose and direction it is easy to flounder and ask vague questions ('what did you think of it?') or ones which are not sufficiently challenging ('what did he find in the box?'). Linking more closely with the programmes of study for reading, an appropriate objective for this particular story might have been either 'to reflect on the motivation and behaviour of characters' or 'to examine the narrative structure'. The story is not written very densely and a focus on language and style would have been less relevant. A more precise objective might have informed the planning of the discussion in more detail; for example, requiring pupils to think about why the mother chose not to tell her son about the identity of his real father (one of the themes of the story). The pupils could then have been given clearer criteria for the written work requirements and the lesson evaluation could have focused on the pupils' fulfilment of the objectives. The fact that two pupils have difficulties with reading is identified in the plan but there is no indication of what the practical consequences are for this lesson.

LESSON B

Class: Year 9 top set

Objectives: to consider how texts are changed when adapted to different media
to assess AT1
to establish working groups
to extend pupils' understanding of drama in performance
to further understanding of *Romeo and Juliet* Act 3, scene 1

Continuity with previous work: Pupils know the plot of the play and are familiar with Act 3, scene 1.

Resources: Copies of *Romeo and Juliet*
Video and play back machine

Lesson Content

Introduction: brief recap of plot of scene establishing that Mercutio was killed by Tybalt (under Romeo's arm) and Romeo took revenge by killing Tybalt.
Divide class into groups of four or five.
Reread the first 33 lines of the scene and give groups five minutes to work out how they would film the introduction to the scene. Prompt questions: where would they set the scene? what actions might accompany the lines? how would they establish that it is a hot day?
Show class the relevant section based on the opening 33 lines from the Zeffirelli film and compare with their versions.
Ask class to continue working in groups deciding how the scene might be filmed (up to death of Tybalt) with a view to giving a brief oral presentation on their ideas at the end of the lesson.
Presentations.
Conclusion: show class entire scene from film and inform them that next lesson the Zeffirelli version will be compared to the Luhrmann film which has a modern setting.

Figure 2.4

The structure of Lesson B is well conceived because it seeks to generate ideas for the subsequent group work by showing an initial extract from the relevant film. The objectives however are more complex than necessary. Assessing pupils may be a purpose of the lesson (although it does not seem to appear in the rest of the plan) but it does not in itself count as a learning outcome. Considering 'how texts are changed when adapted to different media' seems less appropriate than 'understanding of drama in performance' because the focus of the lesson as presented in the plan is more on interpretation than change. Establishing working groups is part of the methodology rather than an objective. What the plan seems to lack is clear guidance for the pupils on how they are to record and present the results of their discussion, which might be in the form of a story board, director's notes added to the text or their own summaries. The plan attempts to cram a great deal into one lesson. 'Brief oral presentation' is vague and giving the pupils more time would also allow the teacher to give them more direction.

Planning lessons and schemes of work, like so many aspects of teaching English, is not a simple mechanical process but requires sensitivity to contexts, an understanding of one's own preferred ways of working as a teacher and a capacity to reflect on and learn from previous experiences. Above all, as the above discussion illustrates, the plans need to be examined critically in relation to what will happen in the classroom.

FURTHER READING

General advice on lesson planning (not just in English) can be found in Capel, Leask and Turner (1995) *Learning to Teach in the Secondary School* and Kyriacou (1991) *Essential Teaching Skills*. Readers interested in pursuing the earlier, more theoretical discussion of objectives and rational planning might consult Stenhouse (1975) *An Introduction to Curriculum Research and Development* and Sockett (1976) *Designing the Curriculum*. Accessible books on learning include Entwistle (1987) *Understanding Classroom Learning* and Claxton (1984) *Live and Learn*. The latter is particularly interesting on the notion of personal and implicit theories. Donaldson (1978) *Children's Minds* is an extremely important publication on language and learning.

RESOURCES

The theme of autobiography is rich in possibilities. Relevant units of work can be found in *From Telling to Selling* (Mathews and Parker), Stanley Thornes, which includes extracts from Fisk, Angelou, Gorky and Olaudeah Equiano (his autobiography, published in 1791, describes the author's experiences as a slave). *Network English for GCSE* (Marigold *et al.*), John Murray, also has a unit on autobiography. Teaching a theme of this kind can be deepened by reading Abbs (1974) *Autobiography in Education*.

3: Writing and Responding

How can I know what I think until I see what I write.

E. M. Forster, *Aspects of the Novel*

The process of writing as undertaken by pupils in schools is the focus of a number of important characteristics, which must at least be acknowledged by teachers – especially English teachers – if effective teaching and learning is to take place. These sometimes contradictory insights could be summarised as follows:

- Writing is often the most painfully and formally *learned* of the three areas of English (misleadingly termed) 'attainment targets' in the National Curriculum.
- At the same time, as E. M. Forster's observation intimates, writing is perhaps the most important and reflective tool of all learning.
- Writing is the most obviously visible aspect of a pupil's learning, which is presumably why it has such central importance in virtually all examinations of attainment.
- Writing is a powerful means of self and social expression, potentially communicating to an increasingly wide audience through formal or informal publication, easy and quick copying, and information and communication technology.
- Writing is an important controlling mechanism, a means of achieving orderly discipline, in many lessons.
- Perhaps because of this, across the curriculum pupils undergo a huge quantity of directed writing for a large proportion of their time in schools.
- Much of this writing has no particular or specified readership in mind, apart from the teacher or the pupil him/herself, and in practice not always even these audiences.
- Compared to the volume of writing completed during school years, most adults write little, and then mostly short, informal pieces.
- Perhaps for a combination of some or all of these reasons, writing is not generally liked by most pupils in secondary schools.

Much of this may read as quite an indictment of the practice of writing in secondary schools, although some of the observations are positive in nature. The list as a whole will inform this discussion on the role of writing as part of the English curriculum. Writing needs to be considered in the context of other aspects of English and of teaching and learning as a whole process, and in relationship to reading on the one hand and speaking and listening on the other. It is also helpful to cast an eye at the same time on the historical conditions which have given rise to the current situation. Monaghan and Saul (1987:91) distinguish writing in schools from reading, characterising the former, potentially at least, as the more active:

However variously reading and writing have been defined, it still remains the case that reading, even when oral, is the receptive skill. . .while writing is the productive skill. The question is relevant when the question of control is considered. The curriculum is, at least in part, the formal statement of what society believes is important for students to know. Society has focused on children as readers because, historically, it has been much more interested in children as receptors than producers of the written word.

Many writers would question whether it is appropriate to view reading purely as a receptive skill but writing is without doubt a potentially liberating, active force: centrally concerned with production as opposed to reception. And yet. . .we keep coming back to this word 'potential'. The reality 'on the ground', as some of the observations on writing listed above suggest, may be quite different, and certainly not liberating. If we compare writing in education to speaking and listening, again with the historical development of the curriculum in mind, a contrasting picture emerges. Green (1993:213), while tracing the imposition of formal schooling and a curriculum based heavily on reading and writing on a centuries-old, all too often unrecognised, oral tradition of learning, shows this process to have been in part at least a means of maintaining social control. He alludes to

> the general shift from 'speech' to 'writing' as the basis of formal education, which needs to be seen as crucial to the emergence and consolidation of modern schooling. The shift went together historically with a new valuation of silence in education and, increasingly, an official emphasis on reading and writing, rather than speaking and listening.

The central tension concerning the role of writing in the classroom is inescapable: a means of control inflicted on a more or less unwilling pupil population, as against a liberating and creative means of expression. The reality of school life may serve to disguise this tension, and indeed the actual experience of most pupils most of the time may lie somewhere between the two poles. It may be instructive, given the opportunity (and it frequently is given, especially to student and beginning teachers), to shadow a group of pupils and observe just how much writing is asked of them, and the nature of the writing activities. This is not to criticise teachers and their curricula, and there is no doubt that writing takes many forms appropriate to different types of learning, as we shall see, but rather to begin to argue for a distinctive role for the English teacher in fostering effective writing.

That role has altered over the years. Writing in English has changed both in the way it has been conceptualised and taught, from a very simple to a more complex formulation and practice. In the traditional classroom, writing tended to take one form (the essay or composition) and had one intended reader (the teacher as evaluator and corrector). The emphasis was largely on a finished product and there was little relationship in practice of writing to reading or speaking and listening. As indicated in Chapter 2 on planning it is not possible to give a precise historical account of the development of English but in broad terms the increase in thematic teaching in the 1960s corresponded to a greater attention to the importance of integrating writing with other language modes. Sometimes the connection was fairly superficial but a fuller form of integration took place when writing arose very specifically from oral activities or reading (for example, writing in role as a character from a novel or using the original text as a model). More attention also started to be paid to the importance of writing for different purposes and in different forms for a variety of audiences (letters, reports, diaries, etc.). Such ideas were clearly embodied in the Bullock Report of 1975. There was also a growing emphasis on the writing process and the role of the teacher intervening on content, presentation, style and accuracy through dialogue with the pupil.

As the conception and practice developed so also did methods of categorising writing. Some authors drew attention to the importance of 'writing to learn' as well as 'learning to write'. Official reports often used the term 'secretarial' to distinguish formal aspects from content; others separated 'compositional' from 'presentational' skills. It was common in the 1970s to distinguish between 'transactional', 'expressive' and 'poetic forms'. The National Curriculum uses three categories and suggests that pupils should be encouraged to write for aesthetic and imaginative purposes, to inform others and to develop thinking. Various authors have preferred different ways of describing different types of writing and criticised others' attempts (the further reading section provides various examples). The important point here, as stated earlier in the Introduction when discussing broad categories of English, is that there is nothing intrinsically correct or wrong with any one form of categorisation. It is necessary, however, to be alert to possible limitations on practice to which different ways of thinking about writing may contribute. It may have been the category of 'creative writing' in the 1960s which encouraged some teachers to instruct pupils not to worry about aspects of punctuation and spelling on the grounds that this would somehow distract from the creative process. It is hardly helpful for pupils who are learning to write and need to acquire positive habits to receive confusing messages of this kind (experienced writers can afford to be more experimental). Distinguishing an 'aesthetic' or 'expressive' category from more functional forms makes obvious sense but may limit the manner in which certain written tasks are set. In Chapter 1 (p.9) the example from 'Badger on the Barge' illustrated how letter writing can be taught from a literary text in a way which focuses on different registers but also gives depth to the writing. When pupils are asked to use language to inform, persuade, argue, give instructions, such tasks do not need to be set in any more narrow a way than when asking them to write a short story. With functional writing sometimes the task is invented purely for the sake of the language use, like writing instructions for replacing the cover on a table tennis bat (one of the tasks on a sample SAT paper at Key Stage 3).

Despite this warning about categorisation, it is clearly helpful to distinguish different purposes for writing. It is best to start with the most positive of the listed characteristics: the ideas of writing as a reflective tool of learning, and as a powerful means of personal and social expression. In order to learn more, let us examine the insights of some accomplished writers from a range of backgrounds and periods.

The story of the genesis of Mary Shelley's *Frankenstein* is probably as well known as the novel itself – if not as popularly infamous as the central idea of the deliberate creation of human life going disastrously wrong. Mary Shelley herself, looking back some years later, recounted, in the introduction to *Frankenstein*, the events of the Byron-inspired competition to write a terrifying ghost story to while away the time beside Lake Geneva, and recalled how for several days she tried hard to 'think of a story' without success. Until one night, not sleeping,

> my imagination, unbidden, possessed and guided me, gifting the successive images that arose in my mind with a vividness far beyond the usual bounds of reverie. I saw
> ...the pale student of unhallowed arts kneeling beside the thing he had put

together. I saw the hideous phantasm of a man stretched out, and then, on the working of some powerful engine, show signs of life, and stir with an uneasy, half vital motion.

This was the image around which the novel was to crystallise, and it is possible and perhaps helpful to see in this vivid picture a metaphor for the process of writing itself. Mary Shelley was able to announce that she had 'thought of a story' – but the extract suggests that her words are ironic: the story was in a sense thinking its own medium, its writer.

Such an experience is not unusual in human creativity: musicians, artists, sportspeople and others testify to the power of the unconscious to perform brilliantly once the conditions are right and it is given space. John Fowles in *The French Lieutenant's Woman* (1969) says much the same thing, as does Ian McEwan (1989:xxv), writing about the inspiration for *The Child in Time* (1987). He relates his experience of daydreaming, when

> my thoughts were narrowed and intensified. I was haunted by the memory of a dream, of a footpath that emerges into a bend on a country road. . .A figure who is me and not me is walking. . .certain that he is about to witness something of overwhelming importance. Writing *The Child in Time*. . .was about the discovery of what that man saw.

A writer more familiar to the secondary English classroom, Nigel Hinton, visiting the school I was then teaching in, explained to an enthralled audience of fifteen year olds how he had begun professional writing. He had himself been an English teacher, and, on his disparaging dismissal of a particular class reader, had been challenged by his class to do better. That night he settled down to try just that, and by the morning his first novel, *Collision Course* (1976), had been virtually written, while he himself remained largely unconscious of what had happened. *Collision Course* remains a favourite in many English classrooms. Clearly, these experiences of writing do not suggest that the images and ideas come from nothing; Mary Shelley realised that 'invention. . .does not consist in creating out of a void, but out of chaos' and that the creative mind must allow Coleridge's 'shaping spirit of the imagination' to do its work.

But where does all this leave the English teacher and his or her perhaps reluctant youthful writers? We must be aware that the sort of writing processes outlined here may not always be appropriate to the realities of the English classroom, and that the insights of the quoted writers refer to a particular type of writing and to themselves as committed, ambitious writers. Nevertheless, despite these caveats, there is a great deal we can learn. Let us try first to summarise some of the conditions which appear to be in place for the creative process to begin and be sustained, although there are differences between the accounts and not all of these conditions apply to all of them:

- a sense of convivial, social engagement as an inspiration;
- an implied contextualising background in reading and in speaking and listening;
- the time and space for the writing process to proceed;
- the incentive of a particular occasion, which may even be competitively challenging;
- the appropriate environment to inspire ideas;
- a provisional sense of audience.

Within the limits and constraints of the classroom and the organisation of the curriculum, there is a great deal that the teacher of English can do to provide conditions which at least approximate to these areas, and we shall look more closely at some of these shortly. The overall intention must be to facilitate pupils' writing by creating the atmosphere of a purposeful workshop, perhaps borrowing on occasion from the traditional apprenticeship model; it is indeed interesting that Nigel Hinton's pupils had some expectation of their English teacher being able to write well, as this would not be as widespread as similar expectations of expertise in teachers of other expressive curricular subjects such as art, music or PE. Maybe English teachers should learn something from these models of frequently good practice: leading by example, practising what we teach.

With this firmly in mind, we may return now to Stead's triangular model of the tensions involved in poetry, which in its original form seems apposite to all forms of writing, and in our adaptation outlined in Chapter 1 (pp.4–5) particularly apt for the teaching of writing in secondary English classrooms. It may be best at this stage to express this multi-layered series of meanings, closely interrelated, in diagrammatic form – at the risk, as always with such things, of gross over-simplification (Figure 3.1).

Again, the points of the triangle must not approach each other too closely, neither must they drift too far apart. Visualising the process – and the product – in this form enables us to see more clearly the relationships between the teaching and learning of writing and the broader aspects of education, as well as showing the originally intended highly specialised focus on the nature of poetic creation. The English classroom at its most effective should be characterised by the atmosphere of a workshop, in which subjectivity is allowed to operate within the tensions of the carefully established objective setting. And arguably the most important element in this setting is the English teacher who establishes and sustains it.

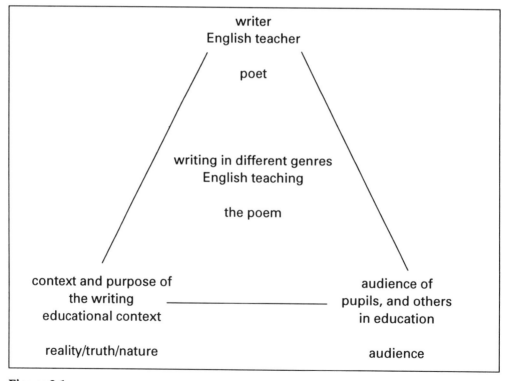

Figure 3.1

Writing, of course, takes many different forms. The curriculum for secondary English has to take this into account, but, to return to the cross-curricular nature of literacy development alluded to in our examination of the National Curriculum, it may well be the responsibility of certain other subject areas to cultivate particular types of writing appropriate to their particular purposes. This is not to excuse the English teacher of responsibility, but it may be a different kind of responsibility: one of involvement in teacher education in the context of whole-school professional development and curriculum organisation rather than attempting actually to teach everything. We need to bear in mind also another of Cox's models of English teaching, that of preparation for adult life, in order to decide precisely which types of writing need to appear in the secondary curriculum and where. It may be helpful to construct a list of types of writing practised in life generally and in school in particular; the one which follows in not intended to be definitive, and you may wish to add to it or take issue with certain parts.

- letter writing, formal or informal;
- poetry composition;
- spider and other types of diagrammatic representation;
- reminder notes: for example, in homework diaries or as lists of tasks/items;
- dialogue and playscript writing;
- assessment sheets – for self or others;
- writing as an aid to presentations: for example, flip charts and OHP slides;
- notes from texts, lectures and other sources;
- narrative, descriptive and discursive writing, including formal essays;
- analytical and empathetic writing based on literature;
- surveys and questionnaires, at all stages of the process and as both creator and respondent;
- mass media-based writing, such as newspapers, magazines and scripts;
- basic transactional writing: requests, memos, reminders, messages;
- diary and journal writing;
- writing distinctively using ICT: word processing, desk-top publishing, e-mail, etc.;
- collaborative writing in a number of possible forms.

To follow up a list such as this, try to work out – if possible with colleagues from both within and outside the English department – where you consider other curriculum areas have responsibility and where the English teacher has a distinctive role to play either as teacher or as a consultant to colleagues. It may well be that the more collaboratively this task is undertaken, the more contentious and contested it will be; certainly this has been our experience of formulating policies and practices for writing in schools. Whatever variations arise, it is often the discussion itself that is most valuable in raising consciousness of what writing is all about, and, where appropriate, challenging its often habitual operation in schools. The English teacher will inevitably wish to safeguard the value of writing in learning and its potential for productive enjoyment; for example, it may be necessary to argue against the all too common practice of using writing as a form of punishment in detention or otherwise, lest the art of writing itself be brought into disrepute. In seeking a guide for what sort of writing should characterise English lessons as distinctive, Kress (1995:90) offers a useful starting point:

In a view of English as central in the making of a culture of innovation the production of subjectivity is at the centre, between social and cultural possibilities and forces on the one hand – available resources, structures of power – and the individual's action in the making of signs on the other. . .[the child's] interest in the making of signs may range from dispositions called 'conformity' to those called 'resistance'. . .Whether in solidarity or subversion, the child's own production of her representational resources is intimately connected, in a relation of reciprocity, with her production of her subjectivity.

The detail, clearly, is a matter for English teachers' judgement, in the context of whole-school policy and practice. However, Kress's phrase 'production of subjectivity' implies forms of writing which set out to achieve precisely that: the expressive, poetic, formative, evaluative, argumentative and imaginatively responsive.

We need now to consider the creation of the appropriate classroom conditions for such writing expertise to develop. Some or all of the following may be in evidence in the teaching of English based on these principles:

- English lessons where it is possible for pupils to take some genuine responsibility for their writing, with different resources designated for different types and stages of writing; for example, ICT, collaborative ventures, silent writing, research, drafting, proof reading and performance. If space allows, it may be that some of these activities could be based in specific areas within and beyond the classroom.
- A sense that, within the inevitable constraints of the curriculum, deadlines and good discipline, pupils may take negotiated responsibility for when and where writing takes place, in recognition of personal preferences.
- An atmosphere where pupils feel secure in trying out new ideas and means of expression through their writing, knowing that it is through experimentation and errors that learning and the development of a distinctive style take place.
- A purposeful attention to the details of accuracy in writing, whether undertaken collaboratively or individually, using available resources and positive, formative responses by the English teacher.
- Constructive but judicial use of drafting as a tool for the development of writing, recognising that it may not always be appropriate, and that for some pupils it may become a tedious chore.
- A sense that creativity through writing is something to be persevered with, celebrated and shared; for example, through attention to:
    completed written assignments;
    performed readings with a range of audiences;
    the English teacher modelling good practice by writing with the rest of the class;
    frequently renewed displays;
    involvement of published writers in a variety of genres.

Before moving on to consider further the sorts of stimuli which could serve to inspire good writing in such conditions, it seems timely to follow our own advice and involve one of the most successful of contemporary writers for children and young people, Anne Fine, in a plea for flexibility. In an interview for the National Association for Writers in Education (1996), she had this to say:

I think there is a little bit too much over-confidence on the part of educationists that they know the way to do it [writing]. I feel extremely distressed at the moment about watching some children being expected to draft and re-draft on the grounds, the very spurious grounds, that that is what a real writer does. That is not what this real writer did when she was young. When this real writer was young she was allowed to sit down, write it, hand it in, get a mark, and never come back to it again. And if she had been going back to it, she would have hated re-drafting it more than I can say. . .I hope this fashion for re-drafting will die out very fast because it's putting an awful lot of really bright, cheerful, happy children off English.

Of course this is but one point of view, albeit one based on successful and influential experience of writing, and there are plenty of other writers who one could use to demonstrate the opposite view: William Blake or Wilfred Owen, for example, wrote poems which improved immeasurably through their painstaking drafting. Anne Fine may have been adept at producing excellent writing at first shot; others may need more target practice and particular expectations may be counter-productive. George (1971) noted that

the teacher and the pupil enter into a true adventure in the exploration of ideas and the language necessary to express these ideas. He [*sic*] cannot do this if he is expected to produce immediate results in the shape of 'creative efforts' worthy of public inspection.

And this is precisely the point: the English teacher needs to be attuned to the specific writing needs of each individual pupil for, to return once more to Blake, 'One law for the lion and the ox is oppression.'

It is, of course, not simply a matter of creating the right conditions, along the lines described above, and then just 'letting it happen'. Indeed, perhaps the most important component of these conditions is the encouragement and stimulation offered by the English teacher in very practical terms, for what good is a 'workshop' when the participants have little idea of how to proceed? Some ideas follow, gleaned from personal experience and observation; they are intended not as 'useful tips' but as possible practical implications of the theoretical context outlined.

Consider accumulating a collection of resources for the stimulation of writing, which should be readily available to pupils. Particularly useful are:

- art postcards available from art galleries (and 'spent' calendars);
- old postcards, perhaps with messages inscribed;
- evocative music, playable, if conditions permit, in 'listening booths';
- fascinating natural objects such as pine cones, shells and curious stones;
- brief magazine articles to inspire discursive writing;
- mounted pictures, advertisements and even 'personal ads'.

The list of possible materials is endless, as are the potential uses, including unlikely combinations woven into writing and empathetic insights.

Vary the audiences for writing, making use of ready readerships such as local primary school children, interest groups within the school (for example, adult visitors or members of particular societies) or, through the use of ICT, pupils in other, perhaps contrasting, schools.

Looking back to the list of possible occasions for writing, it can be interesting to experiment with different genres:

- combining letters, journals and narrative in a particular story;
- challenging the expectations of a particular genre, such as the fairy tale or the detective story, by subverting the normal sequence of events or deliberately mixing apparently incompatible genres;
- using a particular 'class theme', ask pupils to tackle it for a range of contrasting genres, comparing the results and discussing the implications;
- using ICT as a facilitating tool, experiment with moving text around, possibly using published fiction as a model (as with so much writing in English);
- constructing 'choice' fiction where, at appropriate points, the reader must make arbitrary (using dice, for example) or reasoned choices as to where in the text to go next;
- 'cutting up' text, arbitrarily or otherwise, to discover various patterns of sequence in writing;
- trying out different possibilities with the passage of time, from the relatively conventional use of 'flashbacks' to more experimental ideas such as tracing a narrative backwards, as in Martin Amis's disturbing *Time's Arrow* (1991);
- adapting writing for media presentation, using cassette taping to accompany the book (a familiar technique to children's publishers), or writing specifically for the visual image by using storyboards;
- using whole-class or small-group collaborative writing, which could be initially inspired by games such as 'consequences' (using a fold in the paper to hide each individual's entry, except for the last word or two, before passing it around the group), or 'imagining' (for want of a better title), when the teacher, having got the whole class to close their eyes, asks, with carefully directed questions, specific pupils in turn to picture and express what happens next in a narrative sequence.

The point of all these activities is not to entertain with an attractive set of one-off lessons but to vary the inspiration, form and outcome of writing activities in an integrated scheme of work, coherently planned to involve – as most writing activities inevitably do at some point – both reading and oral dimensions also. It is often helpful to provide pupils with templates to help them when they get down to the nitty gritty of what exactly is going to go into a piece of writing: the planning stages. They might be helped to use a story planning sheet as follows:

Setting:	Where does your story take place?
Characters:	Who are your main characters?
	Why are they at a particular place?
Plot:	Where are your characters at the beginning of the story?
	What are they doing there?
	Are there any minor characters who play a part in the story?
	Who are they and what role do they play?
	What happens and why?

More detailed planning specifically on character can also sometimes help pupils get started:

- Give your character a name.
- Explain where they are in some detail, using place names, street names, etc.
- What exactly are they doing? Write down the date and day this is happening.
- What is the weather like?
- What sort of mood are they in?

- What are they thinking about?
- Write down three things they can see, smell, feel, hear.
- Write down one detail of their appearance, item of clothing, etc.
- What are they going to do next?

The English teacher must, of course, keep a clear view of what is actually being achieved through writing activities and must also ensure that each pupil cultivates different forms in the creation of meaning. The diagram in Figure 3.2, from the ill-fated original *Language in the National Curriculum Reader* (Carter 1990), may be a helpful reminder of what exactly is going on: easily forgotten as the detail and entertainment of the activity gather their own momentum.

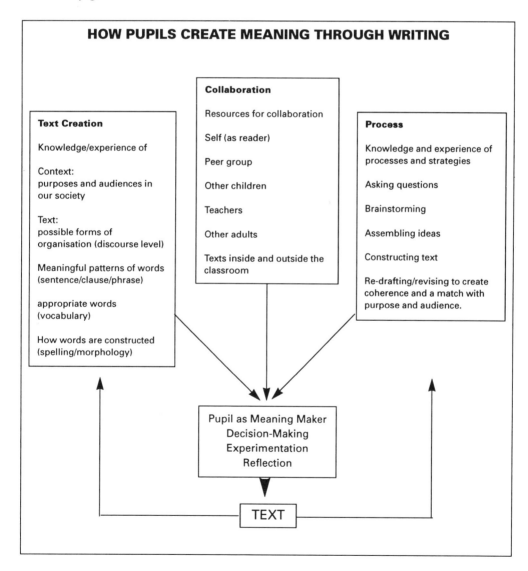

Figure 3.2

It may seem sometimes that the art of effective English teaching is a little like juggling – keeping several balls in the air simultaneously, concentrating hard on the activity while not becoming too conscious of any one ball or part of the process lest the smooth operation of the whole collapses – and the teaching of writing is no exception. In this context, a plan such as that illustrated above may be very useful, almost as a checklist, to ensure that different aspects of writing are sufficiently covered. Not every part, of course, will apply to every stage of each pupil's development or, indeed, to every facet of the teaching of writing: here, as in so much else, the English teacher's professional judgement must remain paramount.

We need now to turn to the English teacher's response to pupils' writing, both during the process and as recognition of the final product, for it is one thing to inspire writing to happen but quite another to sustain, develop and complete it. HMI, incidentally, in conducting English inspections, were keen on examining the range of pupils' completed written assignments, together with evidence of the process such as worked up notes and drafts; such good practice has frequently found its way into LEA and OFSTED inspections, and into the coursework requirements of GCSE examinations. We need to examine in particular how the English teacher may, by judicious response to pupils' writing, guarantee that good progress is made. We need to ensure that learning takes place not only through the writing (as in writing about a particular text or, in other curricular areas, about a certain scientific experiment or historical epoch), but in the quality of the writing itself. Here, surely, lies the special role of the English teacher.

Subsequent chapters on knowledge about language and teaching across the ability range will deal in more detail with the sort of metalanguage required in order to have pupils understand more clearly what exactly is going on when written text is created, and we shall examine which linguistic or semi-linguistic terms are appropriate, at different stages, to bring about a shared, common understanding of text. At this stage, though, we must look at possible approaches that are simultaneously more general, in that they refer to the broad sweep of classroom strategy, and more specific, in that they focus on the particular requirement to improve pupils' expertise in one aspect of English: writing. Again, the work of the Language in the National Curriculum Project proves useful in providing a template for the English teacher to lay against pupils' writing, in the form of a number of questions to ask either with the writer while the task is being undertaken, or as a guide for eventual marking and commenting on the finished piece (Figure 3.3).

As we have suggested, the use of a series of questions like this in the classroom must remain flexible, and there are of course adaptations and additions that could be made for specific purposes. It is worth noting here, however, the concentration on the verb as the engine of the piece of writing in the central series of questions, and this aspect of language is something to which we shall return in Chapter 9. And, of course, the nature of the verb is infinitely variable and by no means peculiar to narrative writing – although it is in this broad genre that its role is perhaps most obvious. On the practical level of operation, one particularly useful adaptation could be for use by pupils themselves, working either collaboratively or individually, in ways such as these:

A FRAMEWORK FOR LOOKING AT WRITING

What do you feel is the writer's purpose or goal? How can you tell?

How is the text structured or organised? What specific features of language show this?

What is the text about?
  e.g. people or things? individuals or groups? concrete or abstract?

What kinds of actions or processes are there?
Are verbs concerned with:

  physical actions?
  ways of behaving?
  thoughts and feelings?
  processes of communication?
  describing things – by what they are? (definition)
                    – by what they have? (attribution)

What tenses are used?

Are verbs concerned with:,

  future possibilities? (e.g. might, could, ought)
  certainties? (e.g. shall, will, must)

What is the relationship between reader and writer? How is this shown?

Does the text read as a coherent whole? What helps it hang together?
  e.g. vocabulary; references forward and back; linking of clauses and sentences.

What kind of text is this?

Figure 3.3

- The development of writing partners in the context of the classroom, helping each other with the processes. As Sawyer *et al.* (1989:234) point out, this approach can be very successful 'provided the partners are empathetic and positive in their response to each other's writing. There needs to be a sense of co-operative relationship between the partners. In the classroom it may take some time for writers to develop the constructive responsiveness necessary for the method's effectiveness'.
- Through the use of ICT (or, more traditionally, the Royal Mail), the extension of writing partnerships beyond the confines of the classroom.
- The deployment of older pupils and other adults as collaborators in the writing and responding processes.
- The encouragement of a writing journal, which is likely to be an individual (and possibly private) enterprise, and, of course, is a way in itself of extending pupils' writing repertoires.

One possible pitfall in the concentration on the form of the writing, implied by many of these guidelines for constructive response, is that the content may be neglected. The two should be inseparable, and, ideally, complement each other: certainly it is this happy union that should be aimed for in the guidance and reception of pupils' writing. One particular question posed in the LINC framework above – 'what tenses are used?' – will serve to remind us of the sort of disastrous situation which may arise if form and content are viewed discretely. Hopefully we have moved a long way since this example occurred, as recounted by the HMI Edward Wilkinson in 1966, but the warning remains apposite:

> A class had been set to write on 'My Father', and one nine-year-old boy entitled his work 'My Real Father', something to be alerted by in itself. This is what he wrote: 'My father is on the broad side and tall side. My father was a hard working man and he had a lot of money. He was not fat or thin. . .His age was about thirty years when he died, he has a good reputation, he is a married man. When he was in hospital I went to see him every Sunday afternoon. . .He likes doing woodwork, my father, for me, and he likes a little game of cards now and then; or a game of darts. He chops the wood and saws the planks and he is a handsome man but he is dead. He worked at the rubber works before he died'.
>
> On this intensely moving piece the teacher commented: 'Tenses. You keep mixing past and present'. This might be the comment of an utterly insensitive teacher, but perhaps it is the comment of an utterly committed one – or an utterly bewildered one, not knowing what he wanted to say, taking refuge in 'grammar'.

This is a timely warning indeed, with the current drive to improve 'basic' literacy, but what exactly do we do when confronted by work like this? The example shows how the process of writing can unleash all sorts of personally painful experiences and, often, fantasies in a way in which oral activities, say, may not. The English teacher is in a highly privileged position – but this privilege carries its own burden of responsibility in terms of sensitivity.

In the final analysis we can agree with Cox that pupils should be praised for writing that is vigorous, committed, honest and interesting, and assert that the proper response to writing should encourage such qualities. Different English departments have developed different marking policies, but it must surely be basic that any marking should be formative, supportive, critical in a positive sense, and unobtrusive. If we summarise the fundamental stages of the writing process to involve

- assembling strategies;
- developing the text;
- editing and proof reading;

then judicious intervention may be appropriate at any one of them, provided the teacher remains true to the principle that pupils should be able to maintain ultimate control over their own writing.

FURTHER READING

Publications by Styles (ed.) (1989) *Collaboration and Writing* and Arnold (1991) *Writing Development* are especially useful for teachers anxious to ensure pupils' progress in writing without hampering spontaneity. Also helpful are Harrison (1983) *Learning through Writing* and Foggin (1992) *Real Writing*. Brindley (ed.) (1994) *Teaching English* contains succinct chapters on several facets of writing in the English curriculum. The English and Media Centre publishes a wide-ranging collection of articles and activities on writing entitled *The English Curriculum: Writing – Material for Discussion*. These titles are also helpful: *Writing: The Drafting Process* (Dawes 1995), *Learning About Punctuation* (Hall and Robinson 1996) and *Words and Images on the Page* (Johnson 1996), the last of which is cross-phase in its subject matter.

RESOURCES

Framework Press publish a most helpful classroom guide, with photocopiable material: *Key Stage 3 Writing: A Language Approach* (Armstrong and Goddard, 1996). For anthologies of young people's original writing try *The Voice Inside* (eds Allard *et al.*, 1994) published by Hackney Education and Leisure, with an accompanying guide. Musical and artistic resources are particularly useful, and many art galleries, including the Tate, the National and the National Portrait offer educational services for visits.

4: Assessment

The new system of weights and measures will be a stumbling block
and the source of difficulties for several generations. . .
It's just tormenting the people with trivia.

Napoleon, Mémoires

Readers who have worked their way through this book systematically will already be familiar with a number of themes and polarities which have emerged in the first three chapters: deep and surface learning, feeling and cognition, mechanical systems and dynamic processes, to name just a few. The likelihood however is that not everyone will have necessarily read the book in a systematic way, chapter by chapter, but will have dipped into sections as the mood has taken them or as the need has arisen. Just as people do not always read books in the logical, linear sequence that one expects them to, neither do they necessarily learn in neat, predictable stages. The system of formal assessment required by the National Curriculum is an attempt to impose an external structure of pre-determined stages on complex, dynamic, idiosyncratic learning processes and this inevitably leads to difficulties.

Another consequence of the emphasis on external systems of assessment designed for accountability is that it can distract from the more important role of assessment in informing and improving teaching and learning. It is often claimed that the different purposes for assessment should be kept in mind and reconciled in practice but this is more difficult than is often assumed. Preparation of pupils for standard tests at Key Stage 3 and external examinations at Key Stage 4 can easily distract from the need to give wide-ranging feedback to pupils to improve their general achievement in the subject. It is as if a driving instructor decides to conduct a driving lesson by waiting at a given destination to which the pupil has been told to drive. The instructor proceeds to look at the time it took, checks the vehicle for any bumps and scratches and then provides the pupils with a report which gives a simple grade and includes comments such as 'could do better', 'go a bit faster next time', or 'watch your steering'. For a teacher to use assessment effectively it is necessary to be thoroughly 'beside the wheel' and involved in the process of learning.

It is easy to get so submerged in the language of assessment (summative/formative; normative/criterion referenced; validity/reliability) that one loses any real insight into the tensions and issues at the heart of the process. Similarly, close involvement with the mechanics of assessment may distract from a real sense of educational purpose. We begin this chapter therefore not with a consideration of technicalities but with a discussion of a sample of a pupil's writing which raises a number of general issues.

This is followed by a brief description of a traditional, narrow approach to assessment in English before considering contemporary developments.

The piece was written by a fourteen-year-old pupil in response to the Wilfred Owen poem, 'Dulce et Decorum est'. As a 'way in' the class were presented with the final Latin phrase from which the poem gets its title ('it is good and noble to die for your country') and set about translating it which they did by various guesses and prompts from the teacher. The poem was read twice aloud and then, with no discussion or analysis, the class were asked to respond in writing to what they had read in any way they wished; they were given no other instructions. This is a revised version of the pupil's work:

Dulce et Decorum est

Flopping down dragging their bodies along the mud and sludge, many half starved with not enough strength to pull the trigger on the gun and half naked and trampling over bodies lying in the trenches and watching people. I heard a shout, 'Help! Help!' I looked down. Just then a plane came. We dived to the ground and as I got up I heard a cry. As the blood was pouring from him, one of the other men began to shout and become hysterical. I slapped him and when he stopped I said, 'Thank your god that that was not you lying there dead'. We began to trample on as a bomb landed nearby. We began to run but it was too late – we lost half our men. Many others had wounds. Some had arms and legs missing. As we sat there in the slum and muck waiting for help we slowly deteriorated into dead bodies. As I was the last one to survive the filth and muck even now I regret joining the army to serve my country.

and this is what the original version looked like:

flopping down draging there bodys along the mud and slut, meny harf starved and not enough strenth to pul the trigger on the gun and harf naked and trampling over bodys lying in the trenches and waching people dye and I heard a shout HELP HELP I looked down gust then a playn come we dived to the ground as I got up I heard a cry as the blud was poring from him one of the uther men began to shout and go hiserikal I slaped him one and when he stop I sed thank your god that hat was not you lying ther ded we began to trammel on as one of the men klapst as a bom landed right near him we began to run but it was to larte we lost harf our men meny others with woonds as the bodys lyed ola over sum wuth arms and legs misson as we sat there in the slum and muick wating four help as we slaoly detereated into ded bodys as is was the last one to surive the filth and muck even now I regret goyning the army to serve my contry

The piece was written many years ago and it has served well in countless in-service and training sessions since, raising questions about approaches to marking, assessment policies and how to deal with special needs pupils' among others. Reading the piece aloud draws attention to the sensitivity and effectiveness of the writing which can easily be missed by concentrating on the surface features. One of the most dramatic responses given by a teacher in one of those very early courses was a red line through the work with 'see me' at the end. Not that mere recognition of its qualities necessarily means that the writing is easy to assess in any formal sense. The achievement can be acknowledged, the piece can be corrected and published, but judging according to pre-determined criteria may mean that it has to receive a low grade, percentage or level.

The performance on this piece of work may not be representative of the pupil's overall standard because the creative effort could well have detracted from the accuracy of the writing. In order to make a proper judgement, a range of pieces would need to be considered. If the writing here is viewed as an initial draft, the judgement may need to be reserved until a final version is seen. Nor is it by any means straightforward how the piece should be corrected. Improving the spelling is reasonably uncontroversial but other matters are open to dispute. Notice in the corrected version the teacher has retained some aspects of the writing which technically are mistakes; the first sentence does not have a main clause. Paradoxically, the stylistic effectiveness of the writing is partly achieved by the limitation of the technical aspects; the absence of punctuation, the repetition of the word 'and' gives the writing a momentum and pace which would be impressive if it had been intended. The question of intention becomes relevant if the piece is used to assess reading rather than writing. There seems to be a genuine, intuitive response to the content and form of the original but whether that counts as 'understanding' is another matter; for that one might argue that an analytic, more cognitive, discursive response is needed.

In the context of a traditional, simple system whereby, for the sake of argument, every written piece was awarded a mark out of ten, a teacher would find some difficulty in knowing how to deal with this piece. At its worst a system of that kind did not give any clear indication of what the mark was for, nor any indication of the strengths and weaknesses of the work. What it did give was a sense of how the individual had performed in relation to other pupils in the class (normative assessment). It is easy to understand why pupils were so concerned to ask each other 'what did you get?' (and often admonished for doing so) because in the absence of any clear criteria to accompany the mark, the only touchstone would be their performance in relation to others in the class. Of course marks would frequently be accompanied by verbal or written comments but these were more often than not bland or predictable; a seven would qualify for a 'very good', a six for 'good' and so on.

The absence of clear criteria meant that pupils were often not significantly motivated by the assessment system to improve performance. In order to achieve a higher grade it is necessary to know what aspects of the work need improvement; if the judgements appear arbitrary then such extrinsic motivation is likely to be minimal. The lack of transparency meant that there was a corresponding lack of useful information for various interested parties: telling a parent that a pupil received a B+ is rather less helpful than telling them what the pupil is able to do and how they can improve performance. The same is true of giving marks to pupils; the emphasis was more on providing judgements than on using the assessment system to provide feedback to pupils of a formative kind.

Through the 1960s and early 1970s positive approaches to marking emerged. The hissing and spitting red pen was in many instances replaced by what was judged to be a more positive and comforting green. Not everyone went for the change of colour but many departments developed enlightened marking policies, recommending that teachers should not be obsessed with grading but should celebrate achievement, respond to content, and be selective when correcting mistakes. Such positive approaches were a considerable improvement and are still central tenets of many assessment policies but there was often a lack of detailed evidence of achievement or detailed feedback on how pupils might make progress.

The limitations of the more traditional model then indicate some of the requirements of a more enlightened system which should:

- motivate pupils;
- provide clear information for pupils, parents and other interested parties;
- provide a diagnosis of pupils' learning needs.

In the light of those demands the emergence of the national system at first looks promising. Specification of eight (or in the original version, ten) levels with specific criteria for each appears to solve the problem at a stroke. Pupils and parents know exactly what needs to be done in order to move from one level to another; the system thus provides formative feedback but also allows more formal, summative judgements to be made at specific times. The approach seems logical enough in theory, until the specific details are examined. Consider, for example, what needs to happen for a pupil to make progress from level 4 to level 5 in reading:

Reading level 4	**Reading level 5**
In responding to a range of texts, pupils show understanding of significant ideas, themes, events and characters, beginning to use inference and deduction.	Pupils show understanding of a range of texts, selecting essential points and using inference and deduction where appropriate.
They refer to the text when explaining their views.	In their responses, they identify key features, themes and characters, and select sentences, phrases and relevant information to support
They locate and use ideas and information.	their views.
	They retrieve and collate information from a range of sources.

In each of the attainment targets, the language used to distinguish one level from another is often vague and indeterminate, sometimes depending on a particular phrase. One solution for teachers is to provide examples of what counts as a particular level (the exemplification materials from SCAA serve that purpose) but this does not necessarily help the pupil for whom the system is meant to be transparent. Nor is the answer to make the statements more specific because that in turn would be a betrayal of the nature of English as a subject and a failure to recognise that language development does not take place in simple, linear fashion. The current broad level descriptors (of which examples are given above) which operate by teachers making 'best fit' judgements are a vast improvement on the original statements which were broken into strands and which led teachers into ticking endless boxes.

Despite the vagueness of the statements, another problem is that the range of attainment being described at any one level is broad. Pupils are expected to move through the levels fairly slowly (just over one a year) and using them to mark progress may prove to be demotivating. A further difficulty is that because the statements of attainment are intended to be objective, measurable indicators of what pupils have achieved, they tend to place more emphasis on surface features of performance. This was acknowledged by Cox (1991:147) in relation to pupils' writing, 'The best writing is vigorous, committed, honest and interesting. We did not include these qualities in our statements of attainment because they cannot be mapped on to levels.'

It is possible to summarise why the (apparently promising) national system of assessing pupils by levels offers only minimal help to teachers in their assessment of pupils' progress as follows:

- the language used to describe the levels does not help to differentiate them (although exemplification helps);
- the range of achievement at any one level is very broad;
- pupils' learning in English does not develop in a simple linear fashion;
- use of levels may be demotivating for pupils;
- there is a tendency for the statements to be reductive.

What the system does offer is a crude method of accountability by comparing the performance of one individual, class, school or local authority with another. In order to compare levels of achievement pupils need to be assessed in a way which produces consistent results or which is 'reliable'. Reliability has to do with the degree to which the form of assessment is likely to yield the same results if repeated on different occasions and judged by different people. A multiple choice test tends to be very reliable because its objectivity is such that it can be marked by a computer.

Imagine trying to produce a highly reliable test for speaking and listening. It would need to be capable of being replicated throughout the country and marked according to a clear scheme so that comparing results would be fair. There would be little point in asking for group discussions or conversations with an examiner (along the lines of traditional CSE and O level oral exams) because the outcomes would be too unpredictable. The closest one might come to a reliable test would be to ask all pupils to read the same passage aloud and award marks for accuracy and expression. Even so, the room for individual interpretation is vast and a considerable degree of moderation would be required.

However, the problem with the construction of the test is that in order to make it as reliable as possible it has ceased to be an appropriate or valid test of speaking and listening. As an assessment of English the test has very little validity. Reliability and validity are key concepts in understanding the tension at the heart of assessing English for they tend to pull in opposite directions. Speaking and listening is extremely difficult to assess because, even more than other aspects of English, performance varies with subject, context and level of motivation. In Barry Hines' novel *Kes* Billy Casper's ability with language seems to be transformed when he speaks about his kestrel. Poor performance in oral work is often to do with the nature of the task which has been devised, the atmosphere of the classroom and the dynamics of the group rather than the ability of the pupils; to provide a valid assessment of speaking and listening evidence needs to be drawn from a variety of situations.

Of course what is true of speaking and listening is also true of reading and writing. A valid test of reading cannot be based on a single set of questions on one passage. A portfolio of evidence with writing for different purposes on a variety of subjects, which shows evidence of process as well as product, is likely to provide a better indication of an individual's aptitude than a narrow paper and pencil test taken under examination conditions. The boycott of the English standard attainment tasks (SATs) which came to a head in the summer of 1993 was precipitated because of the highly reductive conception of the subject embodied in those tests. In order to form reasonably valid judgements of pupils' achievements in English it is necessary to consider a variety of different information drawn from different sources.

The quest for 'objective' and reliable methods of assessment driven by notions of accountability brings with it a number of dangers. So called 'teaching to the test' may not be a problem if the tests are sophisticated and wide-ranging but there may be practical difficulties in administering those that are (the original English SATs at Key Stage 3 took the form of extended projects). Many departments are coming under pressure to teach to the tests to improve league positions and meet national targets. The demand for schemes which will standardise marking has a tendency to place more emphasis on the testing of superficial knowledge with a consequent narrowing of the curriculum. Most significantly, there is danger that the emphasis on summative assessment will distract attention from the important day-to-day monitoring and feedback which is an essential part of the teacher's role.

It was always the intention of the Task Group on Assessment and Testing Report on which the original National Curriculum system of testing was based that assessment should be 'an integral part of teaching and learning' rather than a 'bolt on addition'. The statement is often quoted but the implications of what it might mean in practice need exploration. It may seem fairly obvious to say that teachers are assessing pupils' work and progress all the time but, as indicated above, opportunities for making valuable use of these judgements may be missed if there is too much emphasis on formal assessment and record keeping. Integrated, informal, formative assessment in its widest sense will take the form of advising, giving critical feedback, encouraging peer group evaluation and so on. It is important therefore to recognise that integrated assessment will inform teaching as much as it will provide information about pupils' progress. It is also necessary to recognise that the components of English, speaking and listening, reading and writing, cannot be treated identically.

Speaking develops naturally, whereas reading and writing have to be taught and learned. The extreme version of a 'language in use' approach to English arose because of a failure to distinguish sufficiently between the language modes; it was assumed that reading and writing, like speaking, would develop simply by exposure to language. A policy of providing critical feedback and setting targets is less appropriate in the context of oral work for the same reason. As for the assessment of listening, there is a strong argument that this should be conducted only in a doctor's surgery. Once it is established that people can hear, whether they listen or not will depend on what they are being told. In the National Curriculum what is called 'listening' can more appropriately be described as 'understanding'.

Phrased that bluntly, the argument seems a little crude because it appears not to recognise that speaking takes place in a range of formal as well as informal contexts. Whereas it would look cross to offer advice on how to conduct a conversation with a friend, it may be more appropriate to give formative feedback on how a pupil has delivered a speech. This will be discussed in more detail in Chapter 7. But even in more formal contexts, caution needs to be exercised. Most teachers will be familiar with pupils who have been over-coached as public speakers, who are more interested in style than content, who strive too hard for effect, who are just plain embarrassing. Interviewees who have been 'trained' by over-zealous advisers appear devoid of personality and detached from themselves. It is no surprise that we refer to such people as appearing 'unnatural'. The suggestion in the National Curriculum that pupils should be 'taught to use gesture and intonation' should be treated with considerable circumspection. Unless pupils are waving their arms around like demented seals it is probably safer to leave well alone. Practice, confidence, familiarity and understanding of content will all in time improve performance.

The problem of knowing when it is appropriate to provide formative feedback is illustrated by an example quoted in the Kingman Report. The Committee describes an oral lesson on the theme of smoking with eleven year olds which involved the pupils giving presentations based on group discussions to the rest of the class who were asked to comment on, 'How clear the summary was, whether the speaker kept repeating the same structure or vocabulary, whether the speaker made the discussion appear interesting' and so on. The lesson is intended to be an example of good practice, but the Report makes the rather revealing comment, 'This teacher was aware that some members of the class found the format. . .too stressful.' The point here is not just that teachers should be aware of pupils' sensitivities; it is a more practical one to do with what is effective teaching. Faced with criticism of how they speak, the more confident tend to get defensive, and less secure people become confirmed in their self-image as being inarticulate.

The lesson described above on the theme of smoking could have been set up as a drama on the creation of a television programme called 'No Smoking'. The actual role can afford: some protection ('you may feel nervous if this is your first time in front of the camera'), the legitimisation of direction and comments, the chance to practise ('let's have a run through before filming'), the potential for a richer context (for if it is to work as drama an extra ingredient of dramatic tension would have to be introduced), the opportunity and invitation for teachers to adopt different registers and above all the chance to speak directly about the language being used without feeling personally threatened (Fleming 1989:4). Drama, because it works in fictitious contexts, is the ideal medium to allow self-conscious adolescents the protection to experiment with speaking; it is arguably the only way of 'teaching' standard English.

Planning rich contexts for talk will have more effect on pupils' confidence and performance than assessing and giving feedback. That does not mean that there will not be times when specific instruction and evaluation by peer group, self or teacher are required (for example, how to structure a talk, making use of notes, techniques for conducting an interview), but these should be thought through carefully.

Writing, however, is a different matter because it relies for its development partly on the quality of formative assessment and feedback which pupils receive. It is a very salutary experience to ask a group of English teachers to discuss what advice they would give to pupils about a particular piece of writing. More often than not agreement only extends to matters of punctuation and spelling (even paragraphing can be controversial). Advice on content, style, effectiveness of opening and structure can all be matters for disagreement. That is why entering into a dialogue with pupils about their writing is a more appropriate approach that passing authoritative judgements. The National Writing Project offers a useful set of categories for responding to writing which may feature in formative feedback:

- surface features (spelling, punctuation, handwriting);
- style and structure (appropriateness of language to purpose);
- ideas and content (coherence of and reflection on facts, opinions, action, thoughts);
- writer as writer (comment on process/pupil's understanding and reflection on this);
- writer as person (response to personal content, encouragement, further personal dialogue stemming from the text).

One of the problems in assessing the 'Dulce et Decorum est' piece has to do with the way the task was set. The main criteria for evaluation were not clear in advance, nor was it obvious what the piece was intended to achieve. Although the writing as it stands is effective, the approach in setting the task which emphasised free self-expression caused problems when it came to assessment. Another difficulty is that by the time the piece was submitted for assessment it was almost too late; the teacher needed the opportunity to offer help by intervening in the process.

It was suggested above that it might be difficult to use the 'Dulce et Decorum est' piece as a formal assessment of reading. But the pupil's writing does suggest that there has been quite a significant aesthetic response to the form and content of the poem which might well have been easily articulated either orally or in more analytic writing. Assessment of understanding at a deep rather than surface level is not easy and is achieved in the classroom by the teacher being alert to signs and clues from a variety of sources. The classroom activities listed below give opportunities for assessment of reading other than simply setting written questions on a passage:

- class and group discussion
- individual conversations
- creative responses
- drawings
- active approaches to text (choosing favourite lines)
- dramatic presentations
- representing texts in different forms of media (e.g. narrative to drama; poem to newspaper article).

The following is an example of a nonsense comprehension; the task is to read the passage and answer the questions which follow.

> The blonke was maily, like all the others. Unlike the others, however, it had spiss crinet completely covering its fairney cloots concealing, just below one of them, a small wam. It was quite drumly – lennow, almost samded in fact. When yerden it did not winx, like the other blonkes or even flerk. The other blonkes, which had not been given the same nesh, were by no means leenow or samded. They winxed readily enough. The nesh was quite kexy, had a strong shawk, and was probably venenated. There was only one thing to do with it – gevel in the wong and gaff it in. This would be much better than to sparple it in the flosh as the blonkes that were not drumly could iswonk in the wong but not in the flosh. And in any case, it might not be wise to venenate the flosh.

> What is drumly?
> Why were the other blonkes not lennow and samded?
> In what ways was the drumly like/unlike the others?
> If nesh is venenated, is it wise to gaff it in the wong?

The syntax makes it possible to answer the questions without having very much understanding of what the passage is about. A pupil might be able to 'read' the passage out loud by sounding out the words but this would hardly count as reading in any rich sense of the term. Some of the early reading tests which were simply based on word recognition did little to assess response to meaning. That does not mean that standardised reading tests have no place or value at all as long as they are used with caution and with some insight into their limitations. More sophisticated tests than those which merely asked pupils to articulate words out loud involve pupils in answering comprehension questions, completing sentences from multiple choice alternatives or inserting missing words in a passage (cloze procedure). Such tests can be useful when screening an intake of pupils or in seeking to establish some broad diagnosis of reading ability. It is important however, as with any form of assessment, not to make too many inferences about pupils' abilities or potential on limited evidence.

To return to the 'blonkes' passage, the questions which can be easily answered need not be confined to the literal. It would not be inconceivable to write some sort of reply to the question, 'Are the main ideas in the passage put across clearly and succinctly?' The point is that it is possible to manipulate objective language and concepts at some distance from the self without real engagement or understanding. For some pupils, writing 'It says at the beginning of the play that Romeo and Juliet are a pair of star cross'd lovers' may be no different from answering questions about blonkes.

A key to having a real appreciation of the complexities of assessment is to have a rich notion of 'understanding', a consideration which is often ignored in the debate about assessment. According to Midgley (1979:18), understanding 'is relating; it is fitting things into a context.'

We can easily be deceived into thinking that someone has understood something by their use of language. If in answer to the question 'what is the capital of France?' they answer 'Paris' we might be tempted to draw conclusions which would have to be revised if in answer to 'what is the capital of Spain?' they also answered 'Paris'. Understanding, moreover, is not an 'all or nothing' affair. It can, like learning, take a deep or surface form. When a teacher asks, 'Do you understand or not?' this can be a misleading form of words. It is perhaps worth reiterating that this does not mean that all sorts of tests (even ones which are very simple and focused) do not have their place. It does mean that some caution and humility is required when exercising judgements.

The themes of objectivity and subjectivity which are continuing strands in this book are particularly relevant to assessment. A number of concepts and terms have been used in the course of this chapter and they can be very roughly grouped in the following way:

objective		subjective
summative		formative
mark schemes		feedback
formal tests	moderated	dialogue
reliability	teacher assessment	teacher assessment
grading		validity
accountability		deep
surface		

The two columns on the right and left indicate a tendency towards polarities. The whole quasi-scientific edifice of mark schemes, calculations, percentages and grades can obscure the fact that assessment invariably involves flawed human beings making personal judgements. The myth of measurement, as Broadfoot (1996:218) has described it, is that educational assessment can ever be fully objective:

> Belief in the possibility of educational measurement is part of the more general culture in which the salience of the interpersonal and of individual idiosyncrasies is excluded. By the same token it may be that as the significance of chaos theory and of

'fuzzy logic' in particular becomes increasingly influential in scientific thinking, so the inevitably 'fuzzy' character of assessment will also be both recognised and accepted.

On the other hand, the need for some form of accountability means that assessment has to be seen as a reasonably reliable process and not based purely on individual whims. The two columns are somewhat reconciled by the use of moderated teacher assessment. In this approach (exemplified until recently by the so-called 100 per cent coursework schemes at Key Stage 4) individual teachers make judgements on pupils' progress but these are constantly compared and adjusted by a process of negotiation and consideration of differences of opinion. Agreeing standards in this way allows teacher judgements to be used for other purposes, including certification and accountability. The whole process can be taken to very sophisticated levels (see Chapter 9) and the benefits are considerable in terms of teachers' own professional development.

The use of moderated teacher assessment means that summative and formative assessment coincide more readily and that records can serve the purposes both of providing feedback to pupils and more public information. The importance of formative assessment is emphasised by Black and Wiliam (1998) in a report based on an extensive survey of the research evidence on assessment. They argue very convincingly that the initiatives of the last ten years designed to raise standards have not taken sufficient account of the fact that 'learning is driven by what teachers and pupils do in the classroom'; the changes in policy with regard to National Curriculum testing, GCSE, league tables, management initiatives, target setting and school inspection do not provide enough help and support for teachers in their day-to-day work.

Their view that formative assessment is 'at the heart of effective teaching' is based on a detailed research review which suggests that there is evidence that improving formative assessment raises standards. They suggest improvement can be achieved if formative assessment is used to raise the self-esteem of pupils:

> What is needed is a culture of success, backed by a belief that all can achieve. Formative assessment can be a powerful weapon here if it is communicated in the right way. Whilst it can help all pupils, it gives particularly good results with low achievers where it concentrates on specific problems with their work, and gives them both a clear understanding of what is wrong and achievable targets for putting it right.

Black and Wiliam's report includes the following recommendations:

- *Feedback to pupils should concentrate on the qualities of the individual's work rather than fostering comparison with others.*
  This is a key factor in improving self-esteem. The research evidence suggests that if the prevailing ethos concentrates too much on extrinsic rewards pupils avoid tasks which are too difficult and constantly look for the 'right answer'. In the English classroom it is difficult to foster genuine responses to texts if there is an undue emphasis on comparison with other pupils.
- *Pupils should be trained in self-assessment.*
  Many teachers find that pupils' attempts at self-assessment are not very satisfactory, amounting often to a perfunctory statement that they should 'do

better at punctuation and spelling' or 'try harder'. The problem is that self-assessment is often treated as an added extra to the whole teaching and learning enterprise. Pupils need an awareness of what they are trying to achieve instead of receiving classroom teaching as 'an arbitrary sequence of exercises with no overarching rationale'.

- *Opportunities for pupils to express their understanding should be designed into the teaching.*

  As suggested earlier in this chapter, a wide variety of methods can be used in the classroom to evaluate pupils' progress which can then form a basis for feedback. This includes observation of tasks and activities (e.g. sequencing a poem) as well as pupils' oral and written contributions.

- *Dialogue between pupils and teacher should be thoughtful, reflective and focused.*

  A common method of assessing pupils' understanding has traditionally been through whole-class questioning by the teacher. The limitations of restricting classroom talk in English in this way was well documented in the 1970s through the work of writers like Barnes (1976) who argued for the importance of exploratory talk. The report by Black and Wiliam extends the argument by applying it to assessment. In whole-class questioning it is often only a few pupils who respond and the level of questions is frequently low. Alternative methods of assessing understanding need to be found (for example, asking pupils to jot down answers and read them aloud).

- *Tests and homework exercises must be clear and relevant to learning aims.*

  The conclusion here from the analysis of the research is that 'Feedback has been shown to improve learning when it gives each pupil specific guidance on strengths and weaknesses, preferably without any overall marks.' The use of formative assessment does not necessarily exclude the use of simple (such as spelling) tests but these are employed for very specific purposes.

Moderated teacher assessment provides an indication of the appropriate kind of recording system which might best serve teaching and learning. Time is too precious in schools to duplicate effort. This tended to happen after the first version of the National Curriculum was published. For the purpose of accountability, check lists were needed to record pupils' progress through each strand of each attainment target. These bore little relationship to the kind of day-to-day marking and feedback which was necessary within the classroom. With the revised National Curriculum, portfolios of written work which include the formative feedback given to pupils provide a more detailed record of achievement than separate marks or comments. Records of reading should include details of pupils' preferences, personal responses to plays, poems and novels, and information about their ability to analyse a wide variety of texts; again a portfolio of evidence accompanied by pupils' own self-assessment is an appropriate format. The type of proformas used by GCSE examination boards can be adapted for use at Key Stage 3 showing performance across a range of contexts. As with assessment, recording should serve teaching and learning rather than provide a distraction from it. This chapter concludes with a summary of some features of a successful assessment and recording policy for English:

- Pupils' work is assessed in a range of contexts using a variety of methods.
- The approach to pupils' work is one which recognises achievement *and* identifies

limitations in order to avoid a situation in which high achievers only receive bland praise and low achievers receive little encouragement.

- Criteria for assessment are shared with pupils to give them a sense of overall purpose and direction in their learning.
- Pupils are given specific help and guidance about their progress.
- The reporting system translates easily into reports for parents to avoid duplication of work.

FURTHER READING

For books specifically related to assessment in English see Barrs (1990) *Words Not Numbers: Assessment in English*, Johnstone (1987) *Assessing English: Helping Students to Reflect on Their Work*. Staples (1992) and Protherough and King (eds) (1995) both have a chapter on teaching and assessment. For exploration of the complexities involved in the assessment of reading, see Harrison's chapter 'The Assessment of Response to Reading: Developing a Post-Modern Perspective' in Goodwyn (1995). For broader background reading on assessment the following texts are helpful: Black (1998) *Testing: Friend or Foe? Theory and Practice of Assessment and Testing*, Broadfoot (1996) *Education, Assessment and Society*, Gipps (1994) *Beyond Testing*. Stobart and Gibbs (1990) have produced a teacher's guide with a clear explanation of the issues, including those pertaining to NVQs and GNVQs; a revised edition was published in 1997.

RESOURCES

SCAA (now QCA) have produced portfolios of pupils' work to exemplify grades with commentaries related to National Curriculum levels and criteria. Videos of oral work are also available. Examination boards produce similar materials for Key Stage 4. Sweetman writes an annual guide *Curriculum Confidential*, Courseware Publications, which summarises developments in assessment as well as other areas and is both informative and entertaining.

5: Reading

. . .Read books, repeat quotations,
Draw conclusions on the wall. . .

Bob Dylan, 'Love Minus Zero: No Limit'

Reading, traditionally the first of the three Rs, is currently the focus of hugely energetic enterprise as the central facet of the drive to improve basic literacy. Indeed, for many within and outside the world of education reading has become synonymous with literacy, and there is a good deal of semantic confusion and vagueness on this score. Whether such attention will prove energising rather than energy-draining remains to be seen, but it is against this background that we need to examine the teaching of reading within English in the secondary school. Looking back nearly fifty years, we find one of the standard guides on the teaching of English (Smith, 1954:36) offering the following advice to student teachers:

> Perhaps the most important, and certainly the most dangerous thing we attempt to do with a child in school is to try to teach him [*sic*] to read. On his ability to read, in the widest sense, will depend the ultimate success or failure of all our attempts to educate him. We cannot even proceed far with instruction until we have taught him to do something more than bark at print. Whatever our definition of an educated person might include, we could not omit the requirement that he should be able to make sense of what others write. Most would, one hopes, add the further qualification that he should also find pleasure and inspiration on the printed page.

We could pertinently ask: what has changed since 1954? Certainly some interesting, and still timely, issues arise from the passage:

- Why exactly is reading so important, and what implications does this have on its position in the secondary school?
- In what sense might the teaching of reading be dangerous?
- The use of the masculine form of the personal pronoun is, presumably, a conventional sign of the times; but is there a more significant question lurking here, to do with the question of gender and reading?
- Why does reading predicate all other learning, and, if indeed it does, what does this imply about its specific position as part of the secondary English curriculum?
- What other, perhaps less tangible, aspects of reading are there apart from the ability to 'bark at print', and how do we know if anything else significant is happening in the reading process?

- 'To make sense of what others write' sounds pretty uncontroversial, but one person's (pupil's?) sense may be another's (the teacher's?) nonsense: how far should we give free rein to subjectivity in interpretation?
- What place exactly do 'pleasure and inspiration' have in the reading curriculum in view of the pressure to meet basic literacy targets and achieve examination success at all levels of secondary education?
- What other forms of reading are there – and might there be – apart from the printed page?

The temporal distance of the quotation serves to illustrate both a sense of continuity of concern about reading – some would say *déjà vu* – and, hopefully, a certain progress in our understanding of its nature as a teachable activity. Discussion of these issues will inform our consideration of reading throughout this chapter.

Of course reading can be conducted for a vast range of different purposes and takes a number of different forms. Consider the qualitative difference between reading, say, a railway timetable for specific information, a guidebook for an art exhibition, a magazine read casually while waiting to meet an appointment, and a complex novel read for pleasure. Both in life generally and in school particularly the act of reading decodes and interprets virtually without cease, and is often seamlessly connected to oral and writing activity: consider, for example, the early-morning staffroom routine in many schools of the discovery of lesson supervision – the list is read, talked about (with despair or jubilation as the case may be) and reminder notes and/or complaints are hastily written. Here, as in so much else, the act of reading is primary, and on the initial understanding gained other forms of activity are predicated. In this sense, reading is basic to literacy, but not synonymous with it: literacy implies the ability to use language effectively and appropriately across a wide range of forms. The responsibility of the secondary English teacher is to secure, develop and extend the reading repertoire, including reading for specific information, skim-reading and inference. This can only be achieved through teaching a fully integrated curriculum, not only within English itself but as part of whole-school language practice, with each subject being clear about the types of reading demanded for progress to be made. In the same way as we speak of 'reading a situation', so do many of life's experiences require some sort of reading: reading someone's face, for example, or reading a game of football. Fascinatingly, common vernacular frequently suggests perceptive and subtle truths. In the context of schooling, each curricular area presents its own situations to be read, and not always through the medium of written English; consider, for example, the reading of musical notation, scientific symbols, or works of art.

Reading is at once a highly focused activity and one rooted in an extremely broad cultural context, with the potential to take one or several of many different forms. Focusing with concentration on a text is, for many children, difficult – but that is precisely what effective reading demands and it is hard indeed to imagine paying attention simultaneously to other activities. At the same time, reader response theory, developed largely since the above-quoted advice to student teachers, has shown that there are in fact as many different possible readings of text as there are readers, and that each reader brings to the text a wealth of lived and read experience, including the ability or otherwise to focus with concentration on text. Taking account of and successfully fostering this multiplicity of readings of a fast increasing range of texts, including those based on the media and ICT, is the business of education. As already stated, there can be no escaping the responsibility of the whole school here, especially since each curricular subject demands its own ways of reading, but it is the particular responsibility of the English teacher to teach reading in and *for itself*. This is taken for granted in the primary phase, when the basic ability to read – that is , to make some sort of sense of marks on a page or elsewhere – is taught; we are, though, less familiar and perhaps less comfortable about the responsibility of the secondary English teacher to ensure progress in reading. And this does not simply mean, although it may include, the improvement of a pupil's reading age. The peculiar position of English in this respect is something we shall return to continually in this chapter; however, reading is cross-curricular, the foundation of a good deal of what is learned in school, and this may be the best place to start. Assuming that few secondary colleagues from other disciplines are likely to approach English departments with ideas for collaborative teaching of reading, mutually beneficial though this may be, it is in practice likely to be up to the English teacher to be pro-active here. As an example of good practice, consider the scheme of study in Figure 5.1; it is based on reading both of text and of landscape – and the practised eye does read landscape – devised through the collaboration of English and geography teachers to introduce the topic of Wordsworth and the Lake District landscape.

INTRODUCTION TO WORDSWORTH AND THE LAKE DISTRICT LANDSCAPE: KEY STAGE 4

Resources
- large scale, detailed map of Lake District, with contours and shading;
- pictures/photographs of the Lakes – past and present, industrial and agrarian, 'realistic' and 'romanticised';
- extracts from biography of Wordsworth, and portraits;
- extracts from his poetry (particularly from *The Prelude*);
- extracts from Dorothy Wordsworth's *Journals*, to match subject matter of the verse;
- tourist information 'literature' on the Lakes, taken if possible from different periods and reflecting contrasting presentational styles;
- other written or pictorial records, such as newspaper articles, National Park information, or planning documents (on keeping the appropriate balance between tourism and employment or housing interests, for example).

Activities
- Whole-class work: general discussion on the nature of the different resources used, emphasising the different types of 'reading' involved and the contrasting messages conveyed by the various materials. The stress should also be on the purpose and context of a range of readings, and on similarities and dissimilarities between readers.
- Pairs would examine and then report back briefly on one particular resource in the light of this discussion.
- Small-group activity: to re-present group-chosen information from the above list in a specific form (for example, a magazine article in Country Living, a programme for local radio, or a guidebook for American visitors) for a specific audience. There must be evidence of a wide range of source materials.

Figure 5.1

Important here is the realisation that shared good practice is possible and desirable even within the discrete subject-based curriculum underlined by the structure of the National Curriculum, not simply because it gets people working together in a common cause, but because it concentrates teaching on the range of reading styles to be experienced and developed – taught, in fact – as fundamental to the whole business of learning.

Most people would grant the importance of reading in education – but might balk at the idea of reading as dangerous. But reading, as a fundamental part of literacy, is about power; and power, as this century has surely demonstrated, is potentially dangerous. Just as interpretation through reading is subjective, so too is the notion of power: one person's idea of unjustifiable wielding of power is another's vaunted liberation. Consider these viewpoints:

> Learn the ABC, it's not enough, but
> Learn it. Don't let it get you down!. . . .
> You who are starving, grab hold of the book: it's a weapon.
> You must take over the leadership.
>
> (Bertolt Brecht, 'In Praise of Learning')

or:

> Having created universal literacy, the next task of education is to counter the forces which would make the literate more ignorant than the illiterate by virtue of their (the literate) acquired susceptibility.
>
> Merriam, in Abbs (1976:8)

Brecht suggests that literacy empowers in a Marxist sense, and of course that is likely to be perceived as dangerous to those holding power: his poem is a call to arms born of the class struggle. We do not need to go as far, or indeed to share the revolutionary politics, to see the validity of literacy as empowering; even a cursory examination of classroom activity will show how valuable is the ability to read in gaining control – power – over one's learning and thus one's life. It is a fully democratic force in this sense, and good English teaching fosters its growth in a spirit of open learning. But the very effectiveness of the modern education system in bringing about widespread literacy may have its attendant dangers in that aesthetic and even moral considerations may be neglected. The teaching and learning of reading need to be fully conscious, nurturing a fully social creativity which confronts existential situations and attempts the evaluation and, if appropriate, the transcendence of any received position. Reid (in Ross (ed.) 1985:135) makes the pertinent point:

> The *learning* of, and in, any 'subject' whatsoever, should be a personal *learning experience*, an engagement, an involvement in whatever is being learnt. If, instead, it is as it too often is, merely the 'getting up' of 'knowledge'. . . the educational value of 'learning' that subject has been minimal.

This is indeed a challenge, and it would be ludicrously presumptuous to suggest that the teaching of English – specifically reading – could single-handedly meet it. But it may play a part. It is the process towards full aptitude for words and images which is so vital here, the process of linguistic consciousness described by Dorothy Owen as long ago as 1920 (quoted in Abbs 1976:39):

> Words must first be made the servants of images and the mastery will not be

complete until subconscious thought becomes articulate. The word will then hold in itself the experience and be pregnant with the meaning which it, instead of the images, now encases.

We need now to move on to some of the practicalities in this movement towards articulation through reading: an adventurous and exciting enterprise in response to the challenge noted above – not in the sense of living vicariously through books but, rather, through a full engagement with reading all sorts of formally and informally arranged texts as part of life itself. In formulating some sort of unifying frame of reference for the Cambridge Literature series, the editor, Judith Baxter, and the editorial team came up with five guiding questions, themselves an adaptation of six questions posed in the LINC training manual (1991) referred to earlier. The Cambridge Literature questions are, with minor variations depending on the text and author referred to:

- Who has written this text and why?
- What type of text is it?
- How was it produced?
- How does this text present its subject?
- Who reads this text, and how do they interpret it?

These are pertinent questions to ask, and open up any text to interpretative possibilities both personal and collaborative. The very form of this sort of introduction to a text, as questions rather than statements, implies discovery and invention. Baxter (1995 and subsequently) elaborates, in her general introduction to any one of the series,

This study edition invites you to think about what happens when you read. . .and it suggests that you are not passively responding to words on the page which have only one agreed interpretation, but that you are actively exploring and making new sense of what you read. Your 'reading' will stem partly from you as an individual, from your own experiences and point of view, and to this extent your interpretation will be distinctively your own. But your reading will also stem from the fact that you belong to a culture and a community, rooted in a particular time and place. So, your understanding may have much in common with that of others in your class or study group.

The very fact that a major series intended for use in schools is centred around questions like these suggests that reading can empower, through developing young readers' interpretative tools. The success of the series, and the consultation process with teachers involved, implies that the editorial 'way in' is in tune with good practice, and the range of approaches possible on these premises is liberating. Of course English teachers – and educational series editors – are not so naive as to believe that simply asking the appropriate questions will unlock genuine originality of interpretation, if indeed such a thing exists at all. Rather, the important principle is in the process of discovery and making of meaning. In this context, subjectivity (the intensely personal) and objectivity (the social and cultural context which enables meaning to be found) may be complementary rather than mutually exclusive as often supposed. Traherne, to return for a moment to the seventeenth century, celebrated his own subjectivity all the more for realising that everyone could possess this gift:

You never enjoy the world aright, till the sea itself floweth in your veins, till you are clothed with the heavens, and crowned with the stars: and perceive yourself to be the sole heir of the whole world, and more than so, because men are in it *who are every one sole heirs as well as you.* [My italics]

Some may consider that we have wandered some way from the reality of English in the secondary classroom, but it is precisely this sort of celebration which must give reading its particular flavour and appeal as part of a specifically English curriculum – in other words, as an end in itself as well as a means to other kinds of investigation and learning.

To speak of the act of reading in an English classroom is somewhat misleading, for there are likely to be many different activities, including some or all of these:

- The whole-class reader, with each pupil having a text, read aloud
    by the teacher;
    by pupils 'in turn';
    by pupils reading the dialogue 'in role';
    by pupils having prepared passages beforehand;
    if a drama text, by pupils playing the parts;
    some combination of these styles of reading.
- Paired reading, known also as reading partnerships, whereby fluent readers help other pupils less advanced in their reading skills.
- Reading text in small groups, generally with a view to presenting findings in some sort of appropriate form, which may include drama.
- Guided reading for research, within and outside the classroom, with either the discovery of specific information in mind, or with a more open-ended intention.
- Sustained silent reading on an individual basis, with the English teacher modelling good practice.
- Reading of a particular textbook or worksheet, either individually or collaboratively, in order to carry out a specified task.
- Involvement in one or more of the huge variety of text-related activities, rooted in reading but conceivably developing a range of quite different forms of learning: drama, music, interviews, writing, art, speaking and listening, for example.
- Reading of data generated by ICT and the media.
- Reading of written text in conjunction with other forms of presentation such as illustrations, maps, diagrams, tables and charts.
- Detailed work on inferential comprehension conducted as part of an integrated English scheme of study.

As in so much else, the task of the English teacher is to balance, connect and integrate. There is room for all the forms of reading listed above, and many more, but there is an attendant danger that we become victims of our own success in formulating ever more adventurous ways of reading enacted for their own sake. We need to be all the more acutely focused on the primary requirement that we develop pupils' reading; in this context, we may select appropriately from the repertoire of activities, recognising each for its own particular value and limitations.

The integration of reading into the full English curriculum implies a blurring of the edges between different types of English activity. Take, for example, the plan (Figure 5.2) for connecting a drama sequence to the reading of Penelope Lively's novel *The Whispering Knights* (1971) for a mixed-ability Year 7 group. Clearly reading here is a springboard for diverse activities, including drama, speaking and listening, and writing. Possible extensions are numerous, such as media-based reporting of the controversy and the meeting itself and research-based work on local issues of genuine concern. The two points made at the end of the sequence description are vital, however, if reading is to remain the focus: firstly, that the group be returned to the text itself for enhanced understanding; and secondly, that subsequent discussion concentrates on how reading relates to its contexts and purposes. Combing the text for evidence of a particular pressure group's view, for example, is a different sort of reading from tracing the narrative to find out what happens next.

DRAMA SEQUENCE: *THE WHISPERING KNIGHTS* (YEAR 7)

Background: the novel centres around three children who arouse the malevolent spirit of Morgan le Fay, who then mischievously causes changes to a motorway building project so that it will go through the children's home village, Steeple Hampden, and some beautiful countryside to boot.

Lesson focus: to increase involvement with and understanding of the text, the pupils role-play a public meeting, chaired by the teacher in role, to discuss the motorway's proposed route. In previous lessons, alternative routes, based where possible on textual information, had been drawn up and a map devised. The class then divided into pressure groups for particular views and enacted propaganda campaigns and the collection of signatures in petitions.

In a subsequent lesson, pupils were given role cards, including one representative from each pressure group, for characters from the novel and other teacher-invented characters to enliven the debate. A preparatory lesson was spent making notes on the characters, culminating in a brief introduction from each to the rest of the group, and discussing the nature of public meetings (if possible using the experience of any real local issues).

For the public meeting role-play lesson itself, skilful chairing is required to ensure that each voice is heard, and that the evidence from the text itself is adhered to. The latter consideration may be returned to in future lessons focusing more directly on the novel again, teasing out what new perceptions had been gathered from the entire exercise.

Figure 5.2

Let us continue examining the widely used form of classroom-based reading, that of the shared reading of a text held in common – the 'class reader'. 'Reading around the class' has attracted considerable criticism over the years, and many of us remember, perhaps painfully, desperately trying to work out where our part in a text would fall so that we would not stumble quite as incoherently as some of our classmates. Any meaning tended to get lost, either through sheer boredom of hearing unprepared reading aloud, or through anticipatory panic. In a mixed-ability context these sorts of problems would be exacerbated, and no doubt the first person's patience to snap would be the teacher's. Consider this example, used with teachers by a Special Educational Needs Co-ordinator to illustrate the potential pitfalls (Soloman 1990):

CAN YOU READ THIS?

The boys' arrows were nearly gone so they sat down on the grass and stopped hunting. Over the edge of the wood they saw Henry making a bow to a small girl who was coming down the road. She had tears in her dress and tears in her eyes. She gave Henry a note which he brought over to the group of young hunters. Read to the boys it caused great excitement. After a minute but rapid examination of their weapons they ran down to the valley. Does were standing at the edge of the lake, making an excellent target.

At the very least, reading aloud needs some time for rehearsal: a fluent reader may recover very quickly from hesitation and stumbling in a passage like that above, but how much more difficult might it be for an inexperienced reader? This is not to deny, however, the many positive benefits to a class of sharing a common text and a collaborative reading – benefits which go well beyond the need to give some practice in reading aloud (which, in itself, may be seen as mere 'barking at print' to use the expression of the 1954 handbook quoted on p.54). For one of the early NATE-inspired books dedicated to invigorating English teaching, Calthrop (1971:23) interviewed English teachers who

> felt that the shared experience of reading a common book was something of great value to themselves and to their classes. They regarded it as something quite different from the pleasure to be gained from individual reading and took the view that the feeling of sharing something worth while, the common sense of enjoyment, and the resulting sense of community was a deeply educative process. . .a reciprocal process. . .akin to the experience of a theatre audience. . . The whole process involved a performance by the teacher, a collective, but enjoyed and shared, response from the audience, together with a fair amount of audience participation.

This is reading in a celebratory sense, and requires that we 'awaken our faith' in the possibilities of performance and inspiration as central to English teaching. And like any performance, it needs preparation and rehearsal, not least on the part of the teacher. The rewards, however, can be immense, and more or less distinctive to the English classroom. Neither need the performance stop with the reading, and the use of drama here can be apposite, paradoxically, to halt the narrative in order that reflection may occur. As Grainger (1998:32) points out,

> In reading fiction, the power of the narrative can drive the reader relentlessly onwards, and unless opportunities to pause, consider and reflect upon the text are created and valued, their reading of it may only scratch the surface. Drama is not plot-driven, nor restricted by living time since techniques such as flashbacks, flash forwards and interior monologues provide opportunities to investigate the present moment further, as well as examine precursors and long-term consequences.

Such reflective interruptions need not necessarily take the form of fully-fledged dramatic enterprises, such as hot-seating of characters or a 'talking heads' activity, and are most effective when rooted in reading and response. An English teacher may, for example, choosing the moment carefully, halt the reading to focus on one character in a way similar to that recommended in the chapter on writing, with the instruction to the class to stop reading, close their eyes, and imagine the textual scene just recounted. The teacher could then develop understanding by asking pupils to describe aloud, in first or third person, the character's thoughts and feelings. Alternatively, we may wish to concentrate on the reader as author of interpretation, again interrupting the reading to ask 'if you were writing this, what would you have happening next?' The empathetic and predictive possibilities are infinite, and could easily be explored further through writing, thus cementing the bond between reading, speaking and listening, and writing. The important point is always to return to the text, and this principle is worth bearing in mind whatever is being read, by whom, and however the imaginative nature of the activity is devised.

An approach to shared reading widely and successfully used in the primary phase is that instigated by Aidan Chambers, himself a highly accomplished children's author: the 'Tell Me' method. Chambers (1993) has developed his ideas from W.H.Auden's desire, presented in *Reading in The Dyer's Hand and Other Essays* (1963), that literary critics

1. introduce me to authors or works of which I was hitherto unaware;
2. convince me that I have undervalued an author or a work because I had not read them carefully enough;
3. show me relations between works of different ages and cultures which I could never have seen for myself because I do not know enough and never shall;
4. give a 'reading' of a work which increases my understanding of it;
5. throw light upon the process of artistic 'Making';
6. throw light upon the relation of art to life, to science, economics, ethics, religion, etc.

As guidance for teachers of English, let alone literary critics, this seems excellent advice. Chambers asserts, on these secure foundations, that children can with guidance become judicious critics dedicated to the understanding and enjoyment of texts. The approach is essentially collaborative, and centres on a series of pertinent questions about the experience of books, with the initial warning that the 'Tell Me' approach is not a mechanical textbook programme – it is not meant to be slavishly followed. The basic 'Tell Me' questions are listed below; many others, in a variety of permutations, follow on from them.

- Was there anything you liked about this book?
- What especially caught your attention?
- What would you have liked more of?
- Was there anything you disliked?
- Were there parts that bored you?
- Did you skip parts? Which ones?
- If you gave up, where did you stop and what stopped you?
- Was there anything that puzzled you?
- Was there anything you thought strange?
- Was there anything you'd never found in a book before?
- Was there anything that took you completely by surprise?
- Did you notice any apparent inconsistencies?
- Were there any patterns – any connections – that you noticed?

The details of the subsequent questions are well worth looking up, but we can already see how pertinent is the framework. It may of course need adapting – that is, after all, its purpose – and the questions could be re-interpreted with specific readings in mind for worksheets and long-term schemes of work as well as for more immediate discussions. The reading itself, clearly, does not need to be a shared experience, and some of the questions imply otherwise; but the opening up of interpretative possibilities using the approach must be in some sense social, whether with a whole class, small group (perhaps set a particular book to read with a view to presenting it to the rest of the class), or between the teacher and a single pupil. This flexibility is particularly appropriate to the secondary, 'workshop'-based English classroom. The last of the 'basic questions' may be the most fruitful for interpretation in depth, bringing to mind E. M. Forster's aphoristic 'only connect', within English and in the cross-curricular dimension.

Innovative and detailed approaches to reading texts in school have been well documented elsewhere, most notably in the Cox version of the National Curriculum, which helpfully contained a detailed appendix entitled 'Approaches to the Class Novel', and in the work of Lunzer and Gardner (1984), who pioneered the 'Directed Activities Related to Texts' (DARTS) approach to reading and comprehension. In the years since, published editions of texts for school use (some of which we have looked at), photocopiable ring-binders of accompanying resource materials, influential texts intended for English teachers, INSET workshops led by NATE, LEAs and others, and a rapidly increasing wealth of CD-ROM and media-based stimuli have all inspired excellent English teaching. There is also the possibility that, despite (or perhaps because of) this impressive array of materials, not a little confusion has been inspired. English teachers need to keep a clear sight of the wood of the text among all these magnificent trees, and the best way to do this is to share ideas with colleagues. English departments need to work together, gathering evidence about what works well with whom and when, and adapting resources continually. In such a context, a policy for reading within secondary English will be something of a working document, perpetually under review. Central to such a document would be issues such as these:

- coherent schemes of work to ensure both breadth and depth of reading;
- the use of the school library as a resource for fiction and for text-based and IT/media research;
- the teaching of study skills through reading, including the practical use of the library;
- the development and maintenance of class libraries;
- the continual review of English departmental stock, including multi-cultural authors and titles, non-fiction, women writers, books appealing to boys, questions of suitability of subject matter for age groups;
- the development of resources to aid teaching of reading, including those focused on improving 'basic literacy' in conjunction with SEN staff, pre-reading activities for class texts focusing on expectation, genre and context, activities to teach during the reading of texts, post-reading activities, integrated comprehension materials;
- the assessment of reading, including what Jill Pirrie terms 'the twin spectres of accountability and evidence' (Pirrie 1987);
- humane forms of reading recording such as reading journals, shared and displayed reviews and class folders;
- celebratory reading 'events', perhaps centred on the library, such as teachers talking about favourite childhood books, a book-based 'Blind Date', and visiting authors;
- cross-curricular possibilities for different types of reading;
- the balance of different types of reading within the English curriculum, given the constraints of time and resources;
- reading as an integral part of examination syllabuses;
- INSET and professional development in reading-focused pedagogy.

Presented in this sort of format, the list might appear daunting. In reality it need not be, and some of the best English departmental meetings could take the form of colleagues presenting favourite books and then discussing feasible teaching ideas. As an extension of this, teachers may wish to form their own 'reading circles'; certainly this is an invigorating way of keeping up with personal reading and could of course involve colleagues from other departments.

Some of the thornier issues to do with the place of reading in the English curriculum are concerned with assessment, progress, and what amounts to dictation and even censorship of reading matter. The three are in fact closely related: progress in reading depends on an appropriate assessment of a pupil's current position and can in any case only be ascertained if we use some sort of method of assessment; similarly, progress is likely to mean more demanding texts to read, and the English teacher's intervention here may be crucial. The assessment of reading is problematic, probably more so than either speaking and listening or writing, because it is personal and to a large extent invisible. We can only approach assessment of reading through listening to what pupils say, or looking at their writing – in other words, through some other medium than reading itself. Reading aloud may be merely 'barking at print' and is no guarantee of meaning: it is perfectly possible, in my teaching experience, for a pupil to appear to read aloud fluently but, on questioning, show only scant understanding. The converse may also hold true, and unfortunately has sometimes relegated pupils to low sets and even low achievement. Written comprehension tests may, in the same way, show up more of a pupil's ability to write cleverly formulaic answers – perhaps to what is assumed to be the teacher's expectation of a 'valid' response – than the ability to read with any sensitivity or depth. There are of course many reading tests and great store is set by them, but the fundamental problems remain. In a sense, we need something to grasp hold of, particularly in progress over the key stages, and it may not matter too much which method is used as long as the same format of test is used at the various levels. Even this, however, is hardly universal among partner schools. In practice, assessment of reading takes a great deal of sensitive observation of a pupil's reading across a range of reading activities, and the will to accumulate and record written insights.

In the final analysis the way to achieve progress in reading is to build on enthusiasm – not only for the pleasure of imaginative (generally fiction) reading, but for unlocking the secrets of text because one wants to find out what is there. In the reality of the classroom this means suggesting more demanding, stimulating texts to be read in more sophisticated ways: many of us will remember an English teacher some time in our various educations who took the trouble to recommend a book which changed our experience of reading for the better or revealed an alternative way of reading a favourite which challenged and stretched our understanding. It is precisely this sort of personal touch that can make all the difference, but it needs to be practised in a way which is methodical and rigòrous, not merely haphazard. And sometimes, of course, a pupil is best left alone with yet another Judy Blume or Point Horror: it is a matter of judgement and, even more importantly, recognition and respect for the pupil's own needs. Concern about the quality and subject matter of what children read is important, and Tomkinson's (1921:78) sympathy for English teachers shows it to be nothing new:

Some of the titles will undoubtedly distress the earnest teacher who is anxious that his children should read good literature; but it is not to be expected that the young who have their reading synthesis still before them, should exercise a nice discrimination in their choice of books. If the teacher has a sense of humour, he may divert himself and do his class no harm, by publicly criticising one of the blood and thunder paper-backs which the reading boy usually conceals about his person.

There is indeed something comical about this scenario involving that strange creature 'the reading boy' (all too strange, too often). There are times when the English teacher will need to intervene with reading matter, using 'a nice discrimination'; but there are others, rather more often in my experience, when humour is more appropriate. After all, we tend to forget that reading is meant to be for pleasure.

FURTHER READING

A focused curricular perspective can be found in two publications from the English and Media Centre: *The English Curriculum: Reading 1, Comprehension* and *The English Curriculum: Reading 2, Slow Readers*. Chambers (1993), *Tell Me* although aimed primarily at the primary age range, is very useful. Several publications have sought to adapt recent critical theories to the secondary English classroom and to children's reading generally; among the more accessible are Hunt (1991) *Criticism, Theory and Children's Literature*, and, aimed rather more at university level but still highly relevant, Green and LeBihan (1996) *Critical Theory and Practice – A Coursebook*. Stibbs (1991) *Reading Narrative as Literature: Signs of Life* is a lively, readable and inventive study. Finally, three thoroughly enjoyable, stimulating books by Styles *et al.* provide insights into the ever-expanding world of fiction for children and young people; they are: *The Prose and the Passion* (1994), *After Alice* (1992) and *Voices Off* (1996).

RESOURCES

The widest ranging series of 'educational' fiction is undoubtedly the Heinemann New Windmill series, all of which are hard-wearing hardbacks and represent excellent value for money, but it is worth investigating other publishers' catalogues also, for series such as Collins Cascades, Macmillan M Books, and the low-priced Wordsworth Classics. Accompanying the larger series are ring-bound photocopiable further information and activities. A comparative newcomer is the Cambridge Literature series (Cambridge University Press), a fast-increasing range intended for the 14–18 age range containing impressive resource notes and activities which take into account recent insights in critical theory. There is also impressive choice when it comes to imaginative literary study material and creative approaches. Texts from the English and Media Centre, for Key Stage 3, include *Making Stories*, *Changing Stories* and *Investigating Texts*, all providing excellent stimuli for inventive close reading. (See Chapter 8 for Key Stage 4 suggestions). The *Figures in a Landscape: Writing from Around the World* series (general editor Hayhoe), Cambridge University Press, serves a very useful function in broadening the reading repertoire, as do *True or False? Non-Fiction for Secondary English*, (ed. Ellison), Hodder and Stoughton, and *Pair and Compare 1 and 2* (Bousted and Barton), Collins, – the latter looking at imaginative inter-textual readings. Three excellent, if necessarily expensive, titles from Hodder and Stoughton – *Double Vision*, *Painting with Words* and *Picture Poems* (each by Benton and Benton) explore the possibilities of parallel readings of paintings and texts, and are beautifully illustrated accordingly.

6: Teaching Poetry

Poetry's unnat'ral; no man ever talked poetry
'cept a beadle on boxin' day

Mr Weller in Charles Dickens' *Pickwick Papers*

One of the ideas which has influenced this book is the view that the acquisition of language is largely a natural process. There is also an argument for saying that of all the different forms and uses of language, it is poetry which is the most natural. This may seem to be a strange and controversial claim because one of the characteristic features of poetry, that it is language at its most dense and aesthetically crafted, seems to suggest the opposite view. However, our earliest experiences of language as children could be said to be primarily poetic. A child takes a delight in sounds, rhythms, rhymes, images and textures without being particularly concerned with propositional meaning. The point is made convincingly by Mattenklott (in Thompson (ed.) 1996:13):

> Hans Magnus Enznesberger, the editor of an anthology of children's verse, *Allerleirauh* published in the 1960s, refers to children's verse as *prima poesis*, the first poetry in an individual's life. It accompanies the child from birth, with verses for nappy-changing, bathing and finger games, to the later counting rhymes, word rhymes and jingles which are all part of the independent games of older children. Common to all these forms of poetry is their direct relationship to the body, to movement and gesticulation. . .Other common characteristics of this poetry lie in the predominance of rhythm, alliteration, rhyme and euphony over meaning. In most cases the verses are sheer nonsense.

Young children, without being obsessed by rationality or logic, find pleasure in repetitions, the articulation of sounds and the way words create powerful images; they are not too concerned why it is that the little boy down the lane should need a bag of wool, nor why the dish decided to run away with the spoon. Even if there are objections to the notion that poetry is 'natural', it is difficult to deny that poetry has very strong affinities with the child's earliest experiences of the spoken word.

For this reason, the frequently quoted view that poetry tends to be unpopular in schools is somewhat surprising. In her article Mattenklott states that in Germany 'young people, adolescents and students at universities, even those who study literature, tend to reject poetry. They find that they cannot relate to poetic form and language, and even at times find them tiresome.' (ibid:13). In England in the 1980s similar views were expressed in various reports (by the Assessment of Performance Unit and HMI), books and research papers. Whether the same is true now is difficult to judge. There are many reasons for a greater level of optimism: there has been a steady stream of appealing, modern anthologies for schools; innovative methods for teaching poetry have been developed and widely disseminated; there is a more accepting cultural climate which makes poetry seem less élite (poems on the underground, public performances, publication of the nation's favourite poems, etc.). Many pupils do enjoy the relative freedom of expression and response offered by poetry but many also find this the most 'difficult' aspect of the English curriculum.

A traditional approach to teaching poetry involved the teacher reading the poem aloud and then, through a question and answer session, leading the pupils to an appropriate understanding of the 'meaning' of the work and an appreciation of the formal poetic devices used to create effect. The method is described in the following extract (Dias and Hayhoe 1988:7):

> Such a stance dictates that a teacher's role is to *conduct* the reading of the poem, and hope somehow that his or her reading will be appropriated by pupils. It dictates a classroom procedure which operates primarily through a process of inductive questioning by the teacher and a corresponding developing sense of the poem by the pupils. The teacher is in charge of the meaning that evolves, and the text, rather than the readers' generally unverifiable (it seems) impressions and intuitions, must be adduced in support of the meaning that is 'unlocked' through the teacher's questioning.

This approach was widely criticised in the literature of the 1970s and 1980s because such methods emphasised analysis at the expense of response, and did not give pupils enough responsibility for creating their own meanings. Instead, teachers were advised to use methods such as encouraging pupils to discuss poems in small groups and reading poems aloud without too much analysis in order to emphasise pure enjoyment. Active, directed approaches to reading, such as cloze exercises, sequencing a cut up text, inventing a title for the poem, were also frequently employed. Ideas of this kind did much to enliven the poetry lesson but in the wrong context these methods could be just as alienating and bewildering for pupils as the method of inductive questioning so readily condemned.

The problem with the concept 'poetry' is that it does not describe one simple category of text; it is not possible to offer necessary and sufficient conditions for saying exactly what is to count as 'poetry'. A less philosophical way of making the same point is to say that it is difficult to say very much which claims to be true of all poems for which exceptions cannot be found.

Some modern poems, such as William Carlos Williams' 'This Is Just To Say' with its simple 'prosaic' language and lack of imagery, rhythm and rhyme, appear to flout normal expectations of what poetry should be. Sometimes it is difficult to say to which category particular texts should be assigned. For example, which of the following can be said to count as 'poems': nursery rhymes, song lyrics, acrostics, raps, ballads, limericks? In what category should we place 'poetic prose'? Should concrete poetry really count as poetry? Deceived by language into assuming that there is an entity called 'poetry' which has a single essence, writers often give practical advice about ways of teaching *poetry* which is not universally applicable to all poems. For example, whereas it is often true that readers need time to respond to poems, this is not always the case; many poems are appropriate for reading aloud and responding with instant reactions (many of the humorous, lighter poems in contemporary anthologies for schools are of this kind). It is also not helpful to place too much emphasis on a relativist view, i.e. that readers can never be wrong in their interpretation of a poem.

There have been notable definitions of poetry such as Coleridge's 'the best words in the best order' or Eliot's view that it is not 'a turning loose of emotion but an escape from emotion'. Genuine poetry is 'conceived and composed in the soul' (Gray) and consists of 'noble grounds for noble emotions' (Ruskin). Poetry 'says one thing and means another' (Rifaterre 1978). Some literary theorists have provided useful insights in suggesting for example that poetry is language which most draws attention to itself. Linguistic accounts have attempted to identify the stylistic features which distinguish poetry (for example, patterning of sound, use of contrast, creation of text-intensive meaning). Poets have written about the writing process in ways which give tremendous insight into how they see the art form. The following extract from a radio talk by Ted Hughes (reprinted in Benton and Benton 1995:136) emphasises sensitivity to the texture and feel of language as a prerequisite for poetry:

> as a poet, you have to make sure that all those parts over which you have control, the words and rhythms and images are alive. That is where the difficulties begin. . .Yet the rules to begin with are very simple. Words which are alive are those which we hear, like 'click' or chuckle', or which we see, like 'freckled' or 'veined', or which we taste, like 'vinegar' or 'sugar'. . .'Click' not only gives you a sound, it gives you the notion of a sharp movement. . .such as your tongue makes in saying 'click'. It also gives you feel of something light and brittle – like a snapping twig. Heavy things do not click, nor do soft bedable ones. In the same way tar not only smells strongly. It is sticky to touch with a particular thick and choking stickiness. Also it moves, when it is soft, like a black snake, and has a beautiful black gloss. So it is with most words. They belong to several of the senses at once, as if each one had eyes, ears and tongue, or ears and fingers and a body to move with. It is this little goblin in a word which is its life and its poetry, and it is this goblin which the poet has to have under control.

These aphorisms and descriptions provide useful insights into the genre but do not provide any *definitive* means of saying what is to count as poetry. Some poems are primarily concerned with structure, narrative or ideas rather than the texture of language. A 'found' poem is made up of snippets of language (bits of conversation, graffiti, notices) which are not necessarily 'poetic'. We might want to agree with Johnson who said of poetry that 'it is much easier to say what it is not. We all know what light is but it is not easy to *tell* what it is.'

The somewhat misguided search for a simple definition becomes more complicated because sometimes the term 'poetry' is used in an evaluative way. To say of a piece of text that it is 'not poetry' is simply to state that in the opinion of the reader it is not 'good' poetry. This approach may serve to banish all sorts of doggerel, valentine's verses, slogans and maudlin rhyming couplets from the category but does not help when disagreements occur about the quality of individual texts. The danger in restricting the definition in this way is that pupils' attempts to write poetry may need to be subject to unreasonable criteria.

An alternative approach to defining poetry is to place emphasis on the reader rather than on the text. The idea here is that any text could be read as poetry, depending on the stance the reader takes towards it. Eagleton (1983:7) gave a humorous illustration of this point by describing the way in which a sign on the underground 'Dogs must be carried on the escalator' might be read:

One could let oneself be arrested by the abrupt, minatory staccato of the first ponderous monosyllables; find one's mind drifting, by the time it had reached the rich allusiveness of 'carried', to suggestive resonances of helping lame dogs through life; and perhaps even detect in the very lilt and inflection of the word 'escalator' a miming of the rolling up-and-down motion of the thing itself.

A shopping list may take on more meaning and significance if it is read as a poem, if the reader sees in it an ironic comment on domesticity. As part of a research project on perceptions of poetry, pupils were asked to say whether a number of texts could be described as poetry or not (Fleming 1992). The chosen texts included three versions of a shopping list (Figure 6.1).

	A Woman's Work	
Two pounds of sugar	Two pounds of sugar	Two pounds of sugar
A packet of PG Tips	A packet of PG Tips	A pint of milk, some tea
A pint of milk	A pint of milk	If you buy two packets
Twenty Players	Twenty Players	You get another free.
Box of matches	Box of matches	Half a dozen eggs
A packet of Daz	A packet of Daz	And a cotton reel of thread
Light bulbs	Light bulbs	Half a pound of butter
Tissues	Tissues	And a crusty loaf of
Half a pound of mince	Half a pound of mince	bread.

Figure 6.1

92 per cent of the pupils identified the rhyming shopping list as a poem as opposed to the 32 per cent who thought 'A Woman's Work' could also be described in that way; they seemed to be more influenced by form than content (a result which was replicated elsewhere in the research). In view of this, it was somewhat surprising that as many as 10 per cent were prepared to say that the simple non-rhyming shopping list was a poem. It is likely however that their responses were influenced by having read 'A Woman's Work' first; if they were presented with the simple list first it is unlikely that any of them would have described it as a poem. The view that determining what counts as poetry has more to do with the stance which the reader takes towards the text than any intrinsic characteristics of the text itself is persuasive, but the argument is in danger of being circular for the reader's stance is partly determined by whether the text is seen as a poem. The question still remains as to why a particular individual would read a text in this way other than the fact that it appeared in a poetry anthology or that the lines 'do not go to the end of the line'.

The difficulty of describing precise categories is true not just of the concept of 'poetry' but of language in general. It was a central aspect of Wittgenstein's later philosophy (and a tenet of much twentieth century thought) that words acquire their meaning by use rather than by any simple relationship with reality. Words like 'art' and 'poetry' may appear to describe discrete categories but their relationship with reality is not fixed and determined. All of this discussion may seem purely academic unless the practical implications are explored. These can be summarised as follows:

- it is a mistake to recommend practical methods of teaching *poetry* which may be only appropriate for particular poems or types of poems;
- acceptance of a broad category may mean that the teaching of poetry can usefully be extended to include advertising jingles, song lyrics, headlines, snippets of conversation, etc.;
- the wide concept of 'poetry' may be a source of bewilderment or difficulty for pupils unless the term itself is subject to some discussion.

It was suggested above that poetry is often described by pupils as being the aspect of English they find most difficult. It will be worth examining why this is sometimes the case, before looking at approaches to teaching poetry in the classroom. Steiner (1978) identified several types of difficulties which can be encountered when reading poetry. These may be adapted to make more appropriate links with the practicalities of secondary school teaching.

Some texts present difficulties for pupils simply because they do not understand the vocabulary, allusions or references in them. That does not mean that pupils need to be able to understand every word before making a response to a poem but their lack of comprehension may present barriers which prevent further engagement with the work. This may seem to be a fairly obvious point but can easily be forgotten in the classroom. As described above (p.67), the emphasis, derived from reader response theory, on the role of the pupils in creating meaning meant that small group discussion without teacher intervention was recommended in preference to traditional question and answer sessions. *Young Readers Responding to Poems* (Benton *et al.*, 1988) contains some very convincing examples of the value of this methodology. However, without an appropriate choice of poem and without supplying necessary background information which will allow pupils' discussions to operate within appropriate parameters, they may set off on completely the wrong track. Consider the poem 'Mary, Mary Magdalene' by Charles Causley which begins,

> Mary, Mary Magdalene
> Lying on the wall,
> I throw a pebble on your back.
> Will it lie or fall?

It helps us to know that on the wall of a church in Launceston in Cornwall is a figure of the saint and that the children of the town say that a stone lodged on the figure's back will bring good luck. This simple example is chosen because it is so easy to imagine ingenious pupils thinking up possible explanations without the introductory information. Some readers might argue that their suggestions are as valid as any others. However, there is a pragmatic rather than simply theoretical dimension which needs to be considered. It is not enough to argue that their subjective response should be respected if the pupils themselves are likely to recognise later that they were wrong. In that case the hidden message then becomes for the pupils that poems are problems or puzzles to which someone else usually has the key. Much modern poetry is deliberately ambiguous and invites the reader to speculate about meaning but not all poems are of that kind. When pupils are invited to exercise 'free play' in relation to the meaning and interpretations of poems, appropriate choices of text need to be made.

When choosing a poem for small-group discussion the teacher also needs to decide what kind of background and textual information is necessary. New Criticism may have marginalised the importance of historical and social contexts in relation to literature but reader response theory is in danger of doing the same. The *Cambridge Poetry Workshop* has some useful examples of ways in which pupils can be given information about particular poems while still leaving room for personal response. For example, they are told before reading 'In Memory of God' by Jenny Joseph that the theme of the poem is 'conservation' before reading it but are given room for personal response. All of the poems in the anthology are preceded by activities which are intended to engage the reader in the theme, content or 'emotional territory' of the work prior to reading.

Finding a 'way in' to a poem is sometimes important because the emotional content of the poem does not strike a chord with the reader; this represents another type of 'difficulty'. There may be a surface grasp of objective, semantic meaning but there is no subjective engagement with its deeper significance. This may be true of all readers, not just pupils in school. Response to any text is partly determined by the personal experiences which are brought to bear on the meaning: a reading of a poem about death will have more impact after a recent bereavement. Auden's poem which begins 'Stop all the clocks, cut off the telephone' had considerable impact in the film *Four Weddings and a Funeral* because of the creation of a context which determined response. It is little wonder then that poems based on such themes as cruelty to animals, school and friendship are common in anthologies for pupils because the content is readily accessible. Yeats' 'Lake Isle of Innisfree' has few contingent difficulties (words and allusions which have to be explained) but it may have little impact unless the reader can relate to its central theme: the yearning to return to a place of tranquillity, peace and harmony (perhaps teachers will relate more readily to the poem than pupils). Notice this is not just a matter of relating to the content; only if one can engage with the emotional impact of the idea can one respond to the simple image of peace 'dropping slow, dropping from the veils of the morning to where the cricket sings'. Of course pupils may readily write objectively about the impact of the imagery in an assignment or for examination purposes but that is a different matter.

Being 'grabbed' by a poem is not the same as writing technically about its impact but it is important not to think that the two are necessarily in opposition. Nor is the message here that there are any simple, modern teaching devices which can guarantee that all pupils will respond in a genuine way. One virtue of the traditional O level literature examination was that the rote learning of lengthy quotations and revision notes sometimes brought a level of familiarity which resulted in a deep response to the text almost in spite of, rather than because of, the teaching. In *Angela's Ashes* (McCourt, 1997:223) the naive but authentic response by the young boy Frank to Alfred Noyes' 'The Highwayman' is captured in a poignant account. A verse is recited each day to him while he is in hospital by a young girl, Patricia, who dies before she reaches the end of the poem.

> Every day I can't wait for the doctors and nurses to leave me alone so I can learn a new verse from Patricia and find out what's happening to the highwayman and the landlord's red-lipped daughter. I love the poem because it's exciting and almost as good as my two lines of Shakespeare. The redcoats are after the highwayman because they know he told her, I'll come to thee by moonlight, though hell should bar the way.

Some poems are more easily understood in the wider context of a poet's entire work and with some knowledge of biographical details. As suggested above, New Criticism, on which the teaching of poetry has traditionally been based in schools, tended to marginalise the relevance of background details in favour of a focused concentration on the actual words of the text. Many poems are understood only in the context of the general corpus of the poet's work and most are illuminated by experience of reading beyond the particular text which is the object of study. The example of the shopping list above provides a very modest example of intertexuality – the way in which reading of one text influences the reading of another. Awareness of this type of difficulty will help the teacher decentre when choosing and presenting poems to pupils.

Another type of difficulty relates to poetry as a genre. Readers are likely to have problems if they approach poetry with inappropriate expectations derived from their experience of reading other texts: many poems, particularly those chosen for study in school, need successive readings before they can be properly experienced; form is as important and often more important in evoking response; trying to understand a poem line by line may not be appropriate. If pupils approach the reading of a poem expecting it to yield up meaning in the same way that prose does, it is not surprising that they find the genre difficult. Tolerance of ambiguity and a readiness to accept plurality of meaning are more necessary when reading poetry than other literary genres. The strong contrast between reading poetry and other utilitarian and functional uses of language in the English classroom (to instruct, report, inform, etc.) may be a source of difficulty if poetry only appears at irregular intervals in the classroom.

It was suggested earlier that the broad category which the concept 'poetry' embraces may also be a source of bewilderment for pupils. The early delight in the aesthetics of language which the child experiences may rapidly be replaced by an imperative to analyse and interpret. The family resemblance between writing acrostics, enjoying humorous ditties, joining in with group readings and dissecting for examination purposes may be hard to discern. The argument here is not that poems should never be analysed; it is after all a key means of developing sensitivity to language; appropriate analysis can inform emotional and aesthetic response. The point is that the teacher needs to be aware of the difficulties which may arise and take steps to ensure that they do not become an insurmountable barrier.

It is perhaps more appropriate to think of poetry as being potentially 'bewildering' rather than 'difficult' because the barriers to understanding are more to do with having inappropriate expectations or not quite knowing the 'rules' which apply. Pupils therefore will be helped by some attention to the genre itself, not to pursue strict definitions of poetry but to examine the way different texts require different types of reading. Indeed they are likely to be able to make progress as readers by turning some explicit attention to the particular reading requirements of different discourses. Questions to do with the relevance of the author's intentions and such concepts as ambiguity and plurality of meaning can be addressed in the context of the pupils' own reading and response. Different types of poems can be examined in relation to each other as well as poetry in comparison with other types of written language, such as headlines, posters and advertising. A valuable starting point for such discussion is to give pupils a variety of different types of texts (riddles, jokes, rhymes, etc.) and ask them to say which can be described as poems, as in the research project described above. Alternatively, a modern minimalist poem, for example Stevie Smith's 'Croft' or Williams' 'This Is Just To Say', can be presented in prose and poetry form in order to examine the way in which the poetic form affects the reading and meaning of the text.

Poetry is likely to be bewildering for pupils if it only crops up periodically to fulfil external requirements. A discussion of practical approaches then needs to address not just the teaching of individual poems but the ways in which an appropriate poetry environment can be created in the classroom. The following suggestions are ways of working towards fulfilling that aim:

- include poetry in the classroom library;
- display a 'poem of the week' on a notice board;
- class display of 'our favourite poems';
- have pupils create their own anthologies;
- allow pupils to choose poems to read aloud;
- explore song lyrics with pupils;
- invite poets into the classroom;
- organise poetry festivals with other classes and schools;
- conduct poetry readings;
- publish poetry wall displays and magazines;
- create a supply of audio and video recordings of poems;
- tape-record pupils' discussions of poems for them to review later;
- organise a competition in which pupils have to match poems to titles;
- choose music to accompany the reading of poems;
- create poetry posters of favourite poems;
- pupils learn poems by heart;
- arrange for a poet to visit school.

Not all poetry requires close analysis and study. A classroom collection of accessible, entertaining anthologies with poems from different cultures will provide a valuable resource for some of the above activities. While some poetry, particularly much of the humorous modern poetry written for children, works at a first reading, much poetry needs to be savoured and read closely in order to experience it.

The problem with the traditional inductive question and answer approach to poetry is that it rarely made enough room for pupils to engage with the text. The emphasis was on 'comprehension and criticism' rather than 'reading and response' (Benton et al., 1988:ix). Trying to answer questions which have been set by someone else immediately limits one's own response (Dias and Hayhoe 1988:7):

> To borrow an analogy that Graves (1981) has used in speaking of how writing is often taught, the teacher, the keeper of the poem, 'owns' the poem, the children merely 'rent it'. They live so to speak in the poem on the owner's terms; for the poem is not theirs to 'mess around in'.

It was twenty-eight years ago that Fox and Merrick produced their 'Thirty-Six Things to do with a Poem' and their suggestions are still very useful. The value of such activities is not only that they help pupils to become familiar with texts before premature analysis, they also encourage pupils to take a 'playful' approach to language. Figure 6.2 provides examples of activities which allow pupils to become familiar with texts prior to a close reading and analysis; sometimes the activity (or combined activities) may be sufficient in themselves as an alternative to analysis.

The final 'activity' listed is developed in an interesting way in The Poetry Pack (1995). It resembles the game of consequences in that the dramatic monologue 'My Last Duchess' is given in fragments to groups of students so that they can try to work out the speaker, the person being talked about, the listener, the context. They are also asked

Activity	Purpose	Suitable poems
Invent a title for a poem before being told the actual title.	Allows pupils to respond intuitively to totality of poem prior to analysis. Highlights possible ambiguities.	'Mushrooms' by Sylvia Plath; 'In The Microscope' by Miroslav Holub; 'Space Shot' by Gareth Owen.
Read the poem apart from the final stanza and attempt to write a version before reading the original.	Draws attention to style of writing. Invites pupils to speculate about meaning.	'Meditation on the A30' by John Betjeman; 'My Grandmother' by Elizabeth Jennings.
Restore line lengths and endings to a poem which has been distributed as prose.	Prompts pupils to think about difference between prose and poetry.	'The World is a Beautiful Place' by Lawrence Ferlinghetti; 'Orchids' by Theodore Roethke.
Place stanzas of poem in order.	Draws attention to structure of poem.	'First Blood' by Jon Stallworthy; 'Ballad of the Bread Man' by Charles Causley.
Prepare imaginative readings of poems in groups.	Emphasises importance of reading poems aloud – tone.	'Daniel Jazz' by Vachel Lindsay; 'First Men on Mercury', Edwin Morgan.
Make a collage using pictures, postcards, etc. juxtaposing with words of poem.	Draws attention to visual aspects of poem. May provide new interpretations.	'A Martian Sends a Postcard Home' by Craig Raine;
Create a group tableau of poem or stanza which is then performed as it is read.	Provides concrete focus for understanding and reading.	'My Parents Kept Me From Children Who Were Rough' by Stephen Spender.
Underline favourite/most striking words and phrases/ images.	Emphasises response and exercise of choice prior to analysis.	'Fairground' by Vernon Scannell.
Substitute other words (e.g. colours/verbs/adverbs/ adjectives/metaphors).	Draws attention to effectiveness of poet's choice of words.	'Hard Frost' by Andrew Young; 'Wind' by Ted Hughes.
Examine first (and subsequent) drafts of poems.	Highlights writing process.	'Anthem for Doomed Youth' by Wilfred Owen.
Compare two poems.	Can highlight contrasting content and features of form.	'A Negro Woman' by William Carlos Williams; 'The Fat Black Woman Goes Shopping' by Grace Nichols.
Compare translations of same poem.	Draws attention to nuances of meaning.	'First Ice' by Andrei Voznesensky.
Create storyboard or cartoon strip representing poem.	Highlights structure and narrative content of poem.	'Flannan Isle' by Wilfred Wilson Gibson.
Focus on fragments which have been selected by the teacher before reading the entire poem.	Encourages active reading; useful 'way in'; may focus on particular aspects, e.g. imagery.	'Porphyria's Lover' by Robert Browning.
Present poem gradually, in small sections (e.g. two lines at a time), in sequence.	Deepens response to poem by slowing down reading.	'Futility' by Wilfred Owen; 'The Naming of Parts' by Henry Reed.
Reconstruct two poems which have been cut up. The titles are given.	Focuses on tone and style.	'The Next War' by Wilfred Owen; 'Does It Matter?' by Siegfried Sassoon.
From extracts of direct speech taken from the poem try to work out the speaker and the context.	Arouses interest; raises questions about context.	'My Last Duchess' by Robert Browning.

Figure 6.2

to note down any questions they would like answered. As they receive other fragments they note the ideas of other groups and add their own. When they have seen the whole poem they receive their first fragment and can now add to it or adapt it. After this introductory activity the entire poem can be subject to other different activities; for example, giving it a title, discussing specific questions.

One of the purposes of these tasks is to encourage pupils to be active in their approach to reading, to engage with the form and content. The *Cambridge Critical Workshop* (1995) provides a useful structure for a more formal, systematic approach to texts. Questions could be asked about form (tightly organised, irregular), tone (tender, ironic, harsh), rhythm (steady, irregular), tempo (quick, moderate, slow), diction (formal, colloquial), texture (smooth, coarse), imagery (literal, figurative), impact (dramatic, understated, impersonal).

A central challenge in teaching poetry is to maintain a balance so that due attention is given both to the subjectivity of the reader and the objective text. The same tension is present in approaches to writing poetry. In the belief that creativity (interpreted largely as originality) should be respected, pupils were often told to 'write a poem' with little or no further guidance or direction. The implicit romantic view was of poetry as a 'spontaneous overflow of powerful feelings' or that genuine poetry is 'composed in the soul'; the emphasis was primarily on the expression of private emotion. There was correspondingly an insufficient emphasis on the craft of writing, on the drafting process, and on a sheer delight in language. There is some danger that emphasis on form without sufficient motivation and engagement will promote mechanistic writing devoid of any real sense of meaning or purpose; all teachers will be familiar with the contorted meanings which some pupils produce in the pursuit of a rhyme. However, working with particular formal constraints can be very liberating and expressive because the framework is already given. The following list represents some examples of more structured approaches to writing poetry; a more detailed discussion of these and other methods can be found in the further reading section.

- poems using the form or images suggested by another: 'The Fight of the Year' by Roger McGough; 'Daily London Recipe' by Steve Turner
- list poems
- poems based on tight formal structures (cinquains, haikus)
- group poems
- parody of familiar poems
- pupils given a collection of 15 – 25 words in an envelope and asked to write a poem (Marsh 1988:59)
- found poems (collected writings in the environment, overheard conversations provide the raw material for crafting a poem)
- collections of clichés, catchphrases as the basis for a poem
- dialect poems
- altering perception (e.g. close-up view of an object)
- shape poems
- poems superimposed on pictures (e.g. title and author on the trunk and base of the tree with different lines on each of the leaves)

To summarise, a successful practical approach to poetry in the classroom will involve the following:

- creating a rich poetry environment;
- combining reading with writing of poetry;
- reading a wide variety of poems, some of which are chosen for their accessibility;
- retaining flexibility in approaches to reading and studying poetry;
- choosing appropriate methodologies for particular poems and eschewing any advice which is intended to apply to all poems;
- asking pupils' to do things with poems instead of asking them questions all the time;
- recognising that many poems need familiarity before they can be properly experienced and analysed;
- recognising that close textual study is more fruitful after pupils have experienced the poem;
- focusing pupils attention on poetry as genre in comparison to other forms of writing in a spirit of exploration.

Faced with providing some insight into a defining characteristic of poetry, pupils are able to do little more than agree with Bentham that, 'Prose is when all the lines except the last go on to the end. Poetry is when some of them fall short of it.' Such apparently naive judgements are not wholly inaccurate. The way a poem appears on the page invites us to speculate about meaning, purpose, ambiguities and complexities and makes us think about language itself and respond to it more sensitively.

Poetry is the most 'natural' form of language not just because it has affinities with our experiences as young children but because it provides an insight into its true nature – it is the primary form of language. Common sense can mislead us into thinking that language is a transparent device for conveying meaning in simple ways. In his early philosophy Wittgenstein had argued for a rigorous, exact, logical relationship between language and reality, 'a gospel of icy-cold logical purity, purity of absolute simple names and absolutely simple objects.' (Finch 1995:29) His later philosophy came to reject that view in favour of a richer, more fluid conception of language. We should not expect a simple, logical definition of 'poetry' because poetry itself teaches us that language does not work in that way.

FURTHER READING

Andrews (1991) *The Problem With Poetry*, Dias and Hayhoe (1988) *Developing Response to Poetry*, Benton *et al.* (1988) *Young Readers Responding to Poems* provide excellent discussions of the teaching of poetry drawing on critical theory. The latter publication provides examples of small-scale research projects. Marsh (1988) *Teaching Through Poetry* and Tunnicliffe (1984) *Poetry Experience* are useful books which deal also with the writing of poetry. Buchbinder (1991) *Contemporary Literary Theory and the Reading of Poetry* is stimulating and has helpful sections on further reading. Hayhoe and Parker (1988) *Words Large as Apples* contains useful discussion and practical ideas. Styles and Triggs (1988) *Poetry 0–16* is inspiring and full of valuable information. The HMI publication (DES 1987) *Teaching Poetry in the Secondary School* is still worth reading. For an inspiring book on teaching the writing of poetry see Pirrie (1987) *On Common Ground*.

RESOURCES

Anthologies are too numerous to list but Styles and Triggs' *Poetry 0–16* has an excellent guide to those published up to 1988, including poetry from around the world. See in particular *I Like That Stuff* and *You'll Love This Stuff* (ed. Styles), Cambridge University Press, and *Black Poetry* (ed. Nichols), Blackie. *The Poetry Pack* (ed. Bleiman), English and Media Centre, is full of interesting ideas for exploring poems at GCSE and A level. See also *The Poetry Video* from the same source containing over fifty poetry readings. *The Poetry File* (Ainsworth *et al.*) from Stanley Thornes contains printed poems as well as activities. The anthology *Axed Between the Ears* has an accompanying resource pack, published by Heinemann. *The Forms of Poetry* (Abbs and Richardson), Cambridge University Press, provides a guide to literary forms of English. The *Cambridge Critical Workshop* and the *Cambridge Poetry Workshop* (Wood and Wood) from the same publishers have useful activities and assignments. *Poetry Workshop* (Benton and Benton), Hodder and Stoughton, has a good collection of poems by theme and author; the latter is useful for wider reading.

7: Speaking and Listening

He gave men speech, and speech created thought,
Which is the measure of the universe.

Shelley, *Prometheus Unbound*

Till human voices wake us, and we drown.

T. S. Eliot, 'The Love Song of J. Alfred Prufrock'

Need we drown in a sea of human voices? English teachers are faced with a bewildering array of practical and theoretical possibilities – many of which are alluded to in this book – and it does certainly seem sometimes like drowning. In dealing with speaking and listening, we have at once the oldest, most deeply rooted aspect of human communication and the most recently opened up to adventurous pedagogical possibilities. We have already noted the imposed hegemony of reading and writing over the older, less formal oral tradition of learning with the development of organised schooling; traditionally, this process has relied on the restriction of speaking and listening – especially if in any way spontaneous. This has not escaped the notice of the more astute educational commentators; take, for example, this ironic observation from a fifty-year-old handbook (Lewis 1946:52):

> Before the teacher enters the classroom there is a buzz of conversation; he puts his nose through the door and it stops. The lesson is 'oral composition'; the teacher laboriously squeezes a few reluctant, formal, and stilted sentences from an otherwise dumb class. At length the lesson is over. The teacher has barely closed the door behind him before unauthorised oral composition is again in full swing.

Hopefully, this scenario is not quite as familiar to today's English teachers, but it may well still strike a chord. I remember a colleague explaining to me in my early days of teaching that the reason why teachers feel so tired so often is that they are in fact engaged in damming up and holding back a powerful torrent of youthful energy all their working lives. I have often reflected on this, and clearly such energy is unlikely to be expressed in reading or writing: its principal 'voice' is oral. The idea of education – or more specifically schooling – as a form of control, even opposition, has always been contested too, of course, and increasingly so. 'Energy is eternal delight' wrote Blake: the challenge is to make positive use of this energy and power in our English classrooms.

To return to another of the writers whose words have informed this book, Thomas Traherne, we need more than ever to know for what end we study with matters of speaking and listening, for it is such a vast area, and so deeply personal, that we will surely err in the manner if we do not. By the same token that has reading and writing as formally taught, oral development is the most 'naturally' accomplished of language feats; in this we are presented, as so often, with both an opportunity and a threat. A worthwhile question to pose to a new teaching group is, 'what do you consider to be the point of English lessons in speaking and listening, when you have all become fluent speakers without the need of school?' The responses will vary, but may polarise along the lines of two possibilities:

- to broaden the scope of and opportunities for speaking and listening activities;
- to teach and reinforce 'correct' spoken English, rectifying habitual errors of speech.

The former suggests an enlightened opportunity; the latter, perhaps, is more of a threat and may well reflect a belief among fluent speakers of English that they in fact speak badly or, even worse, that their speech is somehow 'common'. But we have to work with what we have, to start from a realistic appraisal, and maybe even this sort of threat can be converted into something of an opportunity.

Any such realistic appraisal must acknowledge the absolute centrality of speech to language in general, embedded in the very words we use to reflect on practice. For example: we speak of helping pupils find a personal voice in response to literature, perhaps even to discern an authorial voice in the text; but in reality I am here *writing* about what is likely to be a *written* response to *reading*. This is more than just a stylistic nicety: the metaphor of speech brings a suggestion of freshness and spontaneity to language. Surely these are the qualities that we wish to characterise the English classroom? In some ways it may be apt to see each individual pupil as a microcosm of the linguistic development of society as a whole, with a personal reservoir of oral experience pre-dating acquisition of reading and writing: an oral tradition at once social and intensely individual which lays the foundations of all linguistic achievement, and, however sophisticated formal literacy skills may become, continues to give language its 'flavour'. Further, language and thought itself are intrinsically bound up – as Shelley, quoted above, knew full well.

The work of Vygotsky has done much to inform the philosophy and practice of English teaching in this context (see, for example, Britton's illuminating chapter in Brindley 1994). If, following Vygotsky, we see thought as a development of 'interior speech', literally spoken aloud during infancy, then we ignore the delicate relationship between thought and speech at our peril. This is particularly important at adolescence for this is the time of continuing, often accelerating, experimentation: sometimes pupils will 'think before speaking', sometimes not; sometimes we need to go with the spontaneous flow, sometimes intervene to focus on the need to reflect before – or even without – speech. The latter is fundamental to listening, in practice often the neglected partner in the combination of speaking and listening. Carlyle, writing in his highly personal treatise *Sartor Resartus* (1834), realised the intimate relationship between thought and language: 'Language is called the garment of thought; however, it should rather be, language is the flesh-garment, the body, of thought.'

The responsibility of English teachers is enormous and challenging, then, but simultaneously exciting and invigorating. As Quirk and Stein (1990:19) put it:

Not all of us depend to the same extent on words when we are thinking to ourselves, but it is certain that, in general, thinking and decision-making are vastly supported and facilitated by language, even though we may be using the language silently. Most of us can grasp a distinction better when we have the linguistic apparatus to identify it amid the flux and chaos of raw experience around us.

This fusion of language and thought clearly includes reading and writing as well as speaking and listening, but it is the latter facets of language which remain absolutely basic to the process throughout our, and our pupils', development as language users and thinkers.

Quotations from the likes of Shelley and Carlyle testify to the long acknowledged depth of this relationship, but educational practice does not always act accordingly. There can be, for example, a debilitating reliance on 'exercises' in oral 'skills' with the implication that appropriate 'training' will achieve the desired results. It is easy to look back at Tomkinson (1921) and imagine we have left his recommended exercises far behind – 'exercises for beauty of tone', for example, or 'for clear articulation and facility' leading up to the skills of debating for which involvement in the subject matter or personal opinion count for nothing in favour of 'pure' technique. Decontextualised and superficial such activity might be, but the 'presentational skills' demanded by modern oral assessment may in the end amount to much the same thing. The huge interest in speaking and listening during the 1980s gave rise to words such as 'oracy' and 'aural' (which, ironically, nobody was quite sure how to pronounce) and accompanying assessment exercises. A clipboard mentality of 'if it speaks, assess it' swept the English classrooms of the day, often leaving little room for sanity. The National Curriculum served to reinforce this approach, with the lowest attainment level demanding that pupils should be able to communicate a 'simple' message effectively: colleagues I worked with at the time were ready with clipboards to see how quickly a pupil shouting 'Fire!' could empty a school. However, through all this – and perhaps despite much of it – a great deal has been achieved in raising the profile of speaking and listening. Excellent practice is steadily broadening its base, developing an English curriculum in which speaking and listening are fully integrated with the other facets of the subject.

Tensions remain, nevertheless, and it is time to examine them in greater depth. An effective method to use here is to consider nine statements and arrange them into a diamond pattern – either with the most important or agreeable at the top and the others in descending order of priority, or with the most vital statement in the centre and the others around it. This 'Diamond Nine' exercise models good teaching practice, and is most effectively used as a focus for discussion, perhaps for an English department. The statements are as follows:

- a pupil's spoken English should never be 'corrected' by the teacher;
- all classroom talk may be legitimately assessed by the English teacher;
- pupils should be taught that non-standard dialect is inappropriate in some speaking situations;
- speaking and listening should underpin as many English activities as possible;
- pupils should always be made aware of when and how their speaking and listening are being assessed;
- oral English can be broken down into specific skills and taught accordingly;
- formal speaking situations, such as debates and public speaking, should be highly valued in English;
- anything really valuable in speaking and listening cannot be formally assessed;
- sloppy oral expression reflects and/or influences sloppy thought.

You are unlikely to find it easy to fit the statements into a neat pattern, and this in itself testifies to the problematic nature of speaking and listening. Again, some of the statements are mutually exclusive while others are compatible, and it is quite possible to have all of them agreed with by different members of an English department. What matters is that the issues should be openly debated and what matters in this debate is substance rather than style.

On close examination many of the tensions in oral English may be reduced to a basic concern for the nature of its assessment. This was already considered in Chapter 4. English teachers face something of a quandary here, for in today's educational world formal assessment assigns significance to speaking and listening – but at what cost to any real value? Certainly, even if we agree that giving oral performance some sort of accreditation is welcome (and it is still proportionally far less than that given to reading or writing), this is an aspect of English calling for great sensitivity. Some aspects of oral work may demand a detailed and relatively objective set of assessment criteria well known to both pupils and teacher; for example, the delivery of a talk to the rest of the class or the chairing of a small group discussion. At other times, such a public awareness of and concern for the minutiae of assessment may actually hinder the free flow of orally expressed ideas by emphasising the how, the means of delivery, at the expense of the what, the content, the ideas struggling for adequate expression but worth expressing even if imperfectly. In this sort of instance it should be enough for the pupil (and teacher) to be only half consciously aware that oral performance is in the long term assessed. Whole-class discussions, for example, often spontaneous by nature, are generally best assessed in this way. Assessment, then, should match the nature of the activity and should, where possible, involve pupils and teacher in partnership – designing assessment criteria, perhaps, to help each other in the enhancement of the quality of talk. The method of assessment used will arise from the nature of the activity and the logistics involved. Cassette recorders and video cameras can be useful, as can clipboards and checklists – used sparingly. It is of course vital that a clear record is kept over the full range of activities so that a 'snapshot' judgement of a particular pupil may be given if required and so that continuity may be eased between teacher and teacher, year and year.

The dangers of compartmentalisation of speaking and listening into various 'skills' – 'presentational skills', 'listening skills' and so on – for apparent ease of assessment go much further than immediate classroom practice. As with other aspects of education, day-to-day practice both reflects and informs the wider philosophical and cultural context – the English classroom as a microcosm – which is why we have to be so careful. There is a real tension here: we want our pupils to speak confidently, fluently and effectively in the real world of social interaction and work, but do we want to help usher in the Disney Store 'have a nice day!' view of talk where customer-friendly performance is all and serves a sophisticated profit motive? Hornbrook in Holderness (ed.) (1988:156) warned us of the insidious nature of curriculum changes along these lines:

> The worried liberal-left in the teaching profession has been perhaps too easily persuaded to connive at these seemingly beneficient manipulations of the curriculum. . .The smartly turned out hotel receptionists and hypermarket cashiers of TVEI and CPVE and YTS are the compliant service class of tomorrow, non-unionised and badly paid, trained for the telephone and the till, and as doomed in their subordination as the mute congregations of the Middle Ages.

The initials of the initiatives may have changed in ten years, like the names of nuclear power stations, but the dangers are just as real. English teachers need to be fully aware of the implications of what happens in their classrooms; they need to integrate the content with the style of speaking and listening so that values such as honesty, sincerity and respect for others' views are combined with increasing oral lucidity and effectiveness. Indeed, as Harrison (1994) asks, what learning can take place without interaction through talk? It may well be that in a democratic and pluralist society confidently and fluently expressed public opinion is increasingly heard, in interactive radio programmes, for example; and it just might have something to do with the effective teaching of speaking and listening as a major priority in schools over the past three decades. We as English teachers cannot make the agenda, for we operate in the context of powerful social and cultural forces, but we can perhaps offer opportunities and encourage genuine expression.

Harrison (1994:135) offers us an extremely useful summary of the nature of good oral English teaching. Learners need confidence and expertise in talk, he maintains, so that they can

- listen to, convey and share ideas and feelings;
- listen to, convey and share information;
- understand, convey and share the 'story' (their own and others');
- listen to, present, defend and interrogate points of view;
- consider questions, raise questions, work towards answers;
- understand accounts of processes, be able to describe and evaluate processes;
- be sensitive (as listener and as speaker) to appropriate tone and rhythms of voice – for example, sometimes reflective and exploratory, at other times assertive and persuasive;
- be aware (as listener and as speaker) of the need for clear expression;
- know when to be tolerant, when to support, and when to challenge in talk with others;
- be confident in providing a personal presence in talking, without letting self-consciousness intrude on what you want to say – and accept the personal presence of others, while respecting what they have to say (rather than how they say it).

This reflects a holistic and exhaustive view of the nature of speaking and listening in the English classroom with both subtlety and rigour. We shall explore some of the practical implications below and some of the issues concerning self-consciousness of oral performance in Chapter 9. To use the analogy of learning to ride a bicycle, it may be necessary for the learner to know something of the principles of balancing on two narrow strips of rubber, but expertise will only come with practice – with the teacher, in fact, 'letting go'. Indeed, it may well be that too great a knowledge of the laws of gravity – improbable as they seem – may actually cause our rider to wobble and fall off in anxiety.

The role of the audience for talk is a vital one. It is an active role too, for the audience provides the other half of the speaking and listening combination. To fulfil the full range of oral possibilities alluded to above, pupils should be given every opportunity to experience a variety of audiences involving:

- their classmates, as a whole class or as individuals or small groups;
- other pupils of different ages and interests;
- pupils from different schools, particularly cross-phase partnership schools;
- teachers – and not only their English teacher, if feasible opportunities can be found;
- other adults from different walks of life with particularly relevant interests;

- imagined audiences through role-play and media-based oral projects;
- real audiences through the media of audio- and video- taping, and even, as the facility becomes more widely available, video-conferencing.

For listeners too there should be a wide range of meaningful experiences, many of which will be integrated into the sort of activities noted above; we could add, with a specific focus on listening, the use of:

- the teacher as lecturer (let us not forget OFSTED's advice to teachers to rediscover the didactic approach);
- outside speakers, especially if relevant to the particular theme studied, such as representatives from pressure groups, societies, the press, charities, the media and political organisations;
- writers, poets, theatre groups and story-tellers; teachers from different curricular areas with particular information on the topic studied – be aware of the wealth of under-used knowledge and oral expertise in any school.

Throughout all this resourcefulness, the English teacher's own role, as always, is crucial. Apart from creating the conditions of encouragement and stimulation, we too must above all listen attentively and sympathetically. Not all of us are natural listeners, and we are unlikely to be trained counsellors (neither should we be); but we can, nevertheless, 'heal ourselves' in the arts of listening through the focusing of attention on the utterance itself without prejudice. Social intercourse consisting of Pinteresque interrupted monologues is all too common, not least in the classroom, and it may well take a real effort of will to clear one's mind sufficiently of such issues as 'how to respond' or 'what is my view?' to really hear what is being said. If we are to model good practice, however, this is precisely what we need to do. As a practical aid to such reflective learning, it is worth taping an orally-based lesson and analysing the results critically to see how much genuine listening took place and what it resulted in. We as teachers need to learn from our classrooms as do our pupils, and good listening is the key to a great deal of effective teaching right across the curriculum.

Much oral activity will be spontaneous, and quite rightly so. However, the drafting of oral work, where appropriate and with the same provisos we noted for the drafting of written English, should also be actively encouraged. Although, as we argue elsewhere, learning to speak is largely a natural process, the English teacher needs to understand just when drafting may be appropriate as a means of actively teaching speaking and listening as opposed to simply facilitating their occurrence. Oral drafting may well be most apt in different types of planned performance, and the potential and power of the voice to celebrate and accomplish should never be underestimated or under-taught. As for written drafting, the teacher's judicious intervention is vital, and the use of peer support. Thus the stages of drafting should be geared towards effective communication through a polished product, and may well involve, in the process:

- alteration and adaptation of spoken content;
- increased sophistication of delivery;
- greater awareness of the specific audience in mind;
- changes in register, perhaps achieved through reflective use of taping;
- increasing awareness of the precise function of the particular performance – is it, for example, to persuade, to entertain, to instruct, to report, to clarify, to narrate or to describe (to name but a few)?

The nature of the drafting strategy used is dependent upon the type of activity, its context, and its projected audience. In essence, it is the formalisation of preparation, and, as all teachers know full well through their own professional work, many spoken performances require a great deal of painstaking preparation; it would be unfair to expect otherwise of our pupils.

We have already seen just how much scope there is for English teachers to make judgements about the nature of oral activities, audiences, assessment and so on. In the sense that we are concerned to teach children to become better oral practitioners, the making of these judgements begs the question of exactly what constitutes progress in speaking and listening. We have looked at some of the tensions involved in assessment, and much of what actually occurs seems to be based on differentiation by outcome rather than by task. The National Curriculum generally follows this model, and although the levels of attainment are couched in rather generalised terms this may be their saving grace: the only realistic way of assessing oral performance. However, we need also to recognise that different oral tasks will demand in themselves different levels of expertise, without becoming too hidebound by the notion of hierarchical 'skills'. Anderson *et al.* (1984:51) put the case strongly:

> We have found that different types of tasks elicit different types of language and pose different communicative problems for the speaker. . .we have found that there is an ascending scale of difficulty among different task types. Tasks which involve the speaker in describing static relationships among objects are fairly easy to communicate to a hearer, if there are relatively few objects and the relationships between them are fairly simple. Tasks which involve dynamic relationships among people or objects, where a speaker has to describe events which change over time and space, are more difficult. Tasks which require the speaker to communicate abstract notions, for instance in argument or justifications, are more difficult again, for most young speakers.

Some of the terms used here seem to me problematic when they are intended to be taken at face value: when are relationships 'simple' or 'dynamic', for example? Nevertheless, as a reminder that not all oral activities are equally challenging, and that in planning the oral dimension of the English curriculum we have to take this into account, there is a degree of validity in what is expressed here. The issue is further complicated by the realisation that different pupils will have different strengths and weaknesses in different stages of their development and in different social combinations. Variables like this need careful acknowledgement, and it may be that differentiation by outcome is, in the final analysis, the most feasible method. But variety of approach and activity is fundamental. It may be that a non-hierarchical model of oral interaction in the English classroom has greater relevance, such as Howe's 'oracy map' in Brindley (ed.) (1994:47).

Another potentially problematic area, especially relevant in any sort of hierarchical notion of oral 'skills' and deliberately foregrounded in the National Curriculum, is that of standard spoken English. Looking back again to Lewis (1947:51) we find a genuinely humane and egalitarian hope that the spread of standard spoken English might alleviate and erode social class inequalities:

> if it can be shown that it is necessary for the health of our society that there shall be a truly common speech, then we may perhaps hope to bring this about by an appeal to

feeling; by fostering a pride in nothing less than spoken English, speech common to all who live in these islands. . .It is a fantastic transposition of values to wish to preserve 'picturesque' dialects at the expense of the social health of our community.

There is a world of difference in tone between these words, with their understandable post-war optimism, and Rhodes Boyson's hectoring reaction to the debate on National Curriculum English in the late 1980s (originally in The Sun, subsequently in Moon, 1996:44):

Teachers should be putting across proper English and expect to be spoken to in the same way by children. Grammar has to be taught. It is not something children are born with. . .Standard English is the passport to mobility. Sloppiness in speech rules you out for a job.

Taking this notion still further, David Pascall, then chair of the NCC, suggested in 1992 that teachers should not be content to insist on 'correct' expression in their classrooms but should infiltrate the playground, intervening in pupils' speech to enforce standard English. The point is that for all the differences in tone, the ultimate message amounts to much the same. And there is some validity in it, if of rather a simplistic nature, for if a pupil could only speak in a local dialect of English this would undoubtedly close down many vocational and social opportunities. Even if we regret this, we have, among many other things, to prepare our pupils for the realities of adult life, and none is harsher.

In reality, the situation is not as grim, neither need it be as polarised. People – adults and children alike – are adept at speaking many different forms of English according to the context, purpose and audience. For writing, perhaps, the difficulties are fewer, in that writing is a skill learned in a relatively formal fashion and implies in any case a more formal grammar. This is perhaps the root of the confusion, in that it is written English that has largely determined what most regard as 'correct' spoken English – and even a cursory glance over virtually any transcript of spoken English will show the falsehood of a direct correlation. Indeed, any attempt to transfer from one to the other is fraught with problems: the speech sounds stilted, and writing, except in the most informal circumstances, seems imprecise. What matters is the richness of language, whether spoken or written, as Knight (1996) makes abundantly clear in his illuminating chapter entitled 'Standard English and the Spoken Word'. With talk, it is difficult to disentangle the speaker from the spoken: an attack on the nature of a person's speech is an attack on that person's being. Nevertheless, as in writing, it is important that pupils realise that spoken standard English is required for formal situations, such as job interviews, and where necessary the teacher may have to intervene. Any intervention should be carried out with the greatest sensitivity, most effectively through role-play and subsequent open discussion. Other pupils' perceptions may be useful to start debate on the nature of appropriate speech, but the teacher needs to be all the more wary lest prejudice replace realistic appraisal. It is worth noting here the distinction between accent and dialect: a pupil's accent should in no circumstances be tutored or criticised, as it is perfectly possible to speak the standard form of English in any accent, and, indeed, impossible to speak it without one. Effective English teaching thrives on the richness of oral experience, spoken and listened to, and this should be the guiding principle.

So what would this sort of effective English teaching look – or, rather, sound – like? In the context of an integrated English curriculum, we might expect to find a stimulating range of activities and approaches; it would be likely that, whatever the emphasis on reading or writing in any given assignment, some part of it would entail speaking and listening. In fact it would be hard to think up an English activity not involving them, and in this we have an important starting point. Harrison (1994:239) advises the following safeguards on behalf of all learners:

- encourage *flexibility* among all speakers, in mediating between non-standard (usually colloquial) and standard (usually written) forms of the mother tongue;
- *empower* all speakers to range over the whole universe of discourse – intellectual and affective;
- encourage a full sense of *ownership* of all the versions of language that may be required by speakers;
- instil *confidence* in the use of these versions of language;
- encourage *respect* for the variant versions of language that may be used by other individuals and other communities, for their own particular needs.

To which we would add:

- enjoy and celebrate the many possibilities of language use as absolutely fundamental to oral English.

With these principles in mind, the listener may hear some of the following going on:

- Jigsaw technique for group-based research and reporting work: four separate roles, each role combining with pupils from other groups fulfilling the same role to conduct research/discuss a given aspect of a topic for a set period of time, then reporting back to the original 'home' group. Endless variations of context, method, purpose, audience and roles played.
- Fruitbowl method of small-group formation: the teacher assigns each pupil a 'fruit', and then forms groups for effective oral work accordingly – each group usually forming a mixed fruit-salad, sweetened to taste.
- Pair combinations: friendship pairs, working and talking well together for the first part of any activity, are then combined with compatible other pairs to broaden the base of discussion, perhaps mixing genders.
- Rainbow groups: 'random' group formation based on colour combinations, or allocation of numbers to each pupil with all 'ones' and so on then congregating.
- Envoy technique: groups send envoys (or vary to become gossip columnists) to other groups working on the same topic to glean information/gossip and/or be quizzed on their own group's deliberations, with time limits for each stage.
- Goldfish-bowl method: one group member passively observes the group's effectiveness and reports back on the nature of the findings.
- Eavesdropping session: class focuses on the workings of one particular small group's discussion as a model of good practice, perhaps then offering constructive ideas, guided by the teacher.
- Buzz-session: thirty-second (or vary) pair discussions on a given topic before teacher-selected individuals report back to whole class – a good opening for class discussion, ensuring some sort of preparation from all.
- Storytelling: groups of four tell each other autobiographical/fictional stories; each group selects their favourite; another member of the group then relates the tale in first person to the rest of the class who try to guess the identity of the original teller.

- Just a minute: the teacher picks an unlikely topic (e.g. 'the common housefly') and selects a pupil to speak uninterrupted for one minute, with no repetition or hesitation. An elaboration is to insist on the next pupil making a coherent link to the next unlikely topic ('hot-water bottles').
- Statement-arrangement: statements on cards distributed as a stimulus for group discussion on a given theme or issue, as in the 'Diamond Nine' activity.
- Drama-based techniques such as:
  monologues;
  back-to-back alter-ego dialogues;
  hot-seating of pupils (or teacher) in role;
  mock trials;
  role-play, perhaps with assigned characteristics or 'status numbers';
  deliberately inappropriate role-play such as aggressively conducting an interview.
- Chinese whispers: using the whole class to illustrate how oral transmission can change messages/stories/jokes, etc.
- Formal oral activities: such as debates and public speaking sessions – some pupils respond very well to formal structures for oral performance.
- Use of media resources: not merely as an aid to assessment, where they have a use, but as aids to effective oral performance.
- Listening activities: often neglected, but easy to set up, e.g. asking pupils to remember what the salient points were from a taped speech sequence.
- Celebratory performances: e.g. prepared story telling, choral presentation of poetry learned by heart.
- Predictive activities, through which pupils listen to or invent one half of a conversation, implying the other speaker's words, as in the common experience of overhearing one side of a telephone conversation. Wole Soyinka's poem 'Telephone Coversation' is an excellent starting point for this sort of work, as are some of the radio sketches of the American comedian Bob Newhart ('The Driving Instructor' or 'Bringing Tobacco to England').

The list of enterprising activities and approaches is endless, and endlessly adaptable. It may well be that the human voice is an imperfect medium – 'human speech is like a cracked kettle on which we strum out tunes to make a bear dance, when we would move the stars to pity.' (Flaubert, in *Madame Bovary*) – but it is all we have and should be celebrated and cherished. Oral work lies at the very heart of the English curriculum, and the resulting pulse should be the sign of good health.

FURTHER READING

Integrated views of speaking and listening can be found in Jones (1988) *Lipservice: The Story of Talk in Schools*, Tarleton (1988) *Learning and Talking* and Wilkinson *et al.* (1990) *Spoken English Illuminated*. Alan Howe's study in the 'Papers in Education' series, *Making Talk Work* (NATE, 1997) combines theoretical insights with practical activities; the same author has also contributed a stimulating chapter in Goodwyn (1995) *English and Ability* summarising recent developments in oral English. NATE publish four booklets, *Teaching, Talking and Learning*, one for each Key Stage; they have a practical orientation and interesting cross-curricular ideas, drawing positively on the work of the National Oracy Project. Also useful is Holderness and Lalljee (1997) *An*

Introduction to Oracy: Frameworks for Talk, and the 'Speaking and Listening' section of Brindley (ed.) (1994) *Teaching English*.

RESOURCES

NATE publishes materials through Framework Press in the familiar form of ring-bound photocopiable sheets: *Speaking and Listening: Activities at Key Stage 3* (Kilpatrick) and *Speaking and Listening: Integrated Activities for Pupils at Key Stage 4* (Phillips) are up-to-date and inventive. *Exploring Spoken English* (Carter and McCarthy), Cambridge University Press, focuses imaginatively on oral activities, and has the additional benefit of an accompanying cassette. In so far as speaking and listening need to be assessed, the examination boards have produced helpful video guides (vastly improved since the early days of GCSE oral assessment), and SCAA (now QCA) have performed much the same function at Key Stage 3. Rather more distantly, the Assessment of Performance Unit published a still useful audio cassette in 1986, entitled *Speaking and Listening: Assessment at Age 11* (NFER-Nelson).

8: English at Key Stage 4

They are dissolving what is unique in the amiable ocean of their routines.

John Holloway, *The Colours of Clarity*

This book has sought to address the question of how to retain best practice in English teaching within a context of increasing external constraints. These have been felt particularly strongly at Key Stage 4 where the changes in approaches to assessment have had such a significant effect on teachers' day-to-day work. The re-introduction of compulsory examinations, tiering and a tighter control of syllabus content have had a major impact on the teaching and organisation of English in secondary schools. This chapter will discuss some of those specific changes as well as considering some of the broader issues related to working with pupils at this level.

One of the major contentious issues in recent years was the abandonment in the mid 1990s of so-called 100 per cent coursework schemes at GCSE in favour of a system of assessment by combined coursework and external examinations. This issue, perhaps more than any other, outraged many teachers of English and it is important for newcomers to the profession to understand why that was the case. The following discussion is not intended to be mere polemic nor is it simply an exercise in nostalgia; understanding the benefits and tensions associated with particular methods of assessment is not only a valuable means of gaining insight into aspects of teaching English but is also a way of ensuring that current systems are used in ways which are most beneficial for pupils. The change which reduced the coursework component of the GCSE (to a maximum 40 per cent in English and 30 per cent in Literature) had political and ideological motivations but the opposition voiced at the time was based rather more on educational grounds; many teachers felt that coursework schemes allowed the development of more meaningful and worthwhile courses than the ones they replaced.

Chapter 4 described the way in which reliability and validity in assessment can tend to pull in opposite directions. At the risk of oversimplification, reliability is the degree to which a system of assessment yields the same results in different contexts whereas validity refers to the degree to which a method of assessment can be described as an appropriate means of testing what it purports to measure; a multiple choice test in English can be said to have high reliability but poor validity; on the surface it seems that external examinations sacrifice a certain degree of validity for a high level of reliability because pupils are being tested on the same content and tasks. However, even the reliability of external examinations is often overstated. It is relatively easy to ensure a fairly high degree of standardisation with regard to setting examinations by ensuring that the content is the same for everyone and that candidates have the same amount of time to answer questions. Those factors however do not ensure reliability because there is no guarantee that pupils' performance on one or two occasions will be representative of their potential achievement. Also, standardising the marking of the papers is extremely challenging.

Unless English is assessed in a very reductive and mechanistic way (by, for example, judging writing only by surface criteria, and comprehension of reading by the degree to which candidates' answers are correct or incorrect), it is very difficult to standardise marking. The advent of GCSE signalled in all subjects a healthy change of emphasis towards rewarding what pupils were able to do rather than uncovering what they could not. The more complex the examination, the more elaborate mark schemes have had to become in order to ensure comparability of response by examiners. The standardisation of external examinations in English is not much easier than standardising the marking of coursework.

If the degree of reliability of external examinations was overestimated, the reliability of coursework schemes was severely underestimated. Few professionals who were not closely involved in the detailed workings of such schemes had a proper understanding of the rigour with which moderation procedures were carried out. Staples (1992:114) wrote:

> It is only fair to note, though, that many English teachers are passionately committed to 100 per cent coursework, such is their hatred of one-off summative papers coupled with the pride they justifiably feel in the courses they have been able to create under a very open-ended scheme. There must always be severe doubts, however, over a system which allows so little scope for outsiders to assess a pupil's performance, not to mention any positive effects there might be of preparing pupils to think and write under pressure, as they have to do in controlled examinations.

The comment reveals some fairly common misconceptions: teachers generally had more positive educational reasons for favouring coursework schemes than a 'hatred' of other methods of assessment; there was always considerable scope for outsiders to scrutinise pupils' work. Referring to such methods of assessment as *100 per cent coursework* schemes, although common, was somewhat misleading because all of them required at least one submission which was written under controlled examination conditions.

Teachers who knew their pupils well had a good idea of whether other written assignments undertaken at home had received unfair levels of assistance; this was the most frequently quoted objection to such schemes. The thoroughness of the assessment is illustrated by the moderation system for the GCSE literature coursework syllabus run by the NEAB (now AQA) which involved the following stages: compulsory attendance at trial marking meetings where teachers would submit their own marking to scrutiny and improve their expertise; internal moderation within the school which required candidates' work to be carefully graded and ranked to make external scrutiny and sampling easier; computer sampling of a number of scripts which would be sent to an external marker (or inter-school assessor) for blind marking; statistical moderation of a school's submission by comparing internal and external marks; all work sent to the examination board where a large number of scripts from each centre were read by a review panel; written reports and feedback to individual schools on the nature of the assignments set, the accuracy of the marking, etc.

The system of checks and counter checks was extremely impressive with a very high level of attention to detail, so different from the popular assumption that such coursework schemes were casually administered and that results depended purely on the arbitrary judgements of teachers. So far, however, the argument has been phrased in rather negative terms, indicating why it is that such schemes produced more reliable results than was often thought. It is necessary also to consider why they were thought by many teachers to be so much more educationally worthwhile as methods of assessing English at Key Stage 4.

At the time when changes to the examination system were being mooted, teachers gave eloquent testimony to the ways in which coursework assessment influenced their classroom practice for the better. Harrison (1990:3) contrasted the way in which the traditional O level examinations meant that English which had been a 'lively, enjoyable and stimulating subject' in the first three years of secondary school became an exercise in practising repetitive tasks which would gain the necessary grades (writing at speed; practising comprehension papers; completing context questions and essays on set texts which were learned practically by heart). She goes on to describe the varied and dynamic syllabus which the GCSE coursework scheme promoted, requiring

> a climate, a framework. . .within which every pupil has the opportunity to flourish and to excel. The preparation for further study is immeasurably superior as they become self-reliant, independent, forward-looking students, able to organise, revise and view their own work with some objectivity. This is active not passive learning.

Bousted (1992:20) wrote with equal conviction about the value of GCSE coursework syllabuses, drawing on specific examples of her own work on Howker's *The Nature of the Beast* and Shakespeare's *The Merchant of Venice*. She described in detail the work she undertook with a multi-racial, mixed sex class relating their own personal experiences to their reading of the play:

> Teachers could now work with pupils to encourage the confident expression of their initial responses to a text; to then examine the text and see what evidence could be gathered from it to support or challenge these initial responses which, in this process, would often become more considered, and complex. Thus, a more detailed and certainly a more diverse response to the text could be stimulated amongst a class of pupils.

Gabrielle Cliff Hodges (1993:69) described the very wide range of reading and writing which the scheme promoted and used extracts from pupils' work to demonstrate the quality of their responses. She compared her practices as a teacher with her own memories of reading in secondary school where there was 'no connection between reading for pleasure and reading for school purposes.' There were many similar letters and articles bearing testimony to the benefits teachers derived from coursework schemes, which can be summarised as follows:

- teachers were released from the pressures of preparing candidates for examinations and all that entailed (mock exams, teaching exam technique, etc.), which placed severe limits on the time which could be devoted to the actual teaching of English;
- by choosing texts and assignments which were suitable for their own particular pupils (taking into account ability, culture, interests, etc.) teachers were able to ensure more valid forms of assessment;

- a higher level of validity was ensured because the method of assessment was able to judge work which had been produced in more meaningful contexts than the artificial writing and response demanded by timed examinations;
- the trial marking and moderation procedures through which pupils' work and the actual tasks demanded of them were scrutinised and shared, were invaluable sources of professional development for teachers;
- coursework assessment promoted more individual, personal and authentic responses than the writing which tends to ensure success in examinations.

Such schemes were not without their disadvantages. Sometimes schools set inappropriate assignments which did not give pupils sufficient opportunity to demonstrate achievement, or the range of reading and tasks offered to pupils was narrow and insufficiently challenging. However, the professional development for teachers who were involved in such schemes was considerable; each year schools became more adept at creating suitable assessment tasks and grading work accurately. Present schemes of assessment at Key Stage 4 in English which require some elements of coursework appear to be a reasonable compromise but, because of the considerable cost of administering and marking external examinations, do not give the same prominence to review and moderation. As with SATs at Key Stage 3, the money which has been channelled over the years into the pursuit of the holy grail of short tests which are both reliable and valid could have been more usefully diverted to support moderated teacher assessment.

It is not the intention here however to create an unduly pessimistic view of current systems of assessment at Key Stage 4. The challenge for teachers is how to make best use of whatever system is in place (while still exercising the right to lobby for change if that is felt to be an appropriate course of action). Despite the external constraints, it is very evident that syllabuses have been constructed as far as possible in order to preserve best practice in English teaching (some examples of this are given below). It is important therefore for teachers to keep faith in methods which are educationally worthwhile and avoid the narrowing of the curriculum which in the past all too often accompanied examinations. The use of model answers, endless dictated notes on set texts and excessive concentration on examination practice should not be necessary.

A useful exercise for new teachers who are not familiar with the details of syllabuses at Key Stage 4 is to consider how English might be appropriately examined at GCSE given the significant constraints which operate. English syllabuses have to meet the requirements of the National Curriculum and must therefore cover speaking and listening, reading and writing (they must include a substantial amount of literature whether or not the candidates are also taking English literature as a separate examination). Evidence of the following reading therefore has to be shown either in coursework or in terminal examinations:

- prose
- poetry
- drama
- the work of an author published before 1900
- a play by Shakespeare
- the work of an author published after 1900
- non-fiction
- media
- texts from other cultures and traditions

Assessment must include writing to:

- explore/imagine/entertain
- inform/explain/describe
- argue/persuade/instruct
- analyse/review/comment

Other constraints prescribed by the national criteria for GCSE are as follows:

- There must be two tiers of assessment allowing the award of grades G to C and D to A. The GCSE General Criteria which were issued by the then Schools Curriculum and Assessment Authority specified the tiering arrangements which would apply to all GCSE subjects. From 1998 the exceptional award of grades outside the specified range was not possible.
- a minimum of 60% of the final assessment must be by terminal examination; a maximum of 40% of the final assessment must be by coursework; the weighting must be En1 20%; En2 40%; En3 40%. (The proportions in literature are 70% examination and 30% coursework.)

When designing a syllabus, the following decisions need to be made:

- whether to differentiate for the tiers by outcome, by task or by using different stimulus and reading material;
- which aspect of the syllabus is best assessed by coursework, e.g. Shakespeare, poetry, response to non-fiction;
- whether the syllabus can be constructed to integrate with the assessment of literature;
- how the assessment tasks will be combined to fulfil more than one requirement, e.g. the prose work may also fulfil the requirement for an author before 1900, oral work may also constitute an assessment of reading;
- whether set texts should be prescribed.

The complexity of the challenge facing the examination boards is amply illustrated here. It is not the intention to describe various syllabuses in detail (these can be easily accessed) but to illustrate some of the solutions to these problems, and the implications for classroom practice. One of the disadvantages of traditional terminal examinations in English is that writing tends to occur out of context with very little stimulus other than a bald title. One solution offered by several of the boards is to link the reading materials in one section of the examination with the writing in another. Thus in the NEAB specimen paper (foundation tier) pupils are asked to respond to two non-fiction leaflets based on house safety; for example, 'Write down six different things you can do to your house to make it more secure. . .Which of the two leaflets do you think is more likely to get its message across to the reader, and why?' The writing tasks which follow are integrated with the same theme; for example, 'Imagine you are renting a house which you do not feel is very secure from thieves. Write a letter to your landlord explaining in detail what you want him or her to do to make the house more secure. Try to write personally and persuasively.' The paper for pupils taking the higher tier are tested on more demanding reading material based on cosmetic and preventative dentistry.

   The integration of reading and writing here is helpful but the tasks are inevitably thin and two-dimensional. Even a theme such as 'security in the home' has more potential interest than the bland and prosaic treatment forced by the examination context: comparison of attitudes to home security over time (interviewing grandparents) and in different cultures; whether it might be in advertisers' interests to promote a certain degree of paranoia about home safety; examining the extended imagery in the police safety leaflet – 'fortress', 'castle', 'defence'; considering the way films exploit feelings of personal vulnerability in the home (*Home Alone, Cape Fear*); whether a leaflet of this kind may be counter-productive, etc. The theme of cosmetic dentistry has rich potential for exploring cultural concepts of beauty, changing fashions and gender identity by drawing on literature as well as media texts. Classroom teaching needs to foster an active, enquiring approach to meaning and language and the strict division between fiction and non-fiction reading fostered by the examination structure is not always helpful. Analysis of texts with all abilities which probes different levels of meaning is likely to be a more helpful preparation for examinations than constant practice of similar passages in timed contexts.

One of the criticisms of the ways in which traditional examinations assessed reading is that they either required rote learning of set texts or, in the case of language papers, comprehension questions on rather meaningless, decontextualised prose passages. All the current syllabuses inevitably require response to unseen texts of some kind but they also include the use of pre-release material which is studied in advance and can be annotated and taken in to the examination. The current SEG syllabus provides a booklet for advance study containing media texts, non-fiction material and poetry/prose by ethnic minority writers. In the case of the NEAB syllabus the pre-release material takes the form of an anthology of poetry with additional texts for study by pupils who are also taking literature. Differentiation across the two tiers works not by using different stimulus material (as in the case of the safety leaflets described above) but by asking different questions on the same texts. For example, on a collection of poems, the lower tier question is: 'Several of Gillian Clarke's poems show how things have changed. Write about some of the changes she is describing in at least two of the poems.' The higher tier are asked: 'In many of Gillian Clarke's poems there is a sense that the world she knows is being threatened. Looking at the group of poems as a whole, how does she express this sense of threat in different ways?'

In the context of the examinations, the lower tier pupils are not directed to the more interesting aspect of the poetry, the expression of a sense of threat. That is not intended as a criticism of the paper because inevitably in the context of a timed examination the question has to be accessible and easily understood. The important point, however, is that the teaching in the classroom does not have to be similarly limited. The way to help pupils write effectively in answer to the very straightforward question about change is to bring the poetry alive in the classroom by challenging their thinking and through the type of varied activities described in Chapter 6.

Assessment by examination should not divert teachers from varied, active, exploratory approaches in the classroom. Integrated teaching with an emphasis on meaning, the encouragement of personal response to texts, writing with a sense of audience and purpose and the development of confidence in using language will contribute more to a better performance in examinations than rote learning of prepared answers and practice on decontextualised extracts.

Inevitably some practice and specific advice on taking examinations will be necessary but this does not have to dominate the syllabus. General and fairly familiar guidance on sitting examinations will help candidates: read the instructions and questions carefully; leave time to check the paper at the end of the examination; time answers so that all questions are attempted; take heed of the marks which are available for specific questions or sections as these may indicate the relative weighting of time and energy which should be expended on them.

In addition, some specific guidance on approaching the English papers is likely to be helpful: candidates can be helped by examining the structure of the paper in detail so that they know what to expect; they should be prepared for reading stimulus material and advised not to spend too much time on this (some boards specify pre-reading time at the start of the examination); pupils can be advised on making the best use of prompts which give an indication of what should be covered in answers; technical terms can be revised prior to examination (unless these have been acquired in context they will not be understood but some systematic revision prior to an examination is useful); word limits are sometimes set and candidates should be advised not to waste time counting words over and over again – an estimate is all that is necessary; pupils need to be guided in the annotation of texts and anthologies and how to make best use of these in examinations. Specific examination practice and advice is necessary but if it dominates an English syllabus unduly it will become counter-productive.

Coursework is still an element of all syllabuses and some care needs to be taken in setting assignments. In the early days of the coursework syllabuses some assignments set by schools did not allow pupils to demonstrate sufficient achievement of assessment objectives. Creative responses to literature provided some examples of highly innovative work but did not always allow pupils to show more than an elementary grasp of plot. Diaries or letters in role as a character from a novel sometimes prompted pupils to write little more than summaries. One problem was that it was not clear whether pupils were meant to be demonstrating their own understanding of the text or whether the perceptions should be confined to those of the character through whose eyes events were being perceived. Sometimes assignments were inappropriate to the nature of the text; for example, asking the pupils in role as Piggy to write a letter home misses the point that the absence of contact with adults in Golding's *Lord of the Flies* is an essential ingredient of the novel. The point here is not just that assignments should be set carefully but their purpose, assessment criteria and relationship to objectives should be explained clearly to pupils. One of the challenges in creating coursework assignments is to ensure that one assignment fulfils several assessment objectives.

Although the term 'key stages' was introduced fairly recently with the implementation of the National Curriculum, the transition to Years 10 and 11 has traditionally been seen as significant in the pupil's progress through school. It may be that future developments will focus more on the coherence of the 14–18 curriculum; the continued existence of GCSE is by no means certain. GNVQ courses are increasingly being taught at Key Stage 4 (see further reading section). What is certain, however, is that the later years of compulsory secondary schooling do mark a significant period in the development of young people and this chapter needs to consider some of the broader issues which may affect the teaching of English at this level. Some understanding of adolescence will therefore be helpful.

It is important not to make too many over-generalised claims about adolescence. Whereas for some pupils it is marked by emotional upheaval and a crisis of identity, for others it passes relatively smoothly (Head, 1997). The attendant physical and emotional development and uncertainty about roles and relationships may cause no more than fluctuations of mood but for some it involves more serious challenges to authority and deviant behaviour. Nevertheless, it is by definition a time of transition and adjustment so that feelings of personal vulnerability, however these are manifested, may be strong. Because the onset of adolescence varies considerably with individuals, the challenge facing teachers is greater.

Much of the writing on education and adolescence inevitably focuses on more general rather than subject-specific implications. Coleman (1980), for example, in a description of adolescent needs lists the following:

- the importance of a framework of authority in which young people are able to play some part in the decision-making process ('a permissive environment is no more preferable than an authoritarian one');
- the importance of participating as much as possible in the adult world;
- the need to be seen as individuals and not stereotyped;
- the need for help with developing sexuality;
- the importance of involvement in peer group activity.

There are clear implications here for schools: the inclusion of a personal and social education dimension in the curriculum; the value of work experience and extra curricular activities which may be viewed as essential rather than peripheral aspects of school life.

There are also implications for the teaching of English, although these are not clear-cut. Teachers involved in making choices and recommendations for reading for this age group are faced with a paradox which is neatly summed up by Landsberg (1988:183),

> The urgent message of literature's most thoughtful critics. . .is that the reading of good books can work in a mysterious, compelling way to enlarge the reader's life. Vast numbers of books for beginning and middle readers, both the most praised and the most popular, seem to have exactly that effect. On the other hand a tidal wave of books with an obsessively narrow focus on contemporary teenage preoccupations has inundated the market in the last decade, triumphantly carrying with it the majority of readers in this age group. At precisely the moment when a youngster hesitates on the brink of the larger world, the popular literature for him or her is totally given over to navel gazing and trendy 'problems'.

The challenge of both engaging the immediate interests of pupils and helping them know and come to terms with an external world is particularly pronounced at this stage of development. Although teachers may object in principle to the prescription of texts at Key Stage 4, few are likely to disagree with the inclusion of Shakespeare and other pre-twentieth century literature as one way of extending the range of reading which pupils encounter. It is important not to restrict pupils' reading to topics which are seen as 'adolescent', thus stereotyping young people and restricting them from full access to the adult world.

Adolescent cognitive development, under the influence of Piaget, is often associated with the onset of more formal thinking, a more advanced tendency to hypothesise and a more pronounced capacity for 'metacognition' or thinking about thinking. There are implications here for the teaching of English. The type of approach recommended in various chapters in this book, which seeks to develop in pupils a conscious knowledge not just of the way language works but of how different genres and texts operate within different conventions, is well-suited to the developmental needs of young people. Pupils of this age will need opportunities not just for reading and analysing texts but for examining these in their broader cultural contexts and comparing a wide range of types of text (cf. Chapters 5 and 6). They are then more likely to become involved in challenging conventional ideas about reading and literature. These are not alternative models to the 'personal growth' pupils are likely to derive from their reading but ways of extending their understanding to reflect their intellectual development.

Adolescence is also a time of increased focus on beliefs and values with a corresponding emotional disengagement from dependence on adults. Personal and expressive writing therefore may be very important at this age. As with reading, there is a paradox in that the need to give expression to deeply personal thoughts may come at a time when pupils feel least able to voice them. Writing in English should never seek to be an overtly therapeutic process nor should pupils be asked directly to share private experiences. This does not mean however that they will not give expression to matters which are deeply personal to them either directly or though metaphor.

This chapter ends with three extracts from written assignments which were submitted to me in my teaching career and which illustrate the role that writing can play in the young person's growth to maturity. The first piece was written by a pupil in a lower set of a Year 10 class in response to an assignment which asked the group to write a diary in role. She chose to write about a suicide.

> *Monday 10th July God I am sick, I've no-one to talk to. No-body understands. Baby John has done nothing but cry all day. I could kill him never mind myself.*
>
> *Tuesday 11th July Mother came for the day, she never shut up going on about Dave telling me I should of never got married baby or no baby, telling me he wasn't capable as a father. No-body cares about me. No-body understands. I've had enough.*
>
> *Wednesday 12th July Sat in by myself all day no-one came, couldn't be bothered with baby John, I bought tablets at the chemist, I never left them they stayed in my hand all day. I haven't eaten for 3 days now.*
>
> *Thursday 13th July I was up early (5.30 a.m.) Baby John was ill not surprising he hasn't hardly had anything to eat. The rain has never stopped the milkman came for his money but I never answered the door. I bought another bottle of tablets today. One bottle doesn't seem enough.*
>
> *Friday 14th July Went out for a walk it was still raining. I passed the river, too many people fishing there, I wasn't out long frightened in case someone saw me. I bought two more bottles of tablets. I should have enough now.*
>
> *Saturday 15th July I stayed in, closed all my curtains and locked all the doors, before I did all this I took the baby next door and asked if they could look after him till tomorrow. I have wrote a letter to him so when he gets older he will be able to read it and maybe understand why I couldn't live any longer.*
>
> *Sunday 16th July Before I die whoever reads this diary please understand why.*
>
> *My dear son John,*
> *You should now be at an age to understand this letter, I am deeply sorry that I couldn't bring you up, John. I had you at a very young age, in fact I was 15 when I had you, I hope you will grow up to be a fine big lad, someone who knows how to look after thereself not like me I was incapable. John if you go steady with a girl please treat her good and if she was to fall wrong look after her and show that you care for her. Look after yourself John and I hope you have a happy healthy life.*
>
> *Love, Your mam never forgotten and will always be watching over you.*
>
> *P.S. I enclose a photograph of me.*

It appears at first that the pupil used the diary in role to explore situations and feelings which were some considerable distance from her. The piece could be interpreted as an example of a young person using her writing to take a glimpse into an adult world beyond her with its potential difficulties and challenges. The ending borders on the sentimental but the directness and simplicity of the language and the colloquial style give it authenticity. It was in the following year when this girl submitted an autobiography that it became apparent the writing had more a personal relevance: her own mother was only seventeen when she was born and had been unable to look after her. The diary can be seen as an attempt to explore the sense of bereavement and loss her own mother may have felt; the photograph may represent her own wish that a similar memento had been left for her. In the light of the information about her own past life, the diary takes on new meaning. Using the protection of role and metaphor as a means of providing objectivity and distance, she has used her writing to help come to terms with her own personal experiences.

The second example was also submitted by a Year 10 pupil in response to an invitation to write about an occasion when someone felt excluded from a group or situation. I had not asked the pupils to draw directly on their own experience; it was up to them whether they chose to do so and whether they would write in the first or third person. One girl decided to write about her parents' divorce which happened when she was eight years old. The piece is lengthy and written in a very controlled way; there is very little self-pity or heightened emotion and the style is fairly undemonstrative. She writes about her confusion at the time over what divorce meant and the failure of the adults to explain anything:

> When I asked questions about it, or why they were getting divorced I was just told 'You're too young to understand' I think perhaps this hurt me as much as anything else because, true, I did not understand, but I felt I could. I was eight years old.

She continues to describe the fears she felt about the future and of having to be taken into care. After giving an account of the father's departure she describes a first shopping trip for birthday presents without him. The piece ends with a description of the father's first Sunday visit and an outing to the park where at last he explains the divorce to her:

> I saw he was crying, I had never seen him cry before. We arrived back at the car. We did not speak all the way home. When we arrived he kissed us both, we said goodbye; we got out of the car and he went. That was all I needed. Someone should have explained earlier. Two months was too long to wait. Adults should not presume children are too young to understand. They understand more than you think.

The writing is very far from being an indulgent piece of self expression. The pupil uses the task to allow her developing adult self to understand and distance experiences which at the time were bewildering and painful for her.

The same idea of being excluded from and underestimated by the adult world appears in the course of an autobiography written by a Year 11 pupil who had special needs. The pupil concerned was ebullient and witty, very talented at drama but with severe problems throughout his school career with the mechanics of reading and writing. The following extract, which is in contrast to the humorous and more defiant tone of the rest of the piece, is again a retrospective look at childhood with the benefit of a more sophisticated view:

In the third year was good I liked the teacher so I would behive untill one day a sicolligis come to see me and interviewed me made me read ask some silly questions and sent me bake to the classroom. I spent a whole aftrnoon whith her. I did nat know what to think. I was never tould what she whonted.

That night I got no sleep by wondring what they were going to do. I was alwayes the thike one in the class. I thort they were going to sened me away.

And one day a cared was sent to the house.

Saying she was coming to see us. I had a lot of expling to do because I had nere taled my mum or dad. So she came to our house and explaind she wonted to see why I was not progresing at school. This whent on untill the second year of this school.

In the course of the year the group read Daniel Keyes' *Flowers for Algernon,* a science fiction short story in which the main character undergoes an operation to increase his very limited intelligence. The pupil who wrote the autobiography was very taken with this story and, largely inspired by his enthusiasm and leadership, the group worked on a dramatic representation of it. He played the central character and, as someone who had always been considered 'the thike one in the class', it was both ironic and poignant that his own lively intelligence allowed him to play the part before and after the operation so convincingly. It is not necessary for the teacher to have specific knowledge of how pupils' writing and response to reading at this age may relate to their own personal lives; it is enough to be sensitive to the fact that this may be, and often is, the case.

FURTHER READING

Sweetman (1998) *Curriculum Confidential* gives a very clear explanation of developments post-14 including piloting of GNVQs. The book is also a useful source of information on such subjects as national target-setting, the rationalisation of the examination boards and benchmarking. The chapter on English is clear and authoritative. For an interesting discussion of English at Key Stage 4 see Peim in Protherough and King (eds) (1995) *The Challenge of English in the National Curriculum.* Davison and Dowson (1998) *Learning to Teach English in the Secondary School* also has a helpful section on Key Stage 4 English.

RESOURCES

Two NATE publications, *Exploring Pre-Twentieth Century Fiction: A Language Approach* and *The Wider Reading File,* are loose-leaf and photocopiable, focusing on the 14–16 age range. The English and Media Centre also publishes attractively presented guides on *Gulliver's Travels* (including activities on the recent film version), *Under Goliath, The Friends,* Janni Howker's novels, *Animal Farm, Of Mice and Men* and others. Further excellent guides on specific texts accompany *Hodder English 4.* Heinemann, in conjunction with NEAB, have produced a *Teacher's Resource File* (Bennet, Thomas, Buckroyd), written by experienced GCSE examiners, and revision guides to the examination board anthology and other aspects of the syllabus. A wide-ranging Key Stage 4 volume *The Language Book* (Shuttleworth and Mayne) and two packs for Key Stage 4 focusing on language and gender under the title *Language Awareness Project, Years 10 and 11* are available from Hodder and Stoughton.

9: Knowledge About Language

You taught me language, and my profit on't
Is I know how to curse. The red plague rid you
For learning me your language!

Caliban in Shakespeare's *The Tempest*

As indicated in the Introduction, one of the central questions in English is how far should we as teachers seek to decontextualise language, to make it in itself an object of study. The question, as we have already seen in Chapter 7 and will seek to explore further, has very real implications for the practice of English teaching: we may endanger the spontaneity of language through over analysis, in the sense that Wordsworth protested, 'We murder to dissect.' We must also keep our eye on exactly what language is being used for; and Caliban's lament, quoted above, should serve as a timely warning – for Prospero, appropriately both his captor and his teacher, has indeed, wittingly or not, sown the seeds of Caliban's curse.

Imagine again the hapless cyclist first encountered in Chapter 7, already wobbling under the weight of self-conscious knowledge in speaking and listening but, nevertheless, pursued avidly by determined English teachers. How much more unbalanced is this cyclist likely to become if we increase the burden to include knowledge about language as a whole? What started off as a gentle bike ride is in danger of becoming more like a circus balancing act. On the other hand, if our cyclist is to improve, especially when the terrain gets rough and the competition hots up, some knowledge of the theories and techniques of effective cycling is surely helpful. Perhaps here, if we finally abandon the cycling metaphor, is the clue to what constitutes useful knowledge about language: the need to improve language capability for ever more sophisticated purposes and contexts in a complex and demanding – not to mention highly competitive – world. A fundamental tension does remain, between on the one hand the need to perceive the manipulative effects of language in society in order no longer to fall victim to them, and, on the other hand, the understandable but rather less laudable desire to increase one's own manipulative powers of language.

The point is really that effective and interesting knowledge about language is centrally concerned with the integration of analysis with practice. This is not the place to rehearse the well-documented demise of what Mittins (1988) critically termed the 'Naming of Parts' philosophy of teaching about language, for so long the dominant school practice, based on decontextualised exercises and drills. The subsequent abandonment, in the 1960s and 1970s, of this sort of approach did leave something of a vacuum in language teaching, although far less of one than certain commentators would have us believe. An integrated, more holistic and practical approach is now much commoner, despite a politically motivated rearguard action which saw the disgraceful undermining of the recommendations of the Language in the National Curriculum (LINC) working group and constant sniping at any innovative approaches to language teaching. English departments are now able to evaluate pedagogies and accompanying resources forged in the heat of the ideological battles of the 1980s and early 1990s rather more dispassionately than was possible at the time, with a view to implementing a truly holistic teaching of knowledge about language. However, we must also be conscious of the limitations. Towards the end of Brian Friel's play *Translations* (1981) – a marvellous study of language and power which we shall revisit in Chapter 11 – the disconsolate and disillusioned Hugh explains to his pupil Maire, anxious as she is to learn English, 'don't expect too much. I will provide you with the available words and the available grammar. But will that help you to interpret between privacies? I have no idea. But it's all we have.' Ultimately this may well be the case; but 'all we have' may be considerably more than the tragic Hugh realises.

English teachers have an invaluable ally here in what seems to be the intrinsically fascinating nature of language, precisely because it denotes so many things and is open to so many interpretations. It is at once intensely personally subjective in how it feels, and dynamically social in its communicative uses. Class, age, personal identity, peer group membership, locality and nationality all contribute to this fascination, and all of these provide excellent starting points for the examination of language in the English classroom. Such is the overwhelming power of the human feel for language that it may be described as instinctive (although this word itself is problematic in meaning). Pinker (1994:21), already quoted on p.ix, elaborates on this point:

> The workings of language are as far from our awareness as the rationale for egg-laying is from the fly's. Our thoughts come out of our mouths so effortlessly that they often embarrass us, having eluded our mental censors. When we are comprehending sentences, the stream of words is transparent; we see through to the meaning so automatically that we can forget that a movie is in a foreign language and subtitled. . .The effortlessness, the transparency, the automaticity are illusions, masking a system of great richness and beauty.

Knowledge about language should be geared towards uncovering this 'system of great richness and beauty', while at the same time enhancing celebratory spontaneity. This is no easy task, and requires great skill: and here 'skill' does not refer to some blandly reductive going-through-the-motions activity. We are talking rather about the professional expertise, no less, of an English teacher.

To speak of knowledge about language is in some respects misleading, for we all use, and know about, many different languages. English activities, some of which we shall look at below, can explore these different forms of English, depending as they do on context and purpose, and even without the aid of good teaching children are impressively adept at functioning in a vast range of linguistic circumstances and switching painlessly from one to another. We need to build on this 'natural' ability, and we need to pay particular attention to formal and informal modes – to describe them somewhat simplistically. As with so much else, there is nothing especially new in this. Consider Hardy's 1891 presentation of his heroine Tess, in part at least the product of the new national education system, in contrast to her relatively unschooled mother:

> Mrs Durbeyfield habitually spoke the dialect; her daughter, who had passed the Sixth
> Standard in the National School under a London-trained mistress, spoke two languages;
> the dialect at home, more or less; ordinary English abroad and to persons of quality.

Hardy, presumably, intends irony here: Tess's ability to converse in standard English opens the way to two 'persons of quality' in particular, who between them destroy her. Interestingly, Hardy, in his first edition of the novel, wrote of Tess using the local dialect form of English not merely 'at home, more or less' but 'only when excited by joy, surprise, or grief.'

On one level, of course, we need as teachers to ensure that our pupils can function and flourish in the full range of language forms manifested in a pluralist society – a drive towards equality of opportunity. But the reality is far more complex than this: potentially liberating, certainly; but also, as Tess found to her cost, potentially dangerous. The relationship between language, emotions ('joy, surprise, or grief') and social reality is complex and often problematic, and any worthwhile attempt to educate our children in knowledge about language must fully acknowledge this. Neither should the relationship be conceived as static, but rather as dynamic and dialectical, with social opportunities and constraints both influencing and in turn being influenced by the nature of the language(s) involved. In practical terms, as in so much else concerned with English teaching, this is an argument for a fully integrated curriculum both within the subject itself and in relationship with other curricular areas, all of which assuredly deal with manifestations of social reality. One of the strengths of English, however, is its potential use of literature as language in action and in this sense all literature, including *Tess of the D'Urbervilles*, is centrally concerned with (and of course expressed through) language, whatever else it may be about.

With this in mind, a useful practical exercise for an English department could be to consider the texts used as the basis for the curriculum, asking how each lends itself specifically to the teaching of knowledge about language. If the department is large enough, individual or paired teachers could report back to colleagues on their findings, highlighting such possibilities as:

- variety of sentence structure and syntax, including passive and active forms;
- use of connectives and other ways of combining phrases and clauses;
- use of semi-colons, dashes and colons as subtle ways of breaking up language;
- paragraphing and other ways of splitting up text;
- adverbial and adjectival modifiers;
- presentation of dialogue, including its punctuation;
- varieties of dialect, and even accent;
- the uses and limitations of standard English;
- departures from generally-conceived 'correctness' in presentation;
- how characters' language changes in different contexts;
- distinctions between American – and other national forms of – English and our own 'British' English;
- issues of class, race and gender as referring to the nature of language;
- language change over time, and exploration of why changes occur and whether we can apply labels of progress or deterioration to such changes.

A great deal can be achieved through this sort of exploration of literature, and in an increasingly overcrowded English curriculum making full and varied use of any resources is utterly sensible – perhaps essential. The list of possible approaches is very far from exhaustive, but one can see in it a development from what might be termed the formal, presentational aspects of written language towards a consideration of some of the underlying questions about its use. The important point – and an important qualification, perhaps – is that language features should be related to the purpose and context of the literature rather than simply extracted from it in some sort of disjointed fashion. In this respect, pupils may of course be invited to evaluate the effectiveness of language as used by authors, thus further accentuating fresh responses to literature.

Language study based on what is read is but one 'way in'. We need now to consider in more general terms what shape the integration of language knowledge into the English curriculum could begin to take. There are a number of questions to answer, all of which revolve around the central tensions of knowledge about language outlined above:

- How exactly can knowledge about language be integrated into the other aspects of the English curriculum, for example those dealing with literature?
- How may we respect, and encourage respect for, pupils' linguistic experience while preparing them for the realities of language in society?
- How do we deal with the tension between 'correctness' in terms of standard English and 'appropriateness' as preferred by most linguists?
- In seeking to improve pupils' language use, either written or spoken, should we rely principally on a 'remedial' approach, tackling faults and shortcomings as they arise naturally in English activities?
- Should we rather be 'proactive' in teaching methodically aspects of language which we know through experience often give problems, such as speech punctuation, certain spellings, the use of semi-colons, or sentence structure?
- Whichever of the last two approaches is used – and they are not, of course, entirely mutually exclusive – what sort of meta-linguistic vocabulary is needed in order to teach effectively about language?
- How should this meta-linguistic vocabulary itself be taught?
- What opportunities are there for cross-curricular collaboration in terms of language in society (the humanities), expressive forms of language (the arts), language as a communication system (modern foreign languages), etc?
- What opportunities are there also for cross-phase collaboration, so that the often impressive knowledge about language developed in primary schools may be further built on in the secondary phase, and any omissions made good?

These questions must inform our practice, and like the most useful questions in teaching itself they are intended to be open, suggestive of ways forward rather than implying 'correct' answers given by us or anyone else. Brian Cox's descriptions of his Committee's investigations into English teaching as they worked on the original National Curriculum in the mid 1980s are useful here. He noted that while there was often little formal teaching of knowledge about language in English classrooms, meta-linguistic terms such as 'sentence', 'verb' or 'full stop' were constantly and unavoidably being used. This, of course, relates to two of the key questions posed above concerning meta-linguistic terminology, with some implications for other points also. This is just one rather narrow aspect of knowledge about language, but a vital one which may provide a very practical focus for explicit planning of language teaching. To help in contextualising it into English teaching practice a worthwhile exercise may be to consider and list, with colleagues if possible,

- the meta-linguistic terms commonly used;
- whether there is likely to be a shared or widespread understanding of them;
- how they are used (orally, in marking, remedially, prescriptively, descriptively, etc.);
- how these terms are taught or explained;
- which, if any, may be discarded;
- which other terms may be usefully added to the list.

The resulting list should provide a useful starting point for development, but it is the process through which it is arrived at that may well throw up differences in approach. Cox (1991:57) is again helpful in providing a broader context here:

> Two justifications for teaching pupils explicitly about language are, first, the positive effect on aspects of their use of language and, secondly, the general value of such knowledge as an important part of their understanding of their social and cultural environment, since language has vital functions in the life of the individual and of society. . .Language is not merely a neutral medium for the conveying of information; it can trigger emotional responses which may spring from prejudice, stereotyping or misunderstanding. Such attitudes need to be laid open to examination and discussion.

In practical terms, this suggests that the sort of language analysis we are concerned with developing in the classroom, and the attendant terminology, should not be conceived as neutral, decontextualised, or static. Whatever the results of your list, the next stage is rather more time-consuming: the planned implementation of knowledge about language through the curriculum in an integrated and interesting way, bearing in mind the considerations quoted above.

To help further in this process it may be useful to go back a little further, to the Kingman Report (DES 1988) which was intended to provide the theoretical framework for the teaching of language but because it failed to provide a narrowly prescriptive model never really gained the official approval it deserved. Perhaps this has been its strength: certainly there is a great deal of value in it and it is well worth referring back to ten years on. Selective quotations give a flavour of the Report:

> We believe that for children not to be taught anything about their language is seriously to their disadvantage. . .pupils need to have their attention drawn to what they are doing and why they are doing it because this is helpful to their language ability.

> Awareness of the forms of language is an entirely natural development.

> Teaching language must involve talking about language since learning without that activity is slow, inefficient and inequitable (in that it favours those whose ability enables them to generalise without tuition).

> Nor do we see it as part of our task to plead for a return to old fashioned grammar teaching and learning by rote.

> We reject the belief that any notion of correct or incorrect use of language is an affront to personal liberty. We also reject the belief that knowing how to use terminology in which to speak of language is undesirable. There is no positive

advantage in such ignorance. It is just as important to teach about our language environment. The skills, perceptions and knowledge that we are advocating will be of value to all pupils, and should in no way be the exclusive privilege of the more able.

We have met some of these arguments before, particularly those implying an entitlement curriculum, and they – like language itself – may remain somewhat contentious. A further valuable reflective exercise, again conducted collaboratively if possible, might be to consider the validity or otherwise of these statements and how they could be implemented or modified in practical terms of English teaching. One of the explicit recommendations of the Kingman Committee was that knowledge about language should inform teacher education; there has already been significant legislation in this area, and new 'standards' (replacing 'competences', now almost a term of disparagement!) have been developed in initial and continuing teacher education. For English teachers these contain detailed areas of subject knowledge concerning the workings of language, so the practically reflective exercise recommended above has a very real significance in the development of English teaching and should be accorded a high priority. It is essentially a matter of exploring the possibilities of legitimising and subsequently developing the fascination for and considerable knowledge of language brought into any English classroom by the pupils – and, for that matter, their teacher (lest we forget!). This development requires conscious decision making about language use; and as Davies (1996:52) has pointed out,

> This is what English teaching should provide especially well: opportunities for learning about the choices that can and must be made in the use of language, and help for learners in developing explicit understandings and vision of what they can make language do for their own varied and complex needs.

In this context of making informed choices we do need some sort of structure within which to develop the teaching of language. Kingman's four-part model for the consideration of language – its forms; communication and comprehension; its acquisition; its variation – makes a great deal of sense and has been used, in its more detailed form as presented in the Report itself, by some English departments as a convenient model to ensure entitlement.

As with other aspects of the English curriculum, we should as English teachers be ready to look around us as well as examining closely the detail of our own subject teaching. Particularly, we have in mind here the possibilities for cross-phase and cross-curricular co-operation, both of which should serve to emphasise the nature of knowledge about language. For the former, there is a wealth of excellent practice going on in primary schools about which secondary colleagues are sometimes only dimly aware. Pressures of time and curriculum crowding, together with the shrinking of INSET courses, have made it more difficult to share ideas and practices, although the current literacy initiative and the emphasis NATE is placing on attracting primary-based English teachers may do something to alleviate the worst effects in our subject. Successful cross-phase partnerships depend on the willingness of whole school staffs, with the impetus often coming from senior management, but there is still a fair amount achievable by English teachers to build bridges to enhance language teaching. Some possibilities specifically on knowledge about language include:

- cross-phase meetings to discuss which aspects of knowledge about language are taught – including the appropriate terminology – and when;
- projects involving research and interviews on aspects of language, perhaps focusing particularly on acquisition, development and variation;
- teaching specific lessons across the phase divide, perhaps for secondary teachers as 'tasters' of what is to come, and for primary colleagues addressing areas of expertise relevant to a secondary English curriculum such as early years language development;
- primary and secondary pupils using IT programs such as 'Success Maker', probably sited for logistical reasons in the secondary school, to enhance language 'skills';
- sharing of relevant resources, many of which are deliberately cross-phase in nature (see resources list at the end of this chapter);
- the keeping by pupils of a language scrap-book or journal to be carried on from the primary school into the secondary phase;
- pupils in both phases using each other as audiences for language-based activities, such as code making and breaking;
- mutual project study of language as used in either phase, such as teachers' language (a sensitive one, this!) or the language of school brochures and publicity material.

Often it takes the efforts of just one teacher to set the ball rolling, and the advantages, clearly, go well beyond the enhancement of knowledge about language – as the leadership of any school will be quick to realise.

The opportunities for cross-curricular collaboration in this field may seem more readily available; in practice they are often difficult to achieve. Teachers from different curriculum areas often work in quite distinct ways – this in itself can be an opportunity for professional investigation into language use – which are not always easily compatible. English and modern foreign language departments are both centrally concerned with knowledge about language, for example, but often approach it in very different ways with different pedagogical stances. Nevertheless, it is certainly worth attempting to co-operate in establishing a coherent language awareness course across both curriculum areas, perhaps in the early years of Key Stage 3 before the pressure of SATs and second foreign languages becomes too intense, focusing on the common requirements. Cross-fertilisation such as this must have positive outcomes, and an important one, paradoxically, may well be to raise awareness of the differences in style and content across the curriculum – often the first stage in finding common ground. Modern foreign languages may be the obvious first choice for co-operation, but there are other possibilities: special educational needs staff, for example, dealing with learning support and (hopefully) extension may well usefully focus on knowledge about language – feasibly at either end of the academic spectrum – and often in any case work closely with English departments. Consider too the potential of history teachers to collaborate in teaching about language change and its connections with social history; geography for language diversity across the world and, perhaps, the increasing dominance of (American) English today; science and mathematics for the language of precision and for symbolic systems; and music for a non-verbal system of communication and expression. These are just a few of the opportunities available once colleagues start working and thinking together: in fact, virtually any area of learning involves some sort of knowledge about some sort of language. We simply need to make the connections. At a professional development level, such collaboration can make for enterprising opportunities to consider the nature of language used in teaching and learning with a view to formulating a coherent language for learning policy. Often a dynamic starting point for this sort of process is to invite an authority to speak to the whole staff about the nature of language in schools.

Recent publications on English teaching and those aimed at classroom use have positively bristled with imaginative ideas for the teaching of knowledge about language within English. Davies (1996), for example, offers a very useful overview of recommended topics intended as a programme of study that would last the whole of compulsory secondary education at least:

> The history of the English language:
> > the development of dialects of English
> > the development of standard English
> > language change
> Language structures:
> > an introduction to descriptive linguistics
> The nature of language variation:
> > variation according to user: social class and locality
> > variation according to use: register (discourse analysis)
> > attitudes to language variation
> Language development and learning
> Language and power: gender, race, class and education.

This appears to be a comprehensive framework, and could easily be adapted for specific school circumstances – not least for the kinds of activities outlined in the rest of this chapter. Resources are many and varied, and we have attempted to present a selection from those available. Language is all around us, and the English teacher needs to cultivate a 'magpie' attitude towards collecting linguistic resources: junk mail, instruction booklets, tourist guides, health information leaflets, fliers and the like.

As hinted previously, however, the most important resource may be ourselves: teachers and pupils. With this in mind, an appropriate starting point for learning about language, and one to be revisited throughout a course, could be a language autobiography. The sort of experiences and issues which may arise from such an enterprise could each provide a useful stimulus for further, directed, language investigation. They may include, if past experience is a guide:

- 'telling' of language to younger brothers and sisters: learning through teaching;
- experience of early school/nursery language;
- experience of languages other than English, in a vast range of circumstances;
- use of nursery rhymes, games, sayings, proverbs and other examples of the oral language tradition;
- discovery of different accents and dialects: social and geographical mobility;
- trends in language – 'in' words, 'slang' and jargon;
- the influence of the media on language, particularly television, popular music and certain radio stations;
- early experiences of the power of reading and writing;
- memories of parents' use of 'childish' language;
- the impact of 'formal' language requirements and standard English;

- growing awareness of the power of language to express emotions and desires;
- simultaneous, often linked, awareness of the manipulative possibilities in language;
- diverse, often exclusive, 'private languages'.

In planning and realising any language awareness within the English curriculum, the language autobiography may be seen as central, converting itself into something of a journalistic enterprise. It is also worth undertaking as a team of English teachers, not only modelling good practice but, more profoundly, uncovering some of the links between language and experience. Some of these, clearly, may be painful, and a word of warning is apposite here: as language and identity are so closely intertwined, the English teacher needs great sensitivity and humour to bring some aspects of both to consciousness. It may be that some areas are best left uncovered.

The language autobiography, properly introduced and sustained, should give rise to many valuable starting points and resources. To broaden your range of material it may not be necessary to look beyond the staffroom for good examples of diverse accents and dialects, experiences of different languages, and histories of language in use. Again, with sensitivity, here is a wealth of valuable language resources. The guiding principle in all this enterprise must be one of respect for each other's languages, and this is not always easily achieved. Many people feel quite ashamed of their own accent, dialect or command of standard English and, predictably enough, this sense of shame may all too easily be projected into disparagement of others' languages. If knowledge about language is to achieve anything significant, there must be a concerted effort to confront such issues; the general suggestions for activities listed below are intended to be used in this context, and can of course be adapted and extended for particular purposes:

- interviews with older/younger people about language issues and experiences – particularly concerned with acquisition and development;
- subsequent writing of transcripts from taped interviews as a way of exploring the distinctions between written and spoken (standard) English;
- activities based on past examples of language, including the literary, to investigate language change through such activities as cloze and adaptation;
- activities on accent and dialect, including standard English itself, to emphasise the distinction between the two, using local and media examples;
- exploration of language and stereotyping, using comic strip examples (perhaps with blanked out speech bubbles) and characters from TV soaps;
- study of the relationship between gender and language, making use of resources such as advertisements, adapted fairy-tales and gender-specific magazines;
- role-plays presenting appropriate and inappropriate language (spanning such facets as dialect, register and vocabulary) in a range of situations;
- research into and exploration of the connotations of names, including personal names, nicknames, brand names, logos, school names;
- invention of new names along similar lines, perhaps extending into logos, crests, mottoes, names for new soaps or other media products;
- invention of new language systems, codes, sign languages and creoles;
- investigation into animal 'languages' and other non-verbal forms of communication including the apparently endlessly fascinating language of the body and gestures;
- extension of the language autobiography to include a linguistic family tree and, possibly, maps to place variants of language geographically;

- activities based on foreign language instructions with translations withheld (as they often seem to be in any case) to explore the similarities between languages and attempt a translation;
- exploration of jargons, including those around education, and such manifestations as acronyms (no shortage here either);
- investigation of euphemisms and double standards, especially as used in the media (with death of civilians becoming 'collateral damage');
- playing with language through the formation of puns, anagrams, limericks, ambiguous headlines and signs, unlikely name combinations and rhyming slang;
- study of the 'invented' languages of literature, such as those presented in 'Jabberwocky', *1984*, *The Hobbit*, *A Clockwork Orange* and many others.

The study of language is endlessly fascinating, not least because it is so important in defining whatever to be human really is. We should perhaps bear in mind the words of T. S. Eliot in 'Little Gidding' as we undertake the study:

We shall not cease from exploration
And the end of all our exploring
Will be to arrive where we started
And know the place for the first time.

FURTHER READING

Perera (1987) *Understanding Language* is succinct and provocative. Carter (1995) *Key Words in Language and Literature* is a handy reference guide which focuses on language in education, and the same author's *Knowledge About Language and the Curriculum: The LINC Reader* (1991) summarises the excellent work undertaken by the LINC project. Mittins (1990) *Language Awareness for Teachers* and (1988) *English: Not the Naming of Parts* are both humane and de-mystifying texts. Crystal (ed.) – *The Cambridge Encyclopaedia of Language* and *The Cambridge Encyclopaedia of the English Language* are useful reference texts. Another title which refers more directly to the practicalities of the English classroom is Bain *et al.* (1992) *Looking into Language: Classroom Approaches to Knowledge About Language*. For refreshment and extension of subject knowledge, the Penguin English – Applied Linguistics series (eds Carter and Nunan) is excellent, providing insight into a range of language areas such as Woods (1995) *Introducing Grammar* and Wilkinson (1995) *Introducing Standard English*.

RESOURCES

The *Exploring Language* series, Cambridge University Press, is a lively, colourful set of texts for Key Stage 3. Also impressive is the Critical Language Awareness series, Hodder and Stoughton, consisting of six short books on different aspects of language and society. Through Framework Press, NATE has provided excellent resources in photocopiable loose-leaf binders: the *Language Awareness Project, Years 7–9, An Introduction to the Nature and Functions of Language*. For the broad connections between different forms and contexts of language Sweetman's series *Language Links (1,2,3)*, Collins, is well presented and stimulating. *The Grammar Book* (NATE) is an innovative approach and covers the full 11–16 age range with photocopiable activities. *The Cheshire Cat's Guide to English Grammar*, available from Cheshire County Council Education Services, is a similarly adventurous collection of materials, focusing on Key Stages 2 and 3, and David Crystal's book *Discover Grammar*, Longman, 1996, is lively, clear and attractively presented.

10: Teaching Across the Ability Range

Success encourages them;
they can because they think they can.

Virgil, *Aeneid*

One of the major challenges facing teachers of English is how to make provision for the wide range of abilities and aptitudes likely to be encountered in any one class. The problem is not made easier by the fact that invariably class sizes are too large and classrooms under-resourced. It is important to be aware of the degree to which practical constraints of this kind limit what can be achieved. It is all too easy to place the blame for underachievement entirely on pupils' attitudes and motivation or on the teacher's lack of expertise. It is easy, on the other hand, to become defeatist about practical problems and to underestimate the importance of effective teaching, irrespective of the difficulty of the circumstances. As with so many other aspects of teaching English, a balanced perspective is essential.

A combination of factors (school effectiveness research, inspection by external agencies, national target setting, political agendas) has made it less acceptable in recent years to talk about resources as a solution to some of the major challenges facing schools. To restore some balance to the prevailing ethos, try imagining the 'ideal English classroom' created with no expense spared. The final choice of design and content would no doubt vary with the individual's teaching style but it might include: ample space; full fitted carpeting and sound-proofing; one formal, permanent seating area for whole-class teaching and pupil presentations with other tables for individual and group work; enough multi-media computers for one per pupil with Internet access and a collection of CD-ROMs; a comprehensive classroom library with a large selection of modern and classic literature, non-fiction material, newspapers and magazines, and a comfortable seating area; video camera and playback facilities with a library of cassettes, and sound booths for listening to audio cassettes. To complete the fantasy one might include a requirement for significantly reduced class sizes and access to support staff at any time. A teaching environment of this kind is neither sufficient nor necessary for good and effective teaching. However some of the problems of coping with a range of abilities in the class would be significantly reduced by such generous access to resources.

The concept of 'ability' is not straightforward. Much educational writing has questioned whether it makes any sense to talk about generalised ability or intelligence, suggesting instead that there are different types of intelligence (see, for example, Gardner 1984). Many writers have challenged the idea that ability is something fixed or innate, arguing instead that it can be changed by experience. Such 'nature or nurture' debates which used to be so much to the fore in educational writing tend to have less prominence now. For example, many recent handbooks for trainee teachers are more concerned with the mechanics of coping with pupils of different abilities than with examining the concept of 'ability' itself. One of the reasons for the neglect of much of the research on ability and intelligence is that its practical relevance was not always apparent. No matter what explanations might be offered for different levels of achievement (a form of words which avoids making assumptions about pupils' potential), teachers are still faced with the reality of finding strategies to cope in the classroom.

It is important however not to take the term 'ability' too much for granted. The structure and assessment system of the National Curriculum is a reminder that at the very least it is necessary to distinguish between reading, writing, speaking and listening rather than to operate with a global concept of being 'good at English'. Within each attainment target it is possible to make finer distinctions, for example between pupils who excel at different types of writing or at different oral activities. It is also important to recognise that performance can vary with context, level of interest and motivation. The following piece was written by a Year 8 pupil who had learning difficulties. The task was to write a story about a 'bank robbery' (the topic was chosen by the pupils themselves) after a brief discussion with the group of four pupils involved.

One of our freinds gets some keyes of page of the bank. we can get the money out of the trunk an of our freind can go to get the car ready and one can go in a road work and but some dimate in a box that will explored and the van will stop on a dran then we get the money of the van and someone will shout to the men to come with the car and the we come with the car.

The second story was written by the same pupil a week later on the same theme but with a different stimulus. This time the pupils participated in a drama (with the teacher in role as bank manager and then undercover policeman) which became the basis for the writing. The version was over four times the length of the first effort and had considerably more coherence and depth. The second story concluded as follows:

Then I drove it to the back enterence and there went into the bank and Ian was round the conuter buting the money into the bag, and Nathan was holled a gun at the person at the counter and Malcolm was helping Ian to put the money in the bag and I heard a voice say 'you are surround' give yourself up and but your hand above your hand. and I was still in the car, and I was get cound and he put handcuffs on all of us and we went to jail for 20 years for robing a bank. and Ian got away with it with £100 and he went free for the rest of his life. and before we went into jail I said 'I get you when I get out of jail'.

Whereas the first piece of writing was barely comprehensible, the second has a clear narrative structure, includes the use of direct speech, and has more human interest, introducing as it does the theme of revenge. The point here is not to claim that the context which gives rise to language use is all that matters – clearly the pupil has considerable limitations with writing which are still found in the second piece – but the example warns against underestimating the importance of the circumstances which gave rise to the work. The second piece gives more scope for feedback from the teacher and highlights more clearly areas which need to be improved. It is not uncommon for low-achieving pupils to perform at a level which is below their real potential for a variety of reasons: lack of engagement with the task, problems with self-image, peer group pressure or in some cases simply out of habit. The examples of pupils' writing on pages 97–9 also indicate the way in which the context affects achievement.

The concept 'differentiation' is rather more straightforward than 'ability' but there are dangers in its use which can be illustrated by two examples. The first comes from a primary lesson I observed in which the teacher was so preoccupied with the mechanics and organisation of the process that the worksheets designed for the more able were given to the less able and vice versa. Nobody noticed. The second relates to a student teacher who complained that her course had not addressed differentiation but who revealed on further questioning that a considerable amount of time had been spent on how to cope with different abilities in the classroom. Language can deceive and limit thinking. The use of the label 'differentiation' which has a comforting technical ring to it can lead to a narrowing of perspective, to an assumption that there is something which should be going on in the classroom which is somehow different from, and extra to, effective teaching. Imagine the dangers of telling a learner driver that there are four ways of achieving safety (or perhaps 'safetiation'!) when driving. The use of the term can also deceive us into expecting simple, mechanical solutions which can be applied irrespective of context. The challenge in the classroom is how to ensure that pupils make proper connections with whatever task or material they encounter; this requires sensitive judgements and attention to how they are responding or are likely to respond to the lesson.

It is common to distinguish between differentiation 'by task' and 'by outcome'. The latter concept is somewhat strange because it yokes together two rather disparate ideas. The term 'differentiation' implies that something needs to be done in order to take account of individual pupil differences, whereas embedded in the term 'outcome' is the idea that no such action needs to be taken because pupils will be able to respond at their own level to whatever task is set. Differentiation by task makes more sense as a concept because it suggests that different pupils will be given different things to do. However both ideas are in danger of obscuring the fact that the major teaching task may actually lie elsewhere; it may in some cases be more helpful to think about the design of a scheme of work rather than focus exclusively on differentiation in individual lessons. The important question to address is how a teacher's thinking might be influenced by the fact that the class contains pupils with very different levels of achievement.

INTRODUCING TOPICS FOR DIFFERENTIATED WORK

Thinking about how to introduce a new theme, text or aspect of language study is important and has to do with realising that twenty or thirty very different individuals may not necessarily find it easy to focus on the same material at the same time. This idea is not unfamiliar in general accounts of pupil learning and is included in such aphorisms as 'start where the pupils are' or 'relate new knowledge and understanding to what is already familiar', but it is less frequently seen as an important aspect of teaching mixed-ability classes. (The assumption here is that all classes are of mixed ability whether the groups have been set or not.)

Finding an appropriate 'way in' to a theme or literary text which is likely to engage all pupils is helpful for a number of reasons: interest and motivation can to some degree compensate for difficulty of material; having all pupils engaged in a common topic or book (though not necessarily the same tasks) recognises that learning has a social as well as an individual dimension; pupils may be more able to support each other through a shared interest; pupils can be helped to find their own level of work through negotiation within a common framework. Finding a 'way in' is often presented as a mere pedagogical tip but it has a deeper significance related to theories of perception and reading. Phenomenological approaches to reading stress the centrality of consciousness and the convergence of text and reader to create meaning (Iser:1978). The so-called 'objective' world is not perceived transparently but is mediated through consciousness. The teacher's task is in part to mediate whatever text or other content is to be the object of study and to 'frame' the pupils' response. This can be symbolised by the well-known drawing in Figure 10.1. It can be seen as just a set of lines, or the 'reader's' enjoyment can be enhanced by being 'shown' that the drawing contains a picture of both an old and a young woman.

Figure 10.1

Useful 'ways in' to novels include: asking questions about the illustration on the cover and trying to anticipate what the story will be about; exploring the central theme through drama before starting the reading; examining an extract of dialogue from the novel and trying to guess what is going on; reading other related texts (newspaper article, poem, more accessible short story) on a similar theme. Chapter 2 emphasised the importance of *designing* schemes of work rather than just viewing them as collections of ideas for lessons. Often your starting point for introducing a theme which is accessible to all abilities can lead to more differentiated work as the topic progresses, as in Figure 10.2.

Starting point	Development of theme
Discussing what it might it be like to start growing smaller instead of bigger.	Reading extracts from *Gulliver's Travels*; exploring metaphor in expressions like 'feeling small', 'feeling ten feet tall'.
Sharing personal dreams and individual's ideas about dreams.	Reading extracts from Orwell's *1984*, Chaucer's *Nun's Priest's Tale*, *Macbeth*, 'Book of Daniel' in *The Bible*; reading psychological explanations of causes, meaning of dreams.
Sharing anecdotes about being wrongly accused.	Creating a 'Rough Justice' television programme; reading extract from *Othello*.
Ranking a collection of jokes and cartoons from the newspaper in order from funniest to least funny.	Exploring different types of humour; reading and writing examples of parody and satire.
Brainstorming the word 'anger'; sharing anecdotes about being angry; trying to capture anger in an image.	Reading William Blake's 'A Poison Tree'; exploring imagery in *King Lear*, *A Midsummer Night's Dream*, etc.
Looking at pictures of people and trying to guess their occupations, characters, personalities from their appearance.	Reading and studying character portraits in Dickens, Conrad, Joyce, Chaucer, etc. and then looking at extracts to confirm or challenge initial impressions.
Trying to guess the region from a tape recording of different accents.	Studying the difference between accent and dialect. Comparing different uses of the pronoun in different regions and in the past.
Discussing whether it is ever right to tell lies.	Reading Yevtushenko's 'Telling Lies to the Young is Wrong'; studying Miller's *All My Sons*.
Improvising a scene in pairs called 'waiting' in which the place and the object of waiting is not made clear.	Starting to read *Waiting for Godot*.

Figure 10.2

GRADUATED QUESTIONING

The same principle of structuring a scheme of work can be reflected in the design of a worksheet or set of questions in which the more accessible tasks come first followed by those which are more challenging. Traditionally, comprehension exercises distinguished between levels of difficulty in questions: literal (which tested understanding of basic information), inferential (which required pupils to draw conclusions from information presented) and evaluative (which looked for judgement and critical responses). Such hierarchies can be misleading since pupils are often able to express preferences but not necessarily in analytic terms. They often condemned lower-achieving pupils to dealing only with the banal: 'Name the city which John went to when he left home'. The traditional comprehension exercise has largely given way to more active and dynamic approaches to reading texts but the same principle of staging can be employed so that pupils are not alienated by lack of achievement early on. This sometimes has to do with the way tasks are structured rather than necessarily thinking in terms of a hierarchy of skills. Even a traditional set of questions can be graduated in a way which avoids the content being too simplistic: 'Here are three reasons why John left home. Which do you think was the main one?'

PROVIDING INDIVIDUALISED SUPPORT

Differentiating the amount of support given to individual pupils is an effective response to the challenge of working with a range of abilities in the classroom. As an alternative to the more public distribution of different tasks to different pupils which is often recommended as the most appropriate method of differentiation, the low achievers can be given more structured support and higher achievers more challenging extension work in the course of the lesson. This can be formalised by using extra worksheets or may simply involve the teacher giving oral instructions and help. For inexperienced teachers it should be part of the planning process to work out in advance what advice can be given to pupils who are finding it difficult to make progress with the task; for example, suggesting the first line of a piece of writing; breaking a task down into clearer stages; providing a model for pupils to imitate. The following example illustrates how the process of supporting and challenging different groups of pupils can be built into the planning.

As an introduction to a unit of work on writing for young children, a Year 9 class has been set a number of questions and tasks. They are given different types of children's story books and asked to consider

- for which age group each story is suitable;
- which of the stories might be easiest/most difficult for a child who is learning to read;
- what might appeal to children about each of the stories;
- what makes a good story.

The challenge could be extended for some groups by asking them to analyse the language of the stories in more detail; for example, are the sentences simple, complex or compound? Are many subordinate clauses used? What level of difficulty is the vocabulary? Other pupils could be encouraged to focus more on their own memories of reading, stimulated by the examples provided.

A second stage in the project might be to ask pupils to write two versions of the text of a story to accompany a set of pictures – one version for six years olds who are just beginning to read, the other for eight year olds who can read quite fluently. The lower achievers might just be able to write one version without being able to attribute it to a particular reading level; this could be the subject of a later discussion with the teacher or the class. Higher-achieving pupils might be directed to analyse their separate versions of the text, using knowledge acquired in the previous activity.

Making provision for higher-achieving pupils is generally more straightforward because they can be expected to take more responsibility for their own learning and to operate more independently. It is important however not to seek salvation purely in extension worksheets; teacher/pupil relationships are just as important for the more able and you should, for example, make time to discuss and extend their individual reading. There is also a danger that the written work of more able pupils will receive little more than generalised praise; individual feedback either orally or in writing is an important means of challenging all pupils.

The next task on the same project might require pupils to prepare an entry for a catalogue of children's books, including details on language, story, pictures, presentation, format, size, print, likely appeal and value for money. Here differentiation might occur through initial choice of text(s).

The final task of writing and illustrating their own stories to be read to pupils in the local primary school could take place in groups so that pupils support each other in the course of the work. A scheme of work which has been introduced and launched successfully will often allow teachers and pupils to find the appropriate level of work for individuals and groups as the project progresses. A project of this kind can be a useful way of focusing specifically on use of language, punctuation, spelling and reading in a context which has a real sense of meaning and purpose.

One of the most controversial questions in the teaching of English relates to the so-called 'basic skills' and how these should be taught, particularly given that in any one class individual strengths and weaknesses are likely to vary considerably. In the literature on the teaching of English there has been a fair degree of consensus over the years which can be summarised as follows:

- language does not develop simply by instruction and practice in discrete skills;
- exercises and drills do not give pupils sufficient experience of using language;
- viewing English teaching in terms of skills removes the important dimension of values – should reading be seen simply as decoding or should it include valuing books?;
- there is no guarantee that knowledge acquired separately in routine exercises will transfer to actual uses of language;
- language develops primarily by being used in meaningful contexts.

While most teachers would still subscribe to these views, some questions remain: whether, for example, it is ever appropriate to focus on skills as a separate aspect of the English curriculum and whether it is helpful to set exercises. Many books on English teaching are rather vague on both these questions. Advocates of an extreme 'language in use' approach to English made the mistake of assuming that written language was acquired as naturally as the spoken form and as a result they saw little need for specific teaching. By contrast, commentators who clamoured for a 'return to basics' were equally mistaken in that they took a much too simplistic view of how language develops. Both positions underestimated the value of having a conscious awareness and knowledge of the conventions of written language; the concept of a 'basic skill' is very reductive, as may be seen in the discussions of punctuation, spelling and reading which follow.

Punctuation

Punctuation should neither be taught as a completely separate aspect of the curriculum nor should it be so well integrated that it receives no distinct attention. It is desirable to use a variety of methods and strategies which treat punctuation not just as a skill but rather as a convention of the language in its conveyance of meaning. It needs to be related to pupils' developing knowledge about language, including syntax. The following list is a reminder of some of the varied approaches which can be taken.

- Teacher intervention in the writing process: orally or in writing as part of a broad approach to drafting, proof-reading, creating successive drafts. This is likely to be the most productive way of targeting individual needs. Different conventions can be used other than simply correcting work, e.g. underlining mistakes and asking pupils to try to identify what is wrong.
- Examining with pupils 'why punctuation?', e.g. looking at ambiguities, examining texts without punctuation. Creating ambiguous texts can be a useful way of raising awareness of how punctuation can affect meaning.
- Exploration of punctuation in different texts and contexts (adverts, posters, novels, poems, letters) and focusing on changing conventions. In this way work on punctuation can be integrated into other themes and treated as a topic of interest rather than just a skill. The writing of letters, for example, can be confusing to pupils if they are simply taught one approach instead of being shown different conventions.
- Exploration of texts using both essential punctuation and that which is a matter of style and choice. It will help pupils to become more confident if they know when there is and is not flexibility in use.
- Use of games, e.g. with young pupils, creating sentences using sounds for particular punctuation marks.
- Use of exercises as part of a rich and broad approach to language development. Indiscriminate use of exercises can waste the time of those who are already proficient in using punctuation and confuse those pupils who have very little understanding. They are most useful as an occasional method of helping to turn knowledge into regular habit.
- Use of graphics (e.g. cartoons) to reinforce how to punctuate direct speech.
- Use of individual target-setting so that pupils can be selective and do not become overwhelmed by what they have to achieve.
- Asking pupils to read work aloud with the appropriate intonation. This helps to give punctuation meaning and purpose rather than appearing as an arbitrary set of rules.
- Exploiting opportunities to explore the way punctuation affects style and tone, e.g. sentence length.
- Individual, group or class instruction. Class instruction is only rarely of use because of the wide variety of competence in using punctuation in any one class. Many experienced teachers will attest to their experience of teaching the apostrophe, only to find more pupils misusing it after the instruction than before!
- Typing out a corrected copy of a pupil's work. It is clearly invaluable for pupils to word process their own work but the impact of receiving a typed, revised version can be effective.
- Individualised sheets with advice and support. These are more likely to be useful with pupils who simply need reminding of certain conventions, rather than those who are very weak.
- Use of available ICT programmes.

Spelling

Opinions have also been divided in the past on spelling – whether it is 'taught' or 'caught'. As with other aspects of the teaching of English, the reaction against traditional, narrow methods (for example, the rote learning of arbitrary lists) meant that some teachers put too much faith in the hope that merely using language would be enough to ensure that pupils would learn how to spell. Because in the past pupils were inhibited from writing through fear of making mistakes, some teachers reacted against providing any kind of feedback which had negative overtones. Spelling does come very easily to some children but many others (including high achievers in English) need more systematic help.

It is important not to be too dogmatic about different methods; some popular assumptions in the past have proved to be unreliable and books on the teaching of spelling sometimes differ in the advice they provide. The idea that all pupils will learn to spell if they read a great deal is simply not borne out by the research, although fluent readers are often good spellers. Learning rules went out of fashion because English spelling was thought to be so arbitrary; it is in fact regular in over 70 per cent of cases and some writers do recommend the learning of spelling rules. Mudd (1994) prefers to call these 'generalisations' because there are always exceptions to be taken into account, but she warns against their unthinking use and application.

As with punctuation, it is helpful to view spelling not just as a separate skill but as a useful convention which is part of a pupil's general proficiency in and knowledge about language. Spelling can be actively explored in projects which examine

- the way language (and spelling conventions) have changed over time;
- the way spelling gets 'corrupted' in advertising and popular media;
- the differences between English and American spelling;
- the way in which accent and dialect may affect how individuals spell words;
- the significance of social attitudes to spelling;
- the various attempts which have been made to reform spelling;
- the advantages and limitations of spell checkers.

Rather than condemn individual pupils as 'weak spellers' it helps to diagnose more precisely what kind of errors they are making; whether, for example, the problem relates to a difficulty visualising words or has to do with limited phonic awareness. Such pupils may be helped by a multi-sensory approach involving reading, writing and sounding out the word. A particular pattern of errors may reveal that the pupil can be helped by learning a specific rule. Other common methods of helping with spelling include:

- generating lists from pupils' own writing
- informal tests of selected words
- writing words in segments, seeing the patterns within words, e.g. yes/ter/day
- learning spellings rhythmically
- using mnemonics
- using a 'look, cover, write, check' method
- grouping words
- concentrating on learning high frequency words
- using games to reinforce particular spellings.

Reading

It is beyond the scope of this chapter to explore in detail the full implications for classroom teachers of the Special Needs Code of Practice, including working with support teachers and writing individual education plans, matters on which guidance is given in the further reading section. In the past it was common to view the teaching of basic reading skills as a job for the primary school or specialist, and thus of little relevance to the classroom English teacher. Clearly poor readers do need specialist help but that does not mean the English teacher should abdicate responsibility. Effective collaboration with support staff (and acting effectively at times as a support teacher) requires some understanding of the kind of specialised help pupils need. Despite the practical difficulties in giving individuals sufficient attention, it is possible to give weak readers some support within the context of the classroom. Knowledge of the issues involved in developing basic reading skills is helpful because the debate replicates some of the other controversies and unhelpful polarities in the teaching of English; beginning reading is not so dissimilar, in terms of key central issues, to the teaching of reading at a more advanced level.

As with other aspects of the teaching of English the question of 'meaning' was (and to some extent still is) at the heart of the debate over reading and relates to many issues explored in other chapters of this book. Reading is essentially an aspect of using language and as such it must be concerned primarily with a quest for meaning. According to advocates of the 'real books' approach, readers need access to material which makes sense and towards which there is some genuine motivation. The role of the adult is to serve as an experienced guide rather than as an instructor in skills. Children must develop reading in much the same way as they learn so much about language before they get to school (Smith 1988:9):

> How do they learn all this? Not by programs or formal instruction. There are no kits of materials and exercises for teaching children how the world uses reading and writing. They learn – usually without anyone being aware that they are learning – by participating in literate activities with people who know how and why to do these things. They join the literacy club. People write with them and read with them – lists, notes, letters, signs, directions, recipes – any of the routine 'literacy events' of daily life in which the child can share.

It can be seen that the 'real books' approach described here fits comfortably with a 'language in use' philosophy and as such it has some of the same limitations. Reading is treated just like speaking, as an ability which is acquired naturally without explicit teaching. The reason this view was held so vehemently by many educationists is that so many of the more formal approaches to the teaching of reading were arid and lacking in attention to meaning. The emphasis was on teaching the mechanics of reading; children were first taught to decipher words or parts of words and then to put these together in order to read. Phonics (an emphasis on sound/symbol correspondence) and 'look and say' approaches (whereby pupils are taught to recognise whole words) are methods which are based on the belief that children need to work upwards from a grounding in basics. It is not dissimilar to the view that children need to be taught the basic mechanics of punctuation and spelling before they can use language in any meaningful way. The result was sometimes that pupils could enunciate words or 'bark at print' (see Chapter 5) without attention to what the words meant. Artificial reading schemes were produced which paid little heed to pupils' interests or to what motivated them.

As with many aspects of teaching English the polar positions on the teaching of reading are not tenable. A narrow emphasis on the skills of reading without attention to purpose and motivation is unlikely to succeed. On the other hand pupils need to be able to recognise letters, letter sounds and combinations of letters and will not necessarily achieve that ability by simply practising reading. Some specific instruction in the sounds of letters and letter blends may by necessary. The balanced position is usefully summarised by Wray (Wray and Medwell 1994:59):

1. Reading is an extremely complex process. This means that 'simple' approaches to teaching children to read will probably have little chance of success. The approach of 'put children in a roomful of wonderful books and they will learn to read' is just as simplistic as that of 'teach children to recognise and pronounce letters and they will thereby learn to read' and neither is likely to be successful.
2. Teaching reading needs to build upon what children do well (look for meaning, attend first and foremost to functional aspects of print, learn through stories) before introducing aspects which they find more difficult (apply a range of cues simultaneously, respond to text without relying upon its physical context to give them its meaning).
3. Children need to be taught the technicalities of reading but these must be set into a context of meaning.

Wray goes on to quote Adams (1990:422) who has summarised recent research into beginning reading:

In both fluent reading and its acquisition, the reader's knowledge must be aroused interactively and in parallel. Neither understanding nor learning can proceed hierarchically from the bottom up. Phonological awareness, letter recognition facility, familiarity with spelling patterns, spelling–sound relationships and individual words must be developed in concert with real reading and real writing and with deliberate reflection on the forms, functions and meanings of texts.

The teaching of both beginning and advanced reading needs to be based on a view which sees the reader as an active contributor to the meaning of the text. Secondary teachers of English who are confident in handling all types of text in the classroom sometimes claim not to know how to help very weak readers, not realising that many of the same principles apply. The following list provides a reminder of some of the strategies which can be used and considerations to be borne in mind when working with poor readers in the normal classroom:

- use 'ways in' to reading material which may be more helpful than simply presenting a block of challenging text;
- ensure that pupils do not get lost and alienated when reading (a frequent cause of misbehaviour) by checking frequently on understanding;
- remember that asking questions of the whole class which only one or two pupils answer will not provide information on whether all pupils are understanding – try alternative strategies like pairs work or asking pupils to jot down answers in rough;
- take care to use an appropriately large font size when creating worksheets and do not overcrowd them;

- pictures and drawings which accompany text should not be seen as just decorative but may be useful 'cues' to meaning;
- try to create some opportunities for reading with pupils individually – not easy in a crowded classroom;
- try to participate in and support paired or home reading schemes which the school operates so that pupils do not see 'reading' as something completely separate from classroom English;
- take note of mistakes or 'miscues' when pupils read – a guess which bears no relation to the appearance of the word but makes sense may indicate poor phonic awareness; one which takes its cue from the spelling of the word but makes no sense may indicate that the pupil is not reading for meaning;
- motivate reading through interests (including non-fiction).

FURTHER READING

For a useful general introduction to special needs which discusses the code of practice, statementing and individual education plans see Chapter 7 of Capel *et al.* (1995) *Learning to Teach in the Secondary School*. Chapter 8 in Harrison (1994) *The Literate Imagination* focuses specifically on special needs in English. The same author has a chapter in Hayhoe and Parker (eds) (1992) on bilingualism. Edwards, Goodwin and Wellings (eds) (1991) *English 7–14 Every Child's Entitlement* is excellent on making English accessible to all pupils and has very helpful further reading and resources sections on multicultural literature and linguistic diversity. Peters (1985) *Spelling: Caught or Taught?* is still a helpful overview. See also Montgomery (1997) *Spelling*, and Dean (1998) *Teaching the More Able Language User*.

RESOURCES

Hodder English 1,2,3 is an extremely well presented and engaging series of books. Folens English series for Key Stage 3, *Ways of Seeing*, *Discoveries* and *Perceptions* includes photocopiable sheets to support and extend pupils of different abilities. *English Direct 1,2 and 3*, Collins, is well focused. *Shakespeare Without the Boring Bits*, Viking, is an entertaining introduction to Shakespeare at Key Stage 3. See also references in Chapters 3 and 5.

11: English in the Sixth Form

In seed time learn, in harvest teach, in winter enjoy.

William Blake, *The Marriage of Heaven and Hell*

Tensions, you will no doubt have noticed, lie at the heart of every facet of the teaching of English; sixth form work is no exception. A Level English teaching – which constitutes most of post-16 English teaching, in schools at least – is often sought after enthusiastically by newcomers to the profession. However, it is also sometimes withheld by heads of department anxious to safeguard academic teaching, though this happens far less now than it used to. In a sense, this state of affairs mirrored the élitist nature of A Levels generally, intended as they were for university preparation for the minority. There was no alternative qualification available for the less academic: those disinclined towards academic study were simply disqualified and expected to seek apprenticeships or employment. The move away from this élitist concept is a slow, ongoing process. The future of post-16 education is uncertain as we await the government's response to the Dearing recommendations, which might broaden the base of the curriculum at this level.

In many ways, the sixth form seems to provide a most fertile ground for teaching, with the possibility of a genuine and voluntary partnership in teaching and learning based on a greater degree of intimacy than is generally possible in earlier years. Greater maturity, smaller group size, a less formal school/college ethos, and significant subject specialism should also combine to create a convivial ambience. Neither is it a matter only of individual learning, for the combination of these factors may lead to resourceful collaboration. It is widespread practice to 'share' responsibility for A Level groups, thus making collaboration almost inevitable, even if only at the informal level. The opportunities, of course, extend well beyond the informal, and the best departments plan for a balanced curriculum, in terms of both content and teaching style, and regularly monitor the progress of their students.

The intention in this chapter is to look more closely at the creative possibilities open to English teachers in the teaching of A Level courses in English literature and language. There are other qualifications for which English teachers often prepare students, such as Scottish Highers, the expanding but still controversial General National Vocational Qualifications (GNVQ) and other A Levels such as Communications or Theatre Studies, but lack of space precludes a thorough account. There currently exists also a general state of flux, particularly concerning vocational education, which suggests that any such study be postponed for the time being; in the meantime, many English departments have shown a reluctance to become too heavily involved in, say, the communications 'key skills' of GNVQ courses. For better or for worse, A Levels remain the bread and butter of English teaching in sixth forms and the intention rather is to give a 'flavour' of the potential which undoubtedly exists for creative and effective English teaching at this level.

It may be helpful, however, to look a little more closely at the educational context which has such a profound bearing on sixth form English. One issue impossible to avoid is the vast increase in the number of students in sixth forms, most of whom continue to be attracted – often against careers advice – to A Level courses. A glance at some figures illustrates this expansion: in 1939 88 per cent of children left school at fourteen, and even in 1959 only 10 per cent continued schooling beyond sixteen; the growth of A Levels was very much geared to this context, and in many respects the academic basis of the examination-determined curriculum has not been appropriate to the influx of students with quite different needs. At Key Stage 4 the introduction of GCSE has gone some way to bridge the gap between the needs of 'traditionally academic' pupils and those with other aptitudes; but in some respects this has simply pushed the problem up into the post-16 phase. There have been attempts to broaden the base of post-16 education, incorporating both academic and vocational aspects and seeking common ground between the two, but – until now at least – A Levels have remained sacrosanct, sometimes (as in the Dearing Report) referred to as the 'gold standard' of the English education system.

The current very public concern for 'lifelong learning' and entitlement to a broadly-based education has tended to focus on the post-16 curriculum. Increasingly discussed is the possibility of eroding the significance of GCSEs in favour of a seamless continuity in 14–19+ education with qualifications at the age of sixteen seen as no more than a 'staging post' in the process, possibly reduced to an assessment of 'key skills' in literacy, numeracy and ICT. The development of what amounts to three separate strands in education and training should be seen in this context: the academic strand is still to be based on A Levels, with the important development of AS Levels giving a degree of breadth; the vocational, previously often termed the pre-vocational, strand is given expression through GNVQs in both schools and colleges; finally, the occupational route, confusingly once known as the vocational, attains accreditation through National Vocational Qualifications (NVQs) largely outside educational establishments. There is supposed parity between these routes, and the rhetoric of politicians emphasises this. Witness, for example, David Blunkett (in a speech reported in the TES 7.11.97), 'We need to be imaginative. . .We need to challenge this old world obsession with the professions promoted by people who don't want to get their hands dirty.' In reality, however, parity has proved extremely elusive, and some, such as Tomlinson (Ed.) (1997:16), doubt the intentions behind the rhetoric:

> A schizophrenic situation has developed whereby politicians repeat mantras of a learning society in which all are educated enough to want lifelong learning, while cementing a system that cuts off large numbers of young people from education at sixteen, and perpetuates the notion that there are separate types of student suitable for separate tracks.

The situation, then, is problematic, and talk of 'tracks' begs the question of how those born on the wrong side of them are to be educated. It is worth bearing in mind these considerations when planning for the teaching of A Level groups, as it is likely that their composition will reflect a wide range of interest, commitment and aptitude; some indeed may have been advised to select an alternative 'route' but preferred the traditional security of A Levels, perhaps sensing the reality of Tomlinson's words. English is particularly susceptible to these concerns, in that the subject is often taken as a 'safe' second or third option on the basis of enjoyment and a measure of success at GCSE, awareness of the employment market, or even parental insistence on increasing general literacy. These may be sound enough reasons, of course, but not necessarily those of the dedicated, talented student intending to read English at university, who is also likely to be represented in the group and would have been the originally intended client of the A Level dominated system. Diversity presents a challenge, and the chance to innovate accordingly to meet the challenge.

The various tensions, contradictions and concerns may be summarised thus:

- the fundamental distinction between education and training as reflected in the three 'routes';
- the wide-ranging needs and aspirations of students;
- the supposed parity between the three 'routes';
- the transition from compulsory to voluntary participation in education;
- the transition from GCSE courses to A and AS Levels and the position of GCSE English as preparation for further study;
- the competing claims of different institutions: school-based sixth forms, sixth form colleges, tertiary colleges, FE colleges and others;
- the contradictory claims of specialisation, often vociferously endorsed by students, and curricular breadth, reflected in the introduction of 'key skills';
- the perceptions of the alternatives in post-16 education held by the general public, including parents, prospective employers, and higher education;
- methods of assessment – the roles of coursework, modular structures and terminal examinations;
- inter-subject comparisons in terms of possible combinations and perceived difficulty of study.

To these we would add further points relating more immediately to the situation 'on the ground', the day-to-day reality of teaching English at this level:

- implications for selection of students, in that English is often heavily subscribed, and the offering of appropriate guidance and induction;
- pedagogical issues in the teaching of sixth form groups;
- the tension between freedom and restrictions for post-16 students, often particularly keenly felt in school-based sixth forms;
- staffing considerations, including the usual need to work collaboratively;
- students' involvement in their own education and assessment, including such concerns as use of private study time, appraisal, reporting to parents and participatory learning.

Bearing all this in mind may seem rather daunting, but although they are important considerations they should be regarded as secondary to the enthusiasm for the subject with which a teacher of English can inspire sixth form students – often, indeed, the inspiration which has in the first place led teachers to follow that vocation. Given this commitment, much of the rest follows in the collaborative working of a good department; this collaboration should extend to the students themselves, whose involvement may be significant in many of the areas noted above and should serve to alleviate some of the difficulty in keeping all the balls in the air.

It is worth starting this process of participation as early as possible during the course so that it may feed into the teaching and learning from the start, and also establish in the minds of the students the nature of their involvement in their own education. Within the induction period, generally positioned either in the 'fallow' time of June or July previous to the course starting or at the beginning of the new academic year, a survey such as that shown in Figure 11.1 could be used.

As with all research of this kind, the content and format may be adapted for differing circumstances. The important point is that completion of the survey should lead to further discussion of the issues raised, both with the students themselves and as a focus for pedagogical development amongst colleagues. It may well be that few clear-cut conclusions are possible, but this in itself may be a powerful argument for diversity of approach. It is also vital, especially in terms of developing credible co-operation, that the discussions are periodically revisited and that they are seen actually to inform teaching and learning. If conducted properly, this sort of approach may be a fundamental part of the course itself rather than yet another burden.

The suggestions and thoughts arrived at will, of course, differ considerably between individuals, groups and institutions – there would be little point in undertaking such an exercise if not. Nevertheless there are likely to be some key considerations, reinforced by the findings of research (see, for example, that conducted by Morgan at Denbigh School, 1997). My own (unpublished) research in this area, conducted at Thirsk School with both English colleagues and students during 1995–6, corroborated the findings of wider enquiries, and are summarised below.

- Discussion is popularly held to be the most effective teaching method, rather than 'teacher talk'; the related need to listen attentively and encouragingly, and to base discussion on a range of groupings and tasks is also important.
- 'Active' sessions are much valued as 'ways in' to literature and language: using drama, collage-making, booklets, posters, etc.
- Note-taking is regarded as essential, and the preferred method is to have time immediately after discussions and activities, with just the odd *aide mémoire* jotted down during the session itself.
- Notes are the students' own responsibility but should be checked periodically by the teacher, perhaps as the focus of a shared activity and an important aid to examination revision.
- The didactic lecture-style lesson has its place in the context of a balanced curriculum; when vital information has been imparted there is a need to revisit and emphasise, especially in lessons immediately subsequent to the lecture.
- There is a generally perceived need for some work to be done on study skills such as summary making, essay writing, methods of reading, research, use of IT, etc. which may or may not be covered generically by particular sixth forms.
- Related to this point is the expressed liking for collaborative essay planning with a sharing of students' – and particularly the teacher's – expertise, followed by detailed and formative marking; many are acutely aware that the eventual grade depends invariably on how well students write.
- Individual tutorials, either informal or linked to some form of assessment, are widely regarded as useful – especially when focused on specific strengths and weaknesses.
- There are some contradictory views on the nature of deadlines for writing, which

SIXTH FORM INDUCTION: QUESTIONNAIRE FOR ENGLISH

Discuss the following questions with a partner. The aim is to encourage you as students and us as teachers to think about the ways in which teaching and learning best take place.

Circle a number 1 > 5, with 1 denoting 'strongly disagree' and 5 'strongly agree'.

Section 1 Types of learning
(a) I prefer teacher-led lessons to any other   1 2 3 4 5
(b) I like working to given deadlines best   1 2 3 4 5
(c) I like the teacher to give firm discipline, even at sixth form level   1 2 3 4 5
(d) I work best individually   1 2 3 4 5
(e) I work best in a small group   1 2 3 4 5
(f) I thrive on discussion work   1 2 3 4 5
(g) I like to organise my own notes as against teacher direction   1 2 3 4 5

Section 2 Reading
(a) I like to read only for light entertainment   1 2 3 4 5
(b) I like to feel challenged by what I read   1 2 3 4 5
(c) I spend 1=no time, 2=30 mins, 3=1 hour, etc. reading most days   1 2 3 4 5
(d) I like reading poetry   1 2 3 4 5
(e) I enjoy shared reading sessions   1 2 3 4 5
(f) I enjoy reading plays as a group   1 2 3 4 5
(g) I enjoy reading Shakespeare   1 2 3 4 5

Section 3 Writing
(a) I like to draft essays carefully using at least two stages   1 2 3 4 5
(b) I enjoy 'creative writing' best   1 2 3 4 5
(c) I feel confident about writing 'literary critical' essays   1 2 3 4 5
(d) The more coursework-based writing the better   1 2 3 4 5
(e) I write best under examination conditions   1 2 3 4 5
(f) I write for my own personal enjoyment as well as for my studies   1 2 3 4 5
(g) I like a lot of choice in the subjects I write about   1 2 3 4 5

Section 4 I chose English at A Level because:
(a) I have a great interest in literature, language and ideas   1 2 3 4 5
(b) It should lead to good opportunities in employment/HE   1 2 3 4 5
(c) It fits in with my other choices of subject   1 2 3 4 5
(d) Current sixth formers enjoy studying it   1 2 3 4 5
(e) It promises to be the easiest subject on offer   1 2 3 4 5
(f) The results at A Level are consistently good   1 2 3 4 5
(g) It's easier to get in than for some other subjects   1 2 3 4 5

Figure 11.1

really have to be worked out in the context of particular sixth form policies.

- Concern for progression from GCSE to A Level is widespread, and in some ways justified – we are talking about 'advanced' study, after all – but it may also contribute to the unwarranted and even intimidating 'mystique' of A Levels.
- Different teachers have contrasting views on the use of background material and published notes – certainly there is a tension between the need to stimulate a fresh subjective response and the incorporation of recognisably 'literary critical' interpretations and other contextualising information.

Some of these points refer more to literature than to language study, but they have a general validity. English teachers at this level have to be aware that, as McCulloch *et al.* (1993:25) put it,

> Students can be resistant to the suggestion that they take responsibility for their learning. Feeling more secure with the teacher-as-expert, they are content to take the role of listeners and note-takers. Current pressures on teachers may encourage collusion in this model, but. . .this is ultimately counter-productive. . .until students have expressed their understanding in their own words, neither they nor the teacher can say with any certainty what they have or haven't understood.

In the light of this observation, the suggestion concerning the place of 'lecture' sessions is significant, in that many teachers feel vaguely uncomfortable giving this sort of lesson; we need not do so, as there is a great deal of essential information that can be given in this way and, after all, terminal examinations usually account for 80 per cent of the final grade. However, the rider 'in the context of a balanced curriculum' is vital too, and requires reflective thought and planning. In this, as in so much else, A Level teaching is no different from English teaching for previous years: best practice displays a unity of approach across the entire age range and is best characterised by a 'workshop' approach in which all feel able to contribute according to their aptitudes and interests to a full range of activities.

We need now to examine in rather greater depth what all this might mean in terms of real teaching and learning. We will look at ideas for the teaching of Tennessee Williams' play *A Streetcar Named Desire*, Graham Swift's short story 'Learning to Swim', poetry interpretation for the 'critical appreciation' examination, Brian Friel's play *Translations*, and a range of language activities. This may seem like rather a tall order, given the space available in one chapter, but the hope is that approaches are transferable – not only from text to text but across the age and ability ranges in schools – so that summarised ideas will be sufficient to stimulate imaginative teaching.

We start with *A Streetcar Named Desire*, a play containing a mixture of passion, sex and raw energy, occasionally spilling over into violence. As with the reading of any play, it is effective to conjure an atmosphere of a theatre group working towards a shared understanding essential for some sort of performance. The text then becomes a working script; the preliminary group reading raises questions, displays possibilities of interpretation and enactment, and progresses towards a thorough acquaintance with the play itself. During this reading it may be best to avoid too much detailed note-taking in favour of jotted marginalia (an issue here might be whether the students own their own texts or not). During a second, more detailed reading the group should be discovering what works in terms of the drama, acting sections out and receiving guidance towards the key themes, characterisations, and the twists and turns of the plot: this would be the appropriate time for a more extensive accumulation of notes after each session, with the possibility of additional short-term writing tasks. On completion of this reading, probably taking us up to a half term of study, the group should be ready to adopt a variety of approaches to the whole play. There may be options available at this stage, and the activities are often best summarised on a handout such as that in Figure 11.2.

ACTIVITIES BASED ON *A STREETCAR NAMED DESIRE* (a half term's work)

1. Presentations (working in groups of three) given to the rest of the group on themes within the play, with each using a minimum of six carefully chosen quotations to illustrate the presentation. The themes are:
     class conflict and the battle between old and new;
     gender conflict and sexuality;
     psychological issues and the question of insanity;
     setting and atmosphere throughout the play.

2. Tableaux: eleven 'frozen moments', each introduced by the appropriate line(s) – one tableau for each scene, enacted to the minutest detail of facial expression. (See Chapter 12)

3. Theatre programme design (working in the groups established for 1.) to include:
     biographical information;
     themes of the play (see 1. above);
     symbolism and staging;
     design work and illustrations;
     imaginary cast list and 'pen portraits' of the actors.

4. Hot-seating: a drama activity which involves each character, played in role, facing possibly hostile questioning from everyone else. Preparation in researching the nature of each character should be thorough and imaginative. (See Chapter 12)

5. Whole-group writing and illustration of a 'study guide' booklet for future students of the play, assembling the material and insights gathered from the above activities and using ICT and photocopying facilities for the final publication.

6. Essay titles to be based on the themes outlined in 1. above.

Figure 11.2

Various factors will influence the nature of the choices to be made from these approaches. One important consideration is whether understanding of this particular text is assessed by coursework or by terminal examination; if it is the former, the extent of textual knowledge need not be so broad, but the particular assignment chosen for assessment will need to show great depth of insight into the selected aspect of the play.

It is important also, with the arrival of key skills in the A Level syllabuses, that students have the opportunity to work on such areas as giving presentations, using ICT and conducting research.

By way of contrast, Graham Swift's short story 'Learning to Swim' is far narrower in scope and would almost certainly be offered as a coursework option unless combined with other material (possibly the additional stories in the Cambridge edition). This edition, as part of the Cambridge Literature series, presents the text with notes and activities along the lines of the five approaches we noted in Chapter 5; this editorial material is particularly valuable in providing ways into the story for sixth formers. In fact, both literature and language students would benefit from close study of the story, the latter in terms of the linguistic conventions used – such as narrative stance and the interior reflections of three separate but linked characters, and as a possible model for students' own creative writing. It is important to emphasise the creative overlap between literature and language, and innovative English departments are developing exciting teaching opportunities in the light of this cross-fertilisation – cemented as it is by syllabus change incorporating the AS structure, key skills, and modular framework possibilities. To focus again on 'Learning to Swim', additional approaches and activities might include:

- Pre-reading activity: plan a short narrative combining these elements –
  a dysfunctional mother-father-son family relationship
  the family on holiday
  the memories of the adults
  learning to swim
  (the idea here is subsequently to compare students' efforts with Swift's, focusing through discussion and close reading on the similarities and differences).
- Stream of consciousness thoughts, ideally expressed in verse, of the characters – particularly appropriate here in that the story centres on three separate interior monologues distanced partly through the third-person narrative stance.
- Role-played or written re-creation as 'flashbacks' of the incidents presented through memories – thus bringing in the possibility of cinematic conventions.
- Projection of the characters into the future, looking back to the events of the story and presenting these reflections as Alan Bennett-like 'Talking Heads'.
- Focus on the nature of language acquisition, using the metaphor of learning to swim as described in the story.
- Further role-play possibilities such as hot-seating, dream sequences or use of the psychiatrist's chair.
- Wider study of other Swift material, particularly novels like *Waterland* and *Last Orders*.

The 'critical appreciation' section of the literature examination paper, in which candidates respond to poetry or prose under examination conditions without having seen the text beforehand, is now a feature of all literature syllabuses. It attracts controversy: some feel that it genuinely shows what an individual student, unaided, can achieve in understanding and response; others point to the incremental and often collaborative nature of understanding which this paper deliberately precludes, and insist that one slight 'mis-reading', under the pressure of examination conditions, can ruin a student's chances of presenting a coherent response. Whichever view is taken, it is unlikely to be abandoned in the present climate of 'rigour', and English teachers simply have to prepare their students accordingly. It can be done, and adventurously too. The importance of using the entire two years of the course in preparation cannot be over-emphasised: right from the induction period onwards there should be opportunities for engagement with poetry and prose, building confidence to make coherent, informed and subjective responses. Part of this process of confidence building lies in de-mystifying literary criticism while providing the appropriate tools and vocabulary to accomplish the task. It is vital to stimulate peer support here, as A Level groups are mixed-ability in terms of aptitude and confidence: the teacher's selection of working groups and pairs, for example, can be particularly effective. Gradually, using the wealth of excellent resources now available (some of which are discussed in the further reading section), it should be possible for each student to face up to a poem or prose extract alone and unaided – and again there should be plenty of opportunities to practise the skills involved. Perhaps it is not coincidental that this is the very time when many young people take their driving tests, and the combination of nervousness and recklessness may be familiar!

Activities throughout the course, for work on poetry appreciation, may include:

- performance-based interpretations of poems, including mime, music, and role-playing characters;
- 'critics debate' triads, with two students debating opposing interpretations while a third listens carefully, takes notes, and finally reports back with an attempt at consensus;
- playing the poet in role in a hot-seating exercise to face questions, perhaps with a particular teacher-given focus in mind;
- using choral readings with echoes of key words to achieve different effects and understandings, examining through the sound of the verse stylistic features such as rhythm, rhyme and assonance;
- constructing: collages, illustrations for different audiences, brainstorm summaries on sugar paper and animated versions to explore interpretations;
- having groups/pairs construct their own questions, both open and closed, to ask each other on the text, subsequently summarised by the teacher;
- selecting quotations to give weight to an interpretation, using them constructively in the context of many of the above activities and others.

Emerging from this thorough preparation must be a creative combination of close reading, fully endorsed by references and quotations, with a freshness of subjective response. The vital principle, kept in sight throughout the range of activities undertaken, is to return always to the text itself – hopefully with new insights and understanding.

Much of the work on the critical appreciation paper outlined above has direct relevance, with adaptation where appropriate, to advanced English language study also, in the sense that it too demands close textual analysis and response. If we select some of the criteria for achieving an A grade for English Literature (NEAB, 1997), the position is further clarified:

- evidence of an independent free approach;
- detailed understanding and selection of textual detail;
- conceptualised argument, showing insight and flair;
- personal critical response and voice;
- analysis of concepts/language/structure/tone/metre;
- fluent and mature written style with few technical errors.

Our central thesis here is that English remains English, with all its exciting possibilities, whether focusing on literature or language – problematic in any case to differentiate (see Introduction). Teachers educated in the literature tradition, who sometimes feel intimidated by the newer language-based syllabuses, need not do so.

A further text for study focusing on both aspects of English is Brian Friel's *Translations*, a play which imaginatively explores the relationship between language and power. The possibilities for inventive teaching and learning here seem endless; a selection might include:

Contextualisation: historical/cultural

- brainstorm ideas on and impressions of Ireland, contrasted to England;
- directed research activities on aspects of Irish culture;
- cross-curricular possibilities – history, geography, RE, languages, music;
- the Irish dramatic tradition – Yeats, Synge, O'Casey, Behan *et al.*;
- investigation of media presentations of Ireland, past and present.

Language and communication

- investigation of the relationship between languages and imperialism;
- language, dialect and cultural/national identity;
- the nature of translation and interpretation – connotations;
- the associations and characteristics of the featured languages (Greek, Latin, Gaelic, English) and, by extension, other languages;
- the significance of naming in a variety of contexts.

Other possibilities

- active exploration through music and oral culture, making use of the plentiful Irish resources available;
- focus on the nature of education and schooling – the relationship between learning, subversion and control;
- exploration of character and stereotype – challenges to stereotypical expectations;
- learning through drama – performance, role-play, tableaux, etc.;
- nature of maps and mapping – metaphorical significance and ideas of control;
- writing tasks, both empathetic and textually analytical.

Significant here, on reflection, is just how many of these approaches to this particular text embody ideas central to holistic English teaching in more general terms; this serves to underline the idiosyncratic and wide-ranging nature of the subject.

The blurring of the distinction between English literature and language notwithstanding, we need now to examine some of the specific requirements of the language syllabuses. Off-putting to many teachers more used to literature is the extent and depth of the critical terminology; it is as well to remember here that the syllabuses are in English language, not in linguistics. Certainly we need to use the tools of the trade and to impart their appropriate usage to our students; but the context of their usage is far more important. An analogy may be drawn between linguistic terminology for language courses and literary-critical terminology for those based on literature study: in both cases terms are to be used for the purpose of elucidating textual enquiry and understanding, and examiners are explicitly asked not to credit the occasional candidate's attempt to impress by an extensive, if ultimately pointless, display of their knowledge of such vocabulary. As is the case for literature study, there are some excellent published resources now available, to which can be added teachers' – and students' – own magpie-like accumulation of language materials. There is an additional benefit here of being able to use such resources at all levels of English teaching; indeed as language study comes more to the fore throughout the age range, one of the most effective ways to familiarise oneself with the workings of language and its teaching is to read A Level English Language books and then to adapt the approaches and activities for lower-school use. The essential principle, applicable to all English teaching, is that one only really understands language by immersing oneself in it, while at the same time affording a certain critical distance through reflection. In practice this means a close, often analytical, study of language as used, coupled with focused, creative use of language as studied. This parallel approach may be illustrated by some of the activities and teaching ideas below.

- a video or handbook produced by students for a specific audience, e.g. 'A Children's Guide to Grammar', 'An Alien's Guide to Holding a Conversation on Planet Earth';
- role-plays to explore language use in a variety of contexts – the use of jargon at a parents' evening or doctor's surgery, for instance – or to 'test' knowledge of a particular variety of language, such as dialect or creole;
- 'statement games' to spark debate – giving students statements about male or female language use to sort into agree/disagree piles;
- taping of speech in a range of contexts with subsequent detailed transcript analysis and comparison to written English conventions;
- close comparative analysis of contrasting texts, chosen to illustrate language diversity or language change over time;
- study of such features of language as euphemisms, product names, personal names, propaganda, ambiguity and jargon;
- group presentations on researched facets of language, combining if possible the analytical with the active, e.g. a study of the language used for charities' advertising coupled with a simulated (or real?) advertising appeal.

We have examined in this chapter some of the possibilities presented by sixth form English teaching. Perhaps because of the concentrated, intensive nature of the courses on offer in this phase no other area of the English curriculum illustrates so vividly the tension between threats – curricular uncertainty and complex syllabuses amongst them – and plentiful opportunities. Adoption of an adventurous perspective suggests that opportunities may yet win the day.

FURTHER READING

Peach and Burton (1995) *English as a Creative Art* may be used with students or to stimulate teaching ideas. Useful too are Brown and Gifford (1989) *Teaching A Level English Literature*, Scott (1989) *Reconstructing A Level English* and a publication (1990) from NATE's Post-16 Committee, *A Level English: Pressures for Change*, although recent and continuing changes in the sixth form curriculum have lessened their immediate relevance. Canwell and Ogborn have contributed a useful chapter, *Balancing the Books: Modes of Assessment in A Level English Literature*, in Brindley (Ed.) (1994) *Teaching English*. McCulloch *et al.* (1993) *English 16–19: Entitlement at A Level* helpfully links philosophy to pedagogical practice. For a critical overview of the context of post-16 education in general terms, Tomlinson (ed.)(1997) *Education 14–19: Critical Perspectives* is both wide-ranging and succinct.

RESOURCES

As a contextualising aid to literature study, the well-established *Preface* series (gen. ed. Purkiss), Longman, has a wide range of titles dealing with different authors and periods. Macmillans *New Casebook* series (gen. eds Peck and Doyle), also long-standing, provides more detailed literary critical essays, with account taken of recent critical developments; offshoots of this series are the *Critics Debate* texts (gen. ed. Scott) which are particularly useful for summarising contrasting critical interpretations of key texts. Other literary critical studies suited to A Level students' needs include the *Landmarks of World Literature* series (gen. ed. Stern), Cambridge University Press; *Re-reading Literature* titles (gen. ed. Eagleton), which stress recent radical critical positions on well-established books; *Longman Critical Essays* (gen. eds Cookson and Loughrey); and, from NATE, the *Critical Reading at Post 16* series (ed. Dymoke), focusing on practical activities to challenge texts. Three books from the English and Media Centre examine particular areas pertinent to A Level literature courses: *Reading Fictions* (eds Mellor, Patterson, ONeill), comprising twelve short stories; *Literary Terms: A Practical Glossary* (Moon); and *Studying Literature: Theory and Practice for Sixth Form Students* (Moon). *Literature, Criticism, and Style* (Croft and Cross), Oxford University Press, is a comprehensive guide to literary criticism and two books from Cambridge University Press concentrate more particularly on preparation of students for the 'unseen' examination paper: *The Cambridge Critical Workshop* (J. and L. Wood) and *Prose and Poetry* (Shiach). *The Faber Book of Parodies* (ed. Brett) and *Imitations of Immortality: A Book of Literary Parodies* (Parrott) from Viking, are entertaining ways of encouraging stylistic experimentation.

There have been many new texts to aid the teaching of English Language A Level. NATE, through Framework Press, publish a practical 'way in' to introduce aspects of language at this level, *English Language A Level: The Starter Pack* (Goddard *et al.*) as well as invaluable guides to specific aspects of language courses: *Researching Language: English Project Work at A Level and Beyond* (Goddard) and *Original Writing: Structured Activities for A Level and Beyond* (Ross). Three books from the Cambridge University Press address further concerns relevant to language students: *The Structure of English: A Handbook for Students* (Newby); *English as a Global Language* (Crystal); and, with accompanying cassette, *Exploring Spoken English* (Carter and McCarthy). There are several fairly comprehensive language study books also available, which make stimulating reading in themselves and may conceivably be used for supported self-study. Five of the best are: *Issues: A Coursebook for A Level English Language* (Turner), Hodder and Stoughton; *Grammar, Structure and Style* (Russell), Oxford University Press; *Meaning in English Language* (Jeffries), Macmillan; *Living Language* (Keith and Shuttleworth), Hodder and Stoughton; *Understanding Language* (Parry and Allen), Cambridge University Press.

12: Drama

art, though it must have the effect of nature,
is art because it is not nature. . .

W. B. Yeats, *Advice to Playwrights*

The relationship between English and drama has rarely been straightforward. This is partly because the term 'drama' has been used in education to mean different things to different people. The study of plays has invariably been part of the English curriculum but the term 'drama' was more often used to refer to some form of improvised play-making. In the early days of child drama this usually meant having the pupils make up plays in groups to perform for each other at the end of the lesson. In the 1970s and 1980s, as the practice of drama in education became more sophisticated with the teacher intervening in the process to elevate the quality of the work, many English teachers saw the potential for a greater level of integration, using drama to increase pupils' understanding of literature (including scripted plays curiously enough), as a stimulus for writing or to explore a theme in greater depth.

It is not the intention to provide a detailed history of drama teaching in this chapter but some understanding of the debates and tensions which have been associated with the subject will provider a firmer basis for exploring its practical value. The main difference of opinion centred on the distinction made between 'theatre', which was thought to be largely concerned with communication between actors and an audience, and 'drama', which was seen as having more to do with the experience of the participants (Way, 1967). Teachers who were familiar with the negative aspects of performance (pupils showing off and mouthing lines with no sense of purpose) were eager to embrace the new experiential approach which sought to engage pupils in meaningful contexts demanding real thinking and feeling. Rather than seek to educate people *in* and *about* drama, the emphasis was on developing understanding *through* drama.

Instead of teaching pupils how to act, project their voices, design sets and use lights, the emphasis was on the content of the drama, on how to develop insight into human situations through active participation in play-making. Advocates of one or other approach tended to advance their argument by criticising the worst excesses of their opponents. Traditional theatre practice in schools was thought to be superficial, authoritarian, and devoid of educational purpose; 'drama' was accused of being excessively indulgent, undisciplined and devoid of artistic form.

These extreme positions have now largely given way to a more inclusive view of drama which recognises that previous arguments were based on false polarities. Performing in the school play, sharing prepared sketches in the classroom and participating in spontaneous improvised work without an audience can be seen as different manifestations of drama which all have the same 'family resemblance'. Activities of this kind were not always grouped together. While performing to an audience and working from a scripted play belonged in a separate category called 'theatre', improvised drama was more associated with play and dramatic playing. The change of emphasis in categorisation is so fundamental to this chapter that it is worth representing it in diagrammatic form to reinforce the point (Figure 12.1).

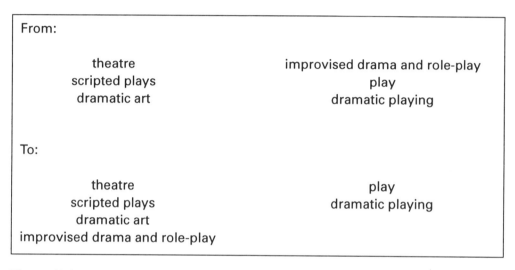

Figure 12.1

Early advocates of drama in education tended to draw on theoretical writings on child play and psychology rather than on the theatre. The emphasis was on the personal growth of the individual through creative self expression and much less on coming to know an external world through its depiction in the art form. It is very easy to see why children's drama was more associated with playing than theatre because of surface appearances. Make-believe play in the home corner of the infant classroom and a small group of Year 8 pupils improvising a play about a bank robbery seem to have more in common with each other than with a performance of *King Lear*. However, the consequences of the conceptual realignment are far-reaching and will inform all the specific practical suggestions in the rest of this chapter. The change in the framework for categorising drama has the following consequences:

- All manifestations of drama in the classroom no matter how simple can draw on insights provided by the nature of drama as art, as in the examples below. Often drama (in the classroom or when used on training courses) is reduced to mere role-play or simulation and fails to exploit the full potential of the art form.
- Although drama appears to come naturally to pupils it should not be assumed they do not have to be taught techniques and conventions. It is reasonable enough to argue that the motivation to engage in drama is part of human nature (a similar argument was advanced in relation to poetry in Chapter 6) but drama as art is not as 'natural' as play.
- The frequently quoted line from *Hamlet* that the purpose of drama is 'to hold a

mirror up to nature' while partially true is potentially misleading if taken too literally. It is self-evidently true in that drama draws on the human condition and is 'grounded in reality' (States 1994) but as an art form it is not entirely representational. Teachers sometimes assume that the purpose of pupils' drama is to replicate real life as far as possible whereas its value in understanding human situations often derives from the way in which it *differs* from real-life situations.

- Whether drama is taught as a separate subject or incorporated into English it makes sense to include the study of plays, including Shakespeare, as part of the drama curriculum. The drama curriculum which at one time was only concerned with creating and making plays needs to include responding to dramatic art as well.

The term 'family resemblance' was used above to indicate that certain concepts *resemble* each other rather than share one or more *identical* characteristics. A minority of writers still persist in arguing that only performing scripted plays to an audience counts as 'dramatic art'. The effect of this type of argument is to view other types of classroom drama in a very reductive way, as mere 'role-play', which is very limiting. Common sense dictates that if a teacher is concerned to use drama in the classroom to explore a poem or short story, placing too much emphasis on performance may limit the involvement of some pupils, change the nature of the experience and simply be a waste of energy. It is a bit like arguing that every piece of writing a pupil produces in school must go on the wall or be published in a magazine instead of being shared informally.

The inclusion of drama in the National Curriculum for English is something of a mixed blessing. It does ensure that some participation in drama is now every pupil's entitlement; and in many schools it continues to flourish as a separate subject and is popular at GCSE and A level. In other schools, however, drama has ceased to be taught as a specialism and is subsumed under English. The purpose of this chapter will be to provide an insight into the way drama as an art form can function in English, while recognising at the same time that the educational potential for drama is considerably enhanced when it is given separate curriculum provision.

It is easy to understand why drama in school became associated more with the play of young children than with scripted plays and the theatre. As stated above, child drama often resembles dramatic playing and draws its popularity partly from that association. Some pupils find it embarrassing to participate in drama but in general it is a very popular activity in schools. For young adolescents, if they can overcome initial inhibitions, it provides an opportunity to experiment with roles and identities which is arguably a developmental need at this stage (see Chapter 8). Drama is a very concrete activity involving intellect, body and emotions which derives its power from the fact that it occurs in the present. If, instead of talking about the fight scene in *Romeo and Juliet,* the teacher starts to interview an eyewitness – 'where were you standing at the time?. . .how did Mercutio get stabbed?. . .are you trying to hide something?' – the mood in the classroom and the level of attention and motivation will often increase dramatically.

It was suggested above that it is rather curious that 'drama' was sometimes used in the course of the English lesson in order to study plays. It can be seen now how this situation arose because the term 'drama' tended to refer exclusively to active play-making. As well as including work on scripted plays as a central aspect of the drama curriculum, active drama approaches can also be used in English in the following ways:

- as a 'way in' to a novel or short story;
- to develop understanding of themes and character in literature;
- in order to engage with a poem prior to or instead of analysis;
- as a stimulus for writing;
- as a means of developing language in all its forms by providing appropriate contexts for different uses, including standard English;
- as a way of exploring genre by transposing from one to another.

Practical books on drama teaching usually take one of two approaches. It is customary either to provide a list of techniques and conventions with examples of their use (tableau, hot-seating, questioning in role, etc.) or to provide some examples of specific lessons or drama projects. Both approaches have considerable value and the further reading section provides some useful examples of each. This chapter, however, will adopt a different method and will seek to offer a set of principles or a way of thinking about drama teaching which is intended to demonstrate how theory can inform practice in very specific ways. Lists of conventions are valuable as long as they are not employed in a mechanistic way; examples of lessons are always necessary but they do not transfer easily to different contexts.

The three general 'principles of practice': use of multi-levels, obliquity, and juxtaposition, will be the main focus of this chapter. These are not discrete categories as will be apparent from the discussion; obliquity is a way of creating distance and juxtaposition is a technique which can create multi-levels. Nevertheless, the principles are useful ways of giving more depth to conventions and approaches which are frequently used in drama. The following discussion will also serve as an introduction to some of the more commonly used conventions and techniques.

MULTI-LEVELS

No matter how uncomplicated the outer form of the drama (a simple piece of improvised dialogue in pairs or work on a few lines of script) the work can usually be given more depth by seeking to highlight or inject below the surface possible different levels of meaning.

Tableau or freeze frame is one of the most common conventions used in the classroom because it is so controlled. Asking pupils to use their bodies to depict a situation, a scene from a short story, an abstract concept or a moment from a play as a still image culminates in a moment of welcome stillness and silence. The technique also has other advantages: pupils are encouraged to think about the way meaning is conveyed through gesture and expression; it can be a useful way of depicting scenes which would otherwise be too difficult or sensitive to act; it slows the drama down and prevents the superficial onward rush of plot which tends to inhibit thinking.

Sometimes the full potential of tableau is not realised because the possibilities of exploring different levels of meaning is not fully exploited. The topic of bullying is one which lends itself to tableau because the approach avoids physical confrontation between pupils. Instead of or in addition to asking pupils to present a scene depicting bullying their work on tableau might include:

- a scene in which the bullying would not at first be obvious to a casual observer;
- two scenes in which the bully in one is the victim in the other;
- a scene which shows on close inspection that one of the bullies is not comfortable with the role;
- a scene in which one of the bullies is a former friend;
- two scenes, one of which shows the consequences of the bullying;
- a scene which is accompanied by characters' thoughts which show that what is happening is different from the way things first appear.

In these cases drama is being used to probe below external appearances. As such it can provide a useful preliminary to reading a short story or a poem such as John Walsh's 'The Bully Asleep'. Tableau can be a valuable activity when reading in class because it demands that pupils' translate their understanding of the text into a concrete form. It can therefore consolidate pupils' grasp of plot and character. The search for different levels of meaning in drama can take place either through looking below the surface or through looking at different interpretations. Asking pupils to create a still image of a moment from the fight scene between Mercutio and Tybalt in Act 3, scene 3 of *Romeo and Juliet* will require some understanding of the scene as a whole. However, asking them to depict the moment in both a serious and a light-hearted way will also focus their thinking on different interpretations and prepare them for contrasting theatre and film representations.

Adding *sub-text* to lines of dialogue is another means of probing hidden meanings either with invented texts or extracts from scripts or novels. Pupils are asked to read the dialogue aloud with the thoughts of the characters included. This technique is used by Brian Friel in *Philadelphia, Here I Come* in which the author has written two parts for the central character, one of which gives voice to his private thoughts throughout the play. A similar technique can be used with dialogue from a novel. In the following extract, adapted from Jane Austen's *Emma*, the characters are discussing their first meeting with Mrs Elton whose truly odious character has yet to be revealed; Emma has her misgivings, in contrast to the more naïve Harriet. Attempting to supply Emma's accompanying thoughts is not straightforward and is likely to provoke discussion about her character.

HARRIET: Well, Miss Woodhouse, what do you think of her? – Is she not charming?

EMMA: Oh! yes – very – a very pleasing young woman.

HARRIET: I think her beautiful, quite beautiful.

EMMA: Very nicely dressed, indeed; a remarkably elegant gown.

HARRIET: I am not at all surprised that he should have fallen in love.

EMMA: Oh! No – there is nothing to surprise one at all. A pretty fortune; and she came in his way.

Sometimes sub-text can refer not just to the characters' private thoughts but to the intended meaning. Emma's final sentence which gives an unromantic view of Elton's motives is not likely to be picked up by Harriet although the meaning is clear to the reader. Asking pupils to create a sub-text which highlights intended meaning provides a complex view of language rather than seeing it as simple and transparent. The following example of a conversation between husband and wife (Fleming 1997) includes a possible intended meaning in brackets:

None of these shirts is ironed. (*Why aren't you doing your proper job as a wife?*)

It's still plugged in downstairs. (*Do it yourself – I'm not a slave.*)

I've got a really important meeting today. (*I'm the one who brings the money in – the least you can do is help.*)

I'll probably tidy another cupboard. (*I wish I had some fulfilment and interest in my life.*)

I'll be late tonight. (*I'm annoyed with you.*)

Fine. (*I'm annoyed with you*).

Pupils can experiment with the way different interpretations of meanings and sub-text affects the acting and the way lines are delivered. The above would have to be acted very differently if the sub-text changed to convey good humour and affection.

Creating sub-text for a few lines of dialogue may also be a useful 'way in' to a scripted play. Pinter's play *Betrayal* opens with the following lines:

JERRY: Well. . .

EMMA: How are you?

JERRY: All right.

EMMA: You look well.

JERRY: Well, I'm not all that well really.

EMMA: Why? What's the matter?

JERRY: Hangover.

The dialogue seems innocent and straightforward enough until we learn that Jerry and Emma have had an affair some time in the past and that Emma's husband was Jerry's best friend. Again, pupils can experiment with different ways of reading and acting just a few lines of dialogue (particularly in the case of this play using pauses) to convey different subtexts.

Arthur Miller's *The Crucible* contains the following exchange near the beginning of the second act:

PROCTOR: If the crop is good I'll buy George Jacob's heifer. How would that please you?

ELIZABETH: Aye, it would.

PROCTOR   (*with a grin*): I mean to please you, Elizabeth.

ELIZABETH   (*it is hard to say*): I know it, John.

(*He gets up, goes to her, kisses her. She receives it. With a certain disappointment, he returns to the table.*)

PROCTOR   (*as gently as he can*): Cider?

ELIZABETH   (*with a sense of reprimanding herself for having forgot*): Aye!

The play contains many scenes which are more obviously dramatic; the previous act culminated in hysteria caused by the 'discovery' of witchcraft in the village. However this simple domestic scene contains much tension below the surface of the words. This is the first time the audience has seen Elizabeth and Proctor together and both of them are living under the strain of his previous affair with the servant girl. Creating a subtext for the characters' lines raises questions about the precise nature of their relationship at this point: there seems to be an excessive politeness, a straining after authenticity.

OBLIQUITY

Before the influence of drama in education in the 1970s and 1980s it was assumed that the only way of approaching literature in the context of drama was to act it out, whether it was a play, short story or extract from a novel. Some writers began to argue that this was the least useful way of working because it did no more than reinforce superficial knowledge of the text. Much however depends on how successfully the dramatised version is realised. The value of acting out a plot was sometimes underestimated; translating a text from one medium to another demands considerable understanding of content and form. It is important, however, to acknowledge that acting out the story is not the only way of using drama to approach a text and it is often desirable to work more obliquely in order to explore character, themes and aspects of the language.

Questioning in role (or hot-seating) is an example of working in this way and is popular because, like tableau, it gives the teacher a considerable degree of control and is a fairly straightforward way of introducing role to a class. The simplest form of the technique involves one pupil or the teacher being questioned as a character from a play or novel. They can be asked about their motivation, attitude, relationships, etc. The approach can be made more oblique by questioning a minor rather than a main character which is helpful when the pupils' knowledge is not sufficiently developed to allow them to be subjected to a full questioning in role. Thus, questioning the guards who lead Cordelia and King Lear away to prison near the end of the play or the servants who wait at the feast at which Banquo appears (*Macbeth*) does not assume a full knowledge of events and understanding of characters' motivation.

Using a teacher to play the role tends to work more successfully in a team-teaching context with the other teacher free to organise the questioning. Sometimes pupils are unable to get beyond the stage of asking very literal questions ('What were you wearing at the time of the murder?') instead of probing deeper issues. Teacher intervention may help to indicate some of the possibilities. Sometimes pupils become confused about the identity of the questioners and this is something which may need to be clarified at the start. Whether they are other characters, newspaper reporters or simply 'readers' of the text who do not have any other clearly defined role will influence the level of knowledge they are supposed to have. For example, are the characters from *Lord of the Flies* being questioned by someone who knows what happened on the island?

Conducting meetings in a dramatic context provides another common method of taking an indirect approach to a theme or text. Often the technique appears to replace action with mere discussion: instead of becoming ghosts or prisoners, the pupils take the roles of investigators of the supernatural who are planning their next mission or guards who are planning how to increase security. This sort of work limits the potential for dramatic action and should not be overused but may provide a useful starting point for a drama project or a useful initial stage for a teacher who is introducing role for the first time. Creating an opportunity for talk in a make-believe context (as opposed to having a discussion or debate) can be liberating for pupils because it allows them the protection of the role to express views which are not necessarily their own. Artificial conflicts can be injected rather than relying simply on pupils' own opinions. In order to elevate such meetings from a simple role-play or simulation it helps to inject an element of dramatic tension; for example, some people at the meeting have hidden motives for their point of view which are not immediately made public. Examples of 'meetings' interpreted in the broadest sense include: press conference given by Mark Antony after Caesar's death; residents' meeting to discuss whether a centre for the homeless should be built in the area; tribunal investigating the deaths of Romeo and Juliet.

Using an oblique approach in drama is one way of creating *aesthetic distance* and can be a useful way of approaching content which for some classes is too emotionally charged to be handled in a naturalistic way: mime, narration, tableau, ritual, reported action and using the perspective of minor characters are all ways of representing a funeral in drama (the scene at Juliet's grave, for example) other than simply acting it out. The objective of creating distance is contrary to the way drama in education was often conceived in the 1970s and 1980s when 'real' feeling and belief were often seen to be the central objects.

An oblique approach is also a useful way of introducing *playwrighting*. Without constraints pupils are often too ambitious in what they try to achieve or are simply overwhelmed by the task. Working within clear guidelines may be liberating rather than the reverse; using reported action rather than trying to create intensely dramatic scenes may be more manageable, as in the following three examples (Fleming 1997:153). The intention here is that the pupils are given the scenario and the first few lines of dialogue to get them started.

- A family are at breakfast when a letter arrives. The person who receives the letter tries at first to conceal its contents from the others. When the contents are finally revealed the consequences for the whole family are considerable.

  MRS JONES: That sounds like the postman – could you see what it is?
  (*John leaves and returns moments later*).
  JOHN: It's for Julie (*handing over a letter*).
  JULIE: Oh, thanks. I'll open it later.

- A group of young people have planned for a bet to stay in a 'haunted house' overnight. One of the party has left the room where they are planning to sleep in order to go to the toilet. The scene begins with the return of the character who is very obviously shaken and ends with the group deciding to leave the house.

  BEN: She's been ages.
  ANGELA: She's got more courage than me staying out that long.
  (*The door opens and Jackie comes in obviously upset and frightened.*)
  MIKE: What's the matter with you?

- The arrival of a stranger in a small village pub shatters the tranquillity of the village because of the news which he gradually reveals in the course of the scene.

  GEORGE: Not many strangers find their way to this pub when they first come here, it's so out of the way.
  STRANGER: It's not my first time here.
  GEORGE: I don't think I've met you before, have I?
  STRANGER: We never actually met but I remember you very well.

Working through *analogy* is another way of approaching a topic or text obliquely. Orwell's *1984* might be introduced by a whole-class improvisation designed to capture the sense of a repressive futuristic society. This could happen in the form of a meeting with teacher in role addressing a group of teenagers who have been arrested for holding an illegal meeting.

JUXTAPOSITION

Juxtaposition refers to the technique of creating meaning by placing two or more dramatic scenes side by side or combining drama with text (poem, letter, novel extract) in a way which provides insight into both. If text is used, the stimulus for the work becomes incorporated into the final product to give it more aesthetic impact, as in the following examples:

- A newspaper article is contrasted with an improvised scene which provides an insight into the truth of what happened, e.g. an article (and headline) which takes a high moral tone in condemning a young woman for shoplifting is contrasted with a scene which shows the domestic pressures which were part of the cause. Notice that placing the article and drama side by side avoids too much heavy didactic moralising; the meaning of the total 'performance' retains some ambiguity.
- A poem is set against a tableau, short piece of scripted dialogue or improvised scene suggested by one of the lines. Alternatively, a long narrative poem or ballad may be represented in tableaux with each group presenting one of the verses.
- Pupils present short scenes based on and incorporating the line, 'Telling lies to the young is wrong' (or other similar expression). The expression (or quotation) acts as more than just a stimulus. Incorporating it into the finished product will give more impact and influence the overall meaning.
- A paragraph from a police list of 'missing persons' is followed by a dramatised version of what might have caused the individual to leave home.
- A diary entry is accompanied by an enacted scene which shows a change (obvious or subtle) in the way it was remembered from the way it was recorded, e.g. a new teacher writes self-deceptively about the first day spent in a new school.
- A monologue or soliloquy is spoken while the rest of the group present a tableau which throws light on its content. The monologue may be one written by the pupils themselves or taken from published works, e.g. by Alan Bennett.
- Different groups are given a few lines of script and they invent and present different possible contexts and interpretations.
- Different groups are given a few lines of script and the same context but each group gives the words a different meaning by changing the tone.

This chapter will conclude with an examination of how these techniques can be used to explore fiction followed by a brief discussion of the teaching of Shakespeare.

The possibilities and limitations of using drama to explore a short story can be illustrated by the following example. Doris Lessing's 'Through the Tunnel' (which is often read at Key Stage 4) deals with the 'rite of passage' of an eleven year old when he plucks up the courage to swim through an underground tunnel while on holiday with his mother. The story does not lend itself immediately to interpretation through drama; there are very few characters and much of the writing consists of intricate descriptions of the beach environment, the sea and the boy's efforts under the water. The density of the description, however, can make it difficult for some pupils to concentrate and engage with the text. Drama could be used to open up the theme rather than to act out the story, as in the following suggestions.

- Before reading the story write the following extract from it on the board:

  He was an only child, eleven years old. She was a widow. She was determined to be neither possessive nor lacking in devotion.

  Ask the pupils to say what they understand by the phrases 'possessive' and 'lacking in devotion'. In pairs, pupils create short scenarios (either improvised or scripted) between parent and eleven year old child which show examples of each.
- Volunteers perform one of their short sketches and the parent in each case is hot-seated to determine more about his/her attitude to their child. The other pupils are asked to say whether the behaviour was reasonable or not. The discussion is directed towards the difficulties for parents of getting the right balance.
- Pupils are given lines of dialogue from the end of the story and asked to create a context, deciding what might have happened. They then read the lines in different ways to create different meanings, and include a sub-text. They explore possible different interpretations, e.g. the parent intends to be caring while the child reacts to the concerns as being over protective:

  'Have a nice morning?.'
  'Oh, yes, thank you.'
  'You look a bit pale. How did you bang your head?.'
  'Oh, just banged it.'

  The class are then given two extra lines of dialogue from the story and asked to speculate further about the context with this new information:

  'I can stay under water for two minutes – three minutes at least.'
  'Can you darling? Well I shouldn't overdo it. I don't think you ought to swim any more today.'

- Pupils read the story. A selection could then be made from the following possible questions and tasks:

  What kind of person is the mother? Is she too possessive?
  To what degree might the mother's attitude be determined by the fact that she is a single parent?
  Why is swimming through the tunnel so important to Jerry?
  Underline any phrases which suggest that the boy has mixed feelings about his mother.
  Underline any phrases from the descriptive passages which give a feeling that the environment is threatening.
  Draw a sketch of the underground tunnel from the description.

- Pupils ask questions of the teacher in role as first the mother and then the boy.
- Pupils create a collage of sounds and words (some derived from the actual text) which represent the boy's dream that night as he sleeps.
- The extract in which Jerry wants to join the older boys is re-read. Groups each create a tableau of a scene not related to this story which shows a young boy trying to join the company of an older crowd. Pupils share the tableaux and say what might be going though the younger boy's mind at that moment in time.

The teaching of Shakespeare has been revolutionised in recent years by the Shakespeare in Schools Project which has used techniques derived from drama in education, theatre and voice training to build up a variety of approaches to Shakespeare texts which are active and accessible to pupils of all ages and abilities. Some new teachers who have been inspired by the rarefied atmosphere of an adult workshop or by reading practical suggestions in one of the many books on the subject become disappointed when the ideas fall flat in the classroom. It is important, however, not to lose faith. Sometimes it helps to explain the purpose of the approach in general terms to pupils so that they do not feel they are just being asked to jump from one rather strange activity to another with little sense of meaning or direction. New teachers sometimes inadvertently send signals that they are not sure about what they are asking pupils to do for the obvious reason that they have not as yet experienced personal success in using the techniques. It is important to try to have confidence and be firm in giving directions and tasks.

One of the central aims is to familiarise pupils with the language of the plays and for them to respond to its rhythms and images prior to any detailed attempt at understanding and analysis of its content. The pupils therefore need to be prepared to engage in tasks without necessarily having a full sense of the context, which is contrary to the way drama usually works. The following examples illustrate the variety of possibilities but readers are advised to consult individual editions of the Cambridge Schools Shakespeare Plays to see how these can be employed in specific contexts.

- choral speaking;
- distributing a speech in sections to pupils so that each individual learns and recites just a few lines;
- speaking lines loudly, in a whisper, angrily, sadly, etc.;
- casting;
- use of music, darkness and light to create scenes (e.g. storm scene in *King Lear*);
- acting out sections (e.g. the play within a play from *A Midsummer Night's Dream*, which lends itself to burlesque);
- tape-record scenes with sound effects (particularly the beginning and ending of contrasting scenes);
- mime while saying words of a speech (e.g. Mercutio's 'Queen Mab' speech);
- practise speaking lines in different ways to change meaning;
- drawing based on description in text (e.g. apothecary's shop in *Romeo and Juliet*);
- improvise scenes not in play;
- unspoken thoughts of characters;
- diagrams of staging, costumes, props;
- identify stage direction in language (e.g. scene in which Katherina has tied up Bianca in *The Taming of the Shrew*);
- focus on insults.

FURTHER READING

For an overview of theory and practice in drama see Fleming (1994) *Starting Drama Teaching* and the further reading sections in that book. Contrasting perspectives on teaching drama can be found in Hornbrook (1989) *Education and Dramatic Art* and Bolton (1992) *New Perspectives on Classroom Drama*; the latter includes examples of lessons. For a detailed discussion of the nature of drama in education see O'Toole (1992) *The Process of Drama* and O'Neill (1995) *Drama Worlds*. For books on teaching Shakespeare see Reynolds (1991) *Practical Approaches to Teaching Shakespeare* and Gibson (1990) *Secondary School Shakespeare*. Useful books on drama and English teaching include Byron (1986) *Drama in the English Classroom* and Neelands (1992) *Learning Through Imagined Experience*.

RESOURCES

Neelands (1990) *Structuring Drama Work* contains a comprehensive guide to conventions used in drama teaching. Fleming (1997) *The Art of Drama Teaching* discusses numerous drama techniques each illustrated by an extract from a scripted play. Taylor (1991) *Drama Strategies* contains examples of lessons. Marson *et al.* (1990) *Drama 14–16* also gives detailed descriptions of a number of drama projects as does Rankin (1995) *Drama 5–14 A Practical Approach to Classroom Drama*. Kempe (1990) *The GCSE Drama Coursebook* is helpful for approaching scripted plays.

13: Media Education

The medium is the message.

Marshall McLuhan

Like drama, media education does not have an independent identity as a curricular subject within the National Curriculum; both subjects are subsumed under the English Orders. Media education particularly, as a relatively recent phenomenon with its own barely established pedagogy and conventions, could be regarded as under threat in this context. There is in fact a striking parallel between this sense of insecurity and that experienced during the early history of English, less than a century ago, in its relationship with classical studies. Some are relieved that media education appears at all in the National Curriculum, pointing out that in the ideological climate of the 1980s its very existence – like society itself in Mrs Thatcher's famous remark – was called into question. Other commentators show concern over this position; Davies (1996:59), for example, protests

> As far as I am concerned, the most extraordinary thing that is currently being said about the latest version of the National Curriculum for English is that it allows far more opportunity for studying the media than had been anticipated and, in this respect, is almost as good as the first version of the National Curriculum for English. Which is fine, except that the first version did not actually do all that much to promote media study and had minimal impact on the practice of English teachers and, if this second version is nearly as good, that means it is nothing like good enough.

Despite Davies' view, the inclusion and promotion of media education in the original National Curriculum for English did achieve significant advances in ensuring at least that all English departments took this area of the subject seriously. It is worth looking back at the Cox (DES 1989) conception of media education, its place in the subsequent official orders, and what commentators made of it. By so doing, we may uncover useful approaches to the rather less detailed – some would say less satisfactory – account in the current orders. Cox was able to make full use of the expertise of the British Film Institute, then as now pioneering the cause of media education, by quoting from its publication (Bazalgette (ed.) 1989:96) of primary phase curriculum policy:

> Media education. . .seeks to increase children's critical understanding of the media. . .How they work, how they produce meaning, how they are organised and how audiences make sense of them, are the issues that media education addresses.

[It] aims to develop systematically children's critical and creative powers through analysis and production of media artefacts. This also deepens their understanding of the pleasure and enjoyment provided by the media. Media education aims to create more active and critical media users who will demand, and could contribute to, a greater range and diversity of media products.

This provides us still with a series of useful guiding principles at once wide-ranging and encouraging depth of study. In terms of the original National Curriculum, published a year later, the fundamental principles were adapted into three approaches (to be found in probably the most useful section entitled 'Non-Statutory Guidance'):

- Approach 1: Media Languages:
    How do we make sense of a media text?
    What conventions are at work in it?
    How do we categorise it in relation to other texts?
- Approach 2: Representation:
    Is this text supposed to be like real life?
    Do you find the characters and setting convincing?
    What roles are there for different groups (e.g. women) in this story?
- Approach 3: Producers and Audiences:
    Who produced this text and why?
    For whom is it made and how will it reach them?
    What will they think of it?

For many involved in promoting media education at a time when the English curriculum certainly appeared like a battleground, this seemed indeed like 'three steps to heaven'. You may notice the similarity to our recommended approaches to the reading of texts in Chapter 5, and this underlines the fundamental unity of English. As the English Orders came to be modified (many would say eroded) English teachers have been determined to safeguard what is most valuable in media education. As ever, this opportunity was and remains elusive, but none the less real. McGuinn in Protherough and King (eds) (1995:157), writing just before the revised English Orders were published, makes an important point:

English teachers must meet a number of important challenges. The first is to treat the English Order as an enabling rather than a restrictive document. The problem is, these opportunities are largely implicit rather than explicit – a series of hints to 'those in the know' rather than clear guidance for the uncertain.

English teachers need to be enterprising and resourceful here; the guiding principle must be that approaches to texts derived from the mass media should not be qualitatively different from those taken to literature, although of course each text – and, more broadly, each genre – will have its own idiosyncrasies.

The term 'media education' implies breadth of teaching and learning, and must be distinguished from 'media studies', which has come to mean rather more specialised syllabus-based study, usually at GCSE or A level. It is the former that we shall be mainly concerned with here, exploring the possibilities of creative media-based activity as central to the English curriculum. In this context there is a cross-phase element, and a great deal of inspiring media education is taking place at Key Stages 1 and 2 in many primary schools which may be successfully built on in the secondary school. There are also strong cross-curricular possibilities and much pioneering work has already been carried out by expressive arts and humanities departments in this field. So media education, perhaps more than most areas of English, may crop up in a variety of times and places. It should be an important part of both Key Stages 3 and 4 of the National Curriculum, and may have further implications as a media studies examination option at GCSE which is often, but not exclusively, taught by English specialists. The place of media studies as a free standing subject in the options system varies considerably between the schools which offer it, and it is well worth keeping a watchful eye on how it is positioned in the all-important options columns at the end of Key Stage 3. An alternative approach, adopted successfully by several schools, is to organise the Key Stage 4 English curriculum around the central 'core' of English GCSE itself with 'satellite' options which may include English literature, media studies and drama, with the teaching groups organised accordingly. There are also some rather more vocationally-orientated alternatives developed in some schools under the general title 'Arts and Media Services' and increasingly subsumed into the GNVQ framework; indeed, given the number of vocational opportunities in the media, it is a little surprising that development here has not been more widespread. Whichever system, if any, is used, there are clear implications for the preparation of pupils in broadly-based media education at Key Stage 3 in a way similar to that generally used for, say, English literature.

As we have already noted in the context of other aspects of the English curriculum, there may be a tension between immersion in the subject and the keeping of a critical distance. The position for media education may exaggerate this tension, in that, almost by definition, it is the area of the curriculum likely to be most familiar to young people (and, by the same token, least familiar to their teachers). The mass media are frequently focused on the young, and are enjoyed by them without too much concern over keeping a critical distance: indeed it would seem strange if otherwise. Traditionally, this may have led to a view of young people as passive victims of cynical media operators; Buckingham and Sefton-Green in Brindley (ed.) (1994) explore this idea:

> The view of young people as 'dupes' of popular media has a long history, and is regularly espoused by critics of all political persuasions. For many on the Right, the media are often seen as a major cause of moral depravity and violence, while they are routinely condemned by many on the Left for their reinforcement of racism, sexism, consumerism and many other objectionable ideologies. Yet what unites these otherwise very different views is a notion of young people as helpless victims of manipulation, and as extremely vulnerable and impressionable. In this account, the text is seen to be all powerful, while the reader is powerless to step back or resist: 'reading' or making sense of media texts is regarded as an automatic process, in which meanings are simply imprinted on passive minds.

This model of passivity, which arises from a rather patronising, dismissive judgement of the very media probably most enjoyed by pupils, needs to be avoided in teaching. It is important to find a way both of being critical and of finding pleasure in the media artefacts being studied. In studying a film the teacher may wish to pause the tape to analyse camera angles, only to be greeted by calls from the class, who are enjoying the film as a change from the rest of the curriculum, to be allowed to continue watching. This may be a familiar scenario, and it would usually be resolved in the give-and-take spirit of good teaching. For example, a simple warning at the start that the watching of the film will be interrupted may be enough.

A worthwhile way in to media education, and one especially suited to an English teacher's fascination for words themselves, is to pose the question, what do we in fact mean by the word 'media'? It is a short step from there to ponder on the idea of the medium in its other contexts: as in 'the happy medium' or as used in spiritualism, for example. Useful discussion may be stimulated on the nature of a medium as a means of transmitting a message, and with carefully chosen examples (the more immediately topical the better) it should be possible to go from there to an exploration of how the medium affects and is affected by the message, the sender of the message, and of course the receiver. We are here in the realms of semiotics, but such an exploration need not be over complex. We need to establish that the medium is not neutral or transparent and is bound up in an intimate and influential relationship with the three other components and with the overall context and purpose.

In discussing these ideas we are laying the foundations of media appreciation which may be at once enjoyable and analytical: the two need not be mutually exclusive. It may be helpful here to consider Brecht's concept of alienation, used by him in relation to the theatre, but undoubtedly applicable to media education in the liberating combination of full enjoyment of the spectacle with critical appraisal. Brecht himself maintained that, 'Alienating an event or character means first of all stripping the event of its self-evident, familiar, obvious quality and creating a sense of astonishment and curiosity about them'.

For Brecht there was a dialectical relationship between theatre and spectator, with meaning arrived at through synthesis. His own term 'Verfremdung' might in this context be better translated as 'de-familiarisation' or 'estrangement', as has been pointed out by Brooker (1994) in his illuminating essay on Brecht's key words, with fewer of the rather negative connotations of the word 'alienation'. Particularly appropriate here is Brecht's insistence that the process of 'Verfremdung' should be thoroughly educational, but also thoroughly engaging, even celebratory, and potentially liberating. In the context of media education this may be an important relationship; a tension between immersion and critical distance may of course remain, but it should be a healthy tension leading to greater understanding and, ultimately, a deeper enjoyment. If we consider other fields of human activity, such as music, sport or motorcycle maintenance, it is surely true that the more we become interested in a particular area, the more we seek to understand its workings – it would be difficult to conceive it otherwise – and the greater the resulting enjoyment. Media education, like other aspects of education, should have greater enjoyment as its end: we are back to Traherne's insistence that we consider always our ultimate ends.

In media education, as with English, there has to be a balance between critical analysis and creative production, with the one constantly influencing the other. Here again, however, the relationship may not be as straightforward or unproblematic as appears at first sight; Medway (1996:131) highlights this:

> Immediately, we are confronted by a striking asymmetry and an apparently insurmountable constraint. . .the semiotic artefacts produced in the one classroom are not the same sort as are analysed in the other. . .There are good reasons for this of course. It would be impossible for students in schools to produce newspapers, advertisements, TV documentaries, commercials, soaps and the like that are in any way equivalent to those produced by the media industries. It is not simply that professional technology is largely unavailable to schools. A more basic problem is that it is impossible for students to experience the sort of economic and institutional environment that informs mainstream mass media production.

In effect this means that we cannot hope to educate our pupils in the ways of the media entirely through 'hands on' experiential learning. It is a fairly common experience for pupils – and their teacher – to be seriously disappointed by the fruits of several lessons' labour in, say, making a video or recording a radio phone-in. In an age of accelerating media sophistication, such disappointment is perhaps inevitable, but it should be confronted as an opportunity to examine exactly what is needed for professional production, not only in terms of technological expertise but also the 'economic and institutional environment' Medway refers to above. The workshop production element in media education remains all the more fundamental in this context, and provides an important taster of the methodologies and technologies involved. For both teacher and pupils, there are important class and equipment management issues here, especially when, as is generally the case, there is not enough equipment to go round. Pupils may well at first need to be convinced that the adage 'successful production is nine-tenths planning and preparation, one-tenth execution' is true, but the results of early failures may be helpful here. We learn from our mistakes, not by simply being told. With careful planning and timed allocation of the resources available it is possible to convert the classroom into a successful media workshop, and the necessary trust shown in allowing pupils to use expensive equipment relatively independently may enhance the spirit of collaborative learning. In the end, it is the production side which many pupils remember most fondly in their media education, and its importance should not be underestimated or avoided through fear of failure or resources management difficulties. The potential to bring together the arts-based and critical-appraisal models of the subject English is perhaps greatest through the agency of media education.

Davies (1996:60) provides a useful statement of intent for media study:

Media study should look at how meanings about the world are:
- made
- sustained
- contested

in *all* forms of human communication. It should study *what* those meanings and beliefs are, *where* they come from, *who* makes them and *why*.

This kind of English operates on the principles that:
- the more those forms or media influence us (by determining our thinking and actions) the more we should study them;
- the more we benefit from them (by gaining understanding, and means of expression) the more we should learn how to use them positively;
- it is not the job of media study to teach people what the right meanings are, or what the right pleasures are – its particular task is to teach people to examine how meanings are made.

This appears to be a positive starting point for the structuring of media education throughout the secondary English curriculum, although we would emphasise more strongly the production side of classroom activity, including the celebratory. Apart from anything else, it is the creative aspect of the curriculum which may usefully counter the danger of a too earnest approach to, for example, the manipulative power of advertising. The sheer size and breadth of the mass media in all their complexity mean that we must keep the underlying structure of media education firmly in mind. Consider the variety of genres that constitute the media or, better still, have a class 'brainstorm' ideas. The list is likely to include:

- popular magazines, increasingly focused on highly specific readerships;
- TV soaps, sit-coms, mini-sagas, drama series and serials;
- popular music in an incredible variety of guises;
- film adaptations of books, including a fast increasing number of 'classics';
- TV commercials, including those loosely based on continuing narrative;
- the vast range of radio programmes, both commercial and BBC;
- advertising in magazines, on hoardings and in other contexts;
- the 'popular' (tabloid) and 'serious' (broadsheet) press;
- computer games and CD-ROM software;
- pulp fiction and non-fiction;
- popular films in a range of genres;
- public information and charity campaigns through the media;
- TV documentaries and news programmes;
- pop music videos;
- 'fanzines' from the worlds of football, other sports, and popular music.

In fact the list is endless, with each item on it capable of infinite subdivisions of ever more subtly distinctive genres. Teachers, clearly, face a genuine learning experience here, adding to the excitement of media education; certainly, in my own experience I have been introduced to some fascinating examples of fanzines and styles of music which would have been otherwise entirely unknown to me. So much for the teacher as expert. As for other areas of the English curriculum previously noted, we have to collect our own resources as well as relying on those available to pupils, and there is no shortage of opportunity if we keep our eyes and ears open.

It is sometimes claimed that media education is particularly relevant to boys, especially the practical, productive side with its range of sophisticated electronic equipment. Thomas (1997) provocatively sees male fascination for such gadgetry as symptomatic of a particular world view unsuited to the reflective and sensitive writing so often called for in English:

> Men like controlling things. They enjoy gizmos like computers and cars and mobile phones because they can operate and control them. Cars are the ultimate in gizmo control, with limitless scope for supplementary gizmodification: turbo, mobile phone, CD HiFi, 4WD and remote control demist on the tinted glass wing mirror. The car, for men, is not simply transport or carriage – it's for driving, a verb which needs no preposition.

Thomas cleverly links this characterisation to styles of narrative writing, but the relevance to media education is clear. There is, of course, a great danger of stereotype reinforcement here if we simply pander to the most overt elements of what is in the end more of a caricature than a characterisation. It is sometimes suggested that boys tend to miss out the reflective stage in learning, preferring to leap straight from the descriptive/informative to the active/speculative. If this is the case, the production of media artefacts is likely to be less than satisfactory, for, as we have already seen, it is the reflective stage – careful planning and preparation – which is all important. Nevertheless, it may well be that pupils – and they are often boys – who are reluctant readers or writers perform creatively with media-based equipment. If a vital part of education is the giving of space, especially to adolescents, then media activities may be particularly valuable.

The English curriculum is now so crowded throughout the years of secondary schooling that any opportunity to cover different requirements through one central area of study must be seized gratefully. Such is the breadth of media education that much of it can be inventively combined with other aspects of English: literature, for example, or language study. In the activities which follow, the idea is to give a 'taste' of what is possible rather than to define a rigorous curriculum. The various connections to other areas of English will be self-evident.

In the early years of the secondary curriculum it may be best to start with a reasonably open-ended project-based introduction to media education, such as the one outlined in Figure 13.1.

A broadly-based scheme of work such as this allows for considerable flexibility, and implies opportunities to assess pupils in all three of the English attainment targets. It also allows for the development of pupils' interests, although the teacher's role will be vital in guiding these into a form of media education through purposeful teaching. At later stages of secondary schooling, similar open-ended investigative and presentational work could be set, considering one aspect of the mass media, on such topics as 'Images of Youth in the Media' or 'The Representation of Women in the Media'. Again, the stimulus and guidance offered by the teacher will be instrumental in ensuring sustained and questioning activity.

A different approach to media education might be to focus on contrasting film versions of literary texts, of which there is certainly no lack. Again, it is clear that a

---

YEAR 7 ENGLISH ASSIGNMENT: MEDIA-BASED ENTERTAINMENT

A four week project on any aspect of media-based entertainment you wish to work on, either individually or in pairs. For this purpose, entertainment includes sport through the media, pop music, radio, television, films, computer games, videos, magazines, or another area of interest by negotiation with the teacher.

- You will need to focus on a particular aspect of your chosen subject which interests you, and plan carefully how you intend to develop the project.
- Your project must include some of the following:
    information researched from books, magazines, CD-ROMs, TV, etc.;
    survey work and interviews, carefully planned and then taped;
    your own views on the subject;
    a detailed description of how the media present the subject of interest, who the intended audience is, and what the effect is.
- Apart from your written and illustrated project, you will need to give an active presentation on your work to the rest of the class. This should include the following:
    a spoken explanation of what your project involved and what particular areas of interest you covered;
    demonstrations and examples illustrating the subject – e.g. songs and music, taped or live; video clips from films etc.; taped interviews; home-produced video material; posters and other large-scale visual material.

Figure 13.1

variety of elements of the syllabus may be covered, including, at Key Stage 4, GCSE coursework and preparation for English and English literature examinations. Film adaptations of Shakespeare can be particularly exciting, and expose the plays to a multiplicity of interpretations. From the media education angle, the question to ask is how a particular interpretation is realised on film. Comparison of the two film versions of Golding's novel *Lord of the Flies*, frequently taught, could focus on questions like these:

- What is the significance of the opening sequence in each film?
- What part does the music play in creating atmosphere?
- Does the fact that the original film was made in monochrome and the more recent one in colour have any implications for our understanding?
- One film emphasises the British public school background of the children, the other places them as American Military School pupils: how are these contrasting portrayals made clear in the films?
- What are the major deviations from the plot and characterisation of the original novel? Are these justified?
- What symbolism is apparent in both films? (e.g. Jack's survival knife or Simon's 'wand' in the later film);
- Which film did you enjoy more? Why?
- Would you try to film the novel differently? How?
- How does either film compare with others you may have seen dealing with similar themes, such as youth interaction, violence, survival, or destruction of a social order?

There are plenty of excellent resources available, some of which are listed at the end of this chapter, to help in teaching the media, including the practical and technical aspects. There is not space here to go into detail, and there is in any case no need to replicate what is readily available elsewhere in an attractive, palatable form for both pupils and teacher. The following list of possible approaches to media education, then, is intended as a stimulus for further exploration and development in the context of a resourceful and inventive English department.

- 'storyboarding' different media texts, either as the planning of a video-film or as an end in itself, using one of the templates available in many publications or created using ICT;
- cross-genre adaptations, such as a film version of events normally portrayed in a documentary – the Comic Strip TV film *Strike* is a marvellous example of a tongue-in-cheek Hollywood version of the miners' strike;
- given a list of a day's 'newsworthy' items, creating an evening news broadcast and subsequently comparing it with what real news programmes made of the material;
- a similar exercise using newspapers, focusing on the distinction between tabloids and broadsheets, and then contrasting newspaper and television presentation of 'news';
- detailed step-by-step analysis of still pictures, starting with one small portion and then progressing to the 'whole' picture, asking how the inclusion of more detail alters interpretation and understanding (along the lines of the British Film Institute's *Reading Pictures* material);

- discursive use of newspaper and documentary presentations of contentious aspects of the world of the mass media, e.g. press intrusion into personal lives; censorship and the relationship between screen and real-life violence; the exploitation of women in tabloid newspapers;
- analysing positive and negative images in TV programmes, as a preliminary to storyboarding and/or shooting a short film focusing on either attractive or unattractive aspects of a school or local area;
- the study of advertising targeted at specific audiences in 'special interest' magazines, and the subsequent creation of a series of ads promoting a product to an unlikely group of consumers;
- role-playing the planning of an evening's TV schedule, given the constraints (such as the 9 o'clock watershed and limits on the number of American or Australian imports) with which schedule planners have to work;
- photo-storying (examples of which may be found in many adolescent girls' magazines) an unlikely subject, such as a 'classic' literary text;
- study of the media promotion of a new pop group (the latest boy band should provide plenty of exemplar material), including the all-important 'image' and the perhaps less important 'music', as preparation for an imaginary promotion campaign;
- analysis of the presentational styles of several disc jockeys for different audiences, programmes, types of music and radio stations, and the planning of a short sequence of linked records for a particular programme;
- cross-curricular possibilities, including expressive arts departments' use of the media for presentational purposes, the humanities' concerns for historical, social and moral aspects of the media, and the technical expertise to be found in science and technology subjects;
- cross-phase approaches, especially appropriate to study and production of media artefacts aimed at younger children.

As with all such approaches and activities, the onus is on the English teacher, working collaboratively with colleagues where feasible, to integrate and develop them as part of a cohesive curriculum. In particular, there needs to be a balance between the responsive and the productive within each activity where possible, and certainly over the whole structure of the course.

This book will conclude with a brief examination of the impact of information and communications technology on the teaching of English. The position of this discussion at the end of the book does not imply any lack of importance attached to it but rather the opposite. It is fitting that we should end with a pointer to the future rather than a neat, definitive conclusion. The way ICT develops in schools will in part depend on access to the technology but increasingly, 'computers should be seen as being as much part of everyday English as is the ball-point pen, the worksheet or textbook' (Davison and Dowson, 1998:188). Tweddle *et al.* (1997:1) provide a succinct summary of the way new technologies for reading and writing have extended the curriculum for English:

Students now need opportunities to understand:

- how the use of wordprocessors, spell checkers and thesauruses affects the processes involved in the different stages of composition and presentation of text;

- how the research opportunities offered by CD-ROM and Internet-based services can be used to support the study of literature and language;
- how the use of electronic sources of information can enhance the processes of comparison and synthesis of information drawn from different texts;
- how the use of the Internet extends and changes possibilities for communicating with, and publishing for, real audiences, across the world.

Perhaps the key word here is 'understand'. Using ICT in English is about employing a useful means to fulfil particular ends but, as with other aspects of the subject, the impact of changing conventions can be the focus of explicit attention. The use of e-mail, for example, provides a new type of communication which is a written form but tends to be almost as informal as speech. Discussion about the distinction between speaking and writing needs to take this into account. New electronic texts are less static and by their combined use of sounds, words and images can express ideas differently from conventional printed texts. Whatever is written in this book about developments in technology is likely to be out of date quickly; the best way to keep informed about the new technologies is through the new technologies themselves. The following 'text-making' tools are identified as being ones commonly used (Tweddle *et al.* 1997:25):

- Word processing: the drafting process is made much easier by the use of such packages. Pupil motivation can be increased greatly by the professional product.
- Desktop publishing: the teaching of layout, design and presentation can be greatly enhanced by the use of such devices.
- Using electronic mail: the possibilities for writing are much extended by the use of e-mail.
- Computer conferencing: the possibilities for discussion and collaborative writing are considerable through grouping e-mail communication.
- CD-ROMS: there are increasing numbers of publications on Shakespeare and other texts which provide potential for interactive study.
- The Internet: the ever expanding access to data bases, texts, museums, libraries has huge potential; pupils need to consider the reliability or otherwise of such sources of information.

One of the themes discussed in the Introduction and implicit in most of the chapters of this book has been the contrast between a world of neat logic, rationality and systems against human reality which is rather more complex, unpredictable and rich. English as an art belongs in the latter domain. How does this leave English teachers in relation to the new technologies which are *par excellence* logical and mechanical? Rather than feel hostile to such developments we believe that teachers should embrace and celebrate their potential. Whether pupils are using a computer programme of spelling tuition and tests, changing the gender pronoun in a short story to see how this impacts on the meaning, searching *King Lear* for references to nature or creating a newspaper front page, the importance of the overarching human context remains the same. We agree wholeheartedly with Finch (1995:170) that what *can* be turned over to machines *should* be turned over to machines so that we can 'wake up to what is not machinelike in us. . .that should leave with us what is much more deeply and importantly human: our immediacy, our spontaneity, our joy and our freedom.'

FURTHER READING

Potter (ed.) (1990) *Reading, Learning and Media Education* gives plenty of helpful background information, as does Inglis (1990) *Media Theory: An Introduction.* Goodwyn (1992) *English Teaching and Media Education* and Bazalgette (1991) *Media Education* make explicit links between English and media education. Less concerned with the English connection, Masterman (1992) *Teaching the Media* has become something of a standard text. Clarke (1987) *Teaching Popular Television* (Heinemann, 1987) is helpful, while the more recent study of the same subject, Goodwyn (ed.) (1997) *Understanding Television* concentrates on the needs of the post-16 student. Two further publications from the English and Media Centre offer practical guidance for teachers: *The English Curriculum: Media Years 7–9* (1991) and Buckingham, Grahame and Sefton-Green (1996) *Making Media: Learning from Media Production.*

RESOURCES

Published material tends to date rather quickly but a great deal is available specifically for classroom use. *Media Studies: Activities for Ages 11–14* (Dahl), Framework Press, is an impressive collection of photocopiable resources and activities for Key Stage 3. There are several other general introductions aimed more at Key Stage 4: *Media Studies: An Introduction* (Dutton), Longman; *Media Choices* (Mills, Mills and Stringer), Oxford University Press; *Media Studies for GCSE* (Wall and Walker), Collins; and *Examining the Media* (Connell, Brigley and Edwards), Hodder and Stoughton. Hodder and Stoughton also publish a wide-ranging series, *Introducing Media Studies* (series ed. Butts) which is both practical and stimulating of further investigation. Other publications focus more directly on specific aspects of media education; the following photocopiable resources are from the English and Media Centre and are all very helpful, with self-explanatory titles: *The Soap Pack: A Study of 'Brookside' from Script to Screen* (with accompanying video); *The Advertising Pack* (with accompanying video); *The News Pack* (with accompanying video); *Production Practices: Media Simulations*; *Picture Power* (also available as a CD-ROM). *Teaching Television: 'The Real World'* (Hart *et al.*), Cambridge University Press, and *The Language of Reporting* (Rumsby), Nelson, are also well worth using when teaching about these areas of the media. For summaries of topical articles from the press – useful as stimuli for discussion about reporting styles and the content itself – Carel Press publish regularly updated *Essential Articles*, while Collins issues articles from The Times on their CD-ROM *Changing Times.*

Apart from publishers, there are plentiful other sources of media education material. Film Education, for example, is a registered charity devoted to the enhanced public understanding of film and provides excellent resources, mainly free of charge, to anyone on their mailing list; especially valuable are their film guides to popular films as they are released, often coinciding with short programmes to video-tape from television. Further resources can be obtained from the two main media-based museums in the UK, The Museum of the Moving Image (MOMI) on the South Bank in London, and The Museum of Film and Photography in Bradford; both make excellent venues to visit with school parties, and have active education departments.

For ICT and English see Tweddle *et al.* (1997) and Shreeve (ed.) (1997). Reviews of CD-ROMS for English are available on the Virtual Teacher Centre at http://vtc.ngfl.gov.uk/vtc/index.htlm.

Bibliography

Abbs, P. (1974) *Autobiography in Education*. London: Heinemann.

Abbs, P. (1976) *Root and Blossom: Essays on The Philosophy, Practice and Politics of English Teaching*. London: Heinemann.

Abbs, P. (1982) *English Within the Arts*. London: Hodder and Stoughton.

Adams, M. (1990) *Beginning to Read*. Cambridge, MA: MIT Press.

Anderson, A., Brown, G., Shillcock, R. and Yule, G. (1984) *Teaching Talk: Strategies for Production and Assessment*. Cambridge: Cambridge University Press.

Andrews, R. (1991) *The Problem With Poetry*. Milton Keynes: Open University Press.

Arnold, R. (1991) *Writing Development: magic in the brain*. Milton Keynes: Open University Press.

Bain, R., Fitzgerald, B. and Taylor, M. (1992) *Looking into Language : classroom approaches to knowledge about language*. London: Hodder and Stoughton.

Barnes, D. (1976) *From Comunication to Curriculum*. Harmondsworth: Penguin.

Barrs, M. (1990) *Words Not Numbers: Assessment in English*. Sheffield: NATE.

Barton, G. (1992) *English into Practice*. London: Longman.

Bazalgette, C. (1991) *Media Education*. London: Hodder and Stoughton.

Bazalgette, C. (ed.) (1989) *Primary Media Education: A Curriculum Statement*. London: BFI Education Department.

Benton, M. and Benton, P. (1995) *Poetry Workshop*. London: Hodder and Stoughton.

Benton, M., Teasy, J., Bell, R. and Hurst, K. (1988) *Young Readers Responding to Poems*. London: Routledge.

Black P. and Wiliam, D. (1998) *Inside the Black Box*, Occasional Paper. London: King's College.

Black, P. (1998) *Testing: Friend or Foe? Theory and Practice of Assessment and Testing*. London: Falmer Press.

Blake, W. (edited by Stevens, D. 1995). *Selected Works* Cambridge: Cambridge University Press.

Bolton, G. (1992) *New Perspectives on Classroom Drama*. Hemel Hempstead: Simon and Schuster Education.

Bousted, M. (1992) 'Praising what is Lost: The Demise of Coursework in GCSE Literature', *Use of English* **44** (1), 15–24.

Bowie, A. (1990) *Aesthetics and Subjectivity from Kant to Nietzsche*. Manchester: Manchester University Press.

Brindley, S. (ed.) (1994) *Teaching English*. London: Routledge.

Britton, J. (1972) *Language and Learning*. Harmondsworth: Penguin.

Britton, J. (1994) 'Vygotsky's Contribution to Pedagogical Theory', in Brindley, S. (ed.) *Teaching English*. London: Routledge.

Broadfoot, P. (1996) *Education, Assessment and Society*. Milton Keynes: Open University Press.

Brooker, P. (1994) 'Key Words in Brecht's Theory and Practice of Theatre', in Thomson, P. and Sacks, G. (eds) *The Cambridge Companion to Brecht*. Cambridge: Cambridge University Press.

Brown, J. and Gifford, T (1989) *Teaching A Level English Literature*. London: Routledge.

Buchbinder, D. (1991) *Contemporary Literary Theory and the Reading of Poetry*. Sydney, Australia: Macmillan.

Buckingham, D. and Sefton-Green, J. (1994) 'Making Sense of the Media: From Reading to Culture', in Brindley, S. (ed) *Teaching English*. London: Routledge.

Buckingham, D., Grahame, J. and Sefton-Green, J. (1996) *Making Media: Learning from Media Production*. London: English and Media Centre.

Burton, M. (ed.) (1989) *Enjoying Texts: Using Literary Theory in the Classroom*. Cheltenham: Stanley Thornes.

Byron, K. (1986) *Drama in the English Classroom*. London: Methuen.

Calthrop, K. (1971) *Reading Together: An Investigation into the Use of the Class Reader*. London: Heinemann (for NATE).

Capel, S., Leask, M. and Turner, T. (1995) *Learning to Teach in the Secondary School*. London: Routledge.

Carter, R. (ed.) (1990) *Knowledge About Language and the Curriculum: the LINC Reader*. London: Hodder and Stoughton.

Carter, R. (1995) *Key Words in Language and Literacy*. London: Routledge.

Carter, R. and Nash, W. (1990) *Seeing Through Language*. Oxford: Blackwell.

Chambers, A. (1993) *Tell Me: Children, Reading and Talk*. Stroud: The Thimble Press.

Clarke, M. (1987) *Teaching Popular Television*. London: Heinemann.

Claxton, G. (1984) *Live and Learn*. London: Harper and Row.

Cliff Hodges, G. (1993) 'Forward-looking thoughts: the study of literary texts at GCSE', *Cambridge Journal of Education* 23 (1), 65–76.

Coleman, J. (1980) *The Nature of Adolescence*. London: Methuen.

Cook, H. C. (1917) *The Play Way*. London:William Heinemann.

Cox, B. (1991) *Cox on Cox: An English Curriculum for the 1990s*. London: Hodder and Stoughton.

Cox, B. (1995) *Cox on the Battle for the English Curriculum*. London: Hodder and Stoughton.

Creber, P. (1990) *Thinking Through English*. Milton Keynes: Open University Press.

Crystal, D. (1987) *The Cambridge Encyclopedia of English*. Cambridge: Cambridge University Press.

Crystal, D. (1995) *The Cambridge Encyclopedia of the English Language*. Cambridge: Cambridge University Press.

Cullingford, C. (1990) *The Nature of Learning*. London: Cassell.

Curtis, D. (1993) *Teaching Secondary English*. Milton Keynes: Open University Press.

Davies, C. (1996) *What is English Teaching?* Milton Keynes: Open University Press.

Davison, J. and Dowson, J. (1998) *Learning to Teach English in the Secondary School*. London: Routledge.

Dawes, L. (1995) *Writing – The Drafting Process: an examination of drafting in pupils' writing*. Sheffield; NATE.

DES (1975) *A Language for Life* (The Bullock Report). London: HMSO.

DES (1987) *Teaching Poetry in the Secondary School – an HMI View*. London: HMSO.

DES (1988) *Report of the Inquiry into the Teaching of English Language* (The Kingman Report). London: HMSO.

DES (1989) *English for Ages 5–16* (The Cox Report). London: HMSO.

Dias, P. and Hayhoe, M. (1988) *Developing Response to Poetry*. Milton Keynes: Open University Press.

Donaldson, M.(1978) *Children's Minds*. London: Fontana.

Eagleton, T. (1983) *Literary Theory – An Introduction*. Oxford: Basil Blackwell.

Edwards, V., Goodwin, J., and Wellings, A. (1991) *English 7–14: Every Child's Entitlement*. London: David Fulton Publishers.

Eliot, T.S. (1954) *Selected Poems*. London: Faber and Faber.

Entwistle, N. (1987) *Understanding Classroom Learning*. London: Hodder and Stoughton.

Finch, H.L. (1995) *Wittgenstein*. Shaftesbury: Element Books.

Fine, A. (1996) Interview given for NAWE: 'Another Little Spanner?', *Writing in Education*, Spring, 1996.

Flaubert, G. (translated and edited by Russell, A., 1956) *Madame Bovary*. London: Penguin.

Fleming, M. (1992) 'Pupils' Perceptions of the Nature of Poetry', *Cambridge Journal of Education*, 22 (1), 31–41.

Fleming, M. (1989) 'Drama, Kingman and Cox', *Drama Broadsheet*, Spring 6 (1), 2–5.

Fleming, M. (1994) *Starting Drama Teaching*. London: David Fulton Publishers.

Fleming, M. (1997) *The Art of Drama Teaching*. London: David Fulton Publishers.

Foggin, J. (1992) *Teaching English in the National Curriculm: Real Writing*. London: Hodder and Stoughton.

Forster, E.M. (1927) *Aspects of the Novel*. London: Edward Arnold.

Fox, G. and Merrick, B. (1982) 'Thirty-Six Things to do With a Poem', in Lee, V. (ed.) *English Literature in Schools*. Milton Keynes: Open University Press.

Friel, B. (1981) *Translations*. London: Faber and Faber.

Fullan, M. and Hargreaves, A. (1992) *What's Worth Fighting for in Your School?* Milton Keynes: Open University Press.

Furlong, T. and Ogborn, J. (1995) *The English Department: Organisation and Management*. London: The English and Media Centre.

Gardner, H. (1984) *Frames of Mind*. London: Heinmann, first published 1983, New York: Basic Books.

George, N. (1971) 'Creativity in Theory and Practice', *Aspects of Education*, **13**.

Gibson, R. (1986) *Critical Theory and Education*. London: Hodder and Stoughton.

Gibson, R. (1990) *Secondary School Shakespeare*. Cambridge: Cambridge Institute of Education.

Gipps, C. (1994) *Beyond Testing*. London: The Falmer Press.

Goodson, I. (1997) '"Trendy Theory" and Teacher Professionalism', *Cambridge Journal of Education* **27** (1), 7–21.

Goodson, I. and Medway, P. (1990) *Bringing English to Order*. London: Falmer Press.

Goodwyn, A. (1992) *English Teaching and Media Education*. Milton Keynes: Open University Press.

Goodwyn, A. (ed.) (1995) *English and Ability*. London: David Fulton Publishers.

Goodwyn, A. (1997) *Developing English Teachers: the Role of Mentorship in a Reflective Profession*. Milton Keynes: Open University Press.

Goodwyn, A.(ed.) (1997) *Understanding Television*. London: Routledge.

Grainger, T. (1998) 'Drama and Reading: Illuminating their Interaction', *English in Education* Spring **32** (1).

Green, B. (1993) 'Literacy Studies and Curriculum Theorizing; or, The Insistence of the Letter', in Green, B. (ed.) *The Insistence of the Letter: Literacy Studies and Curriculum Theorizing*. London: The Falmer Press.

Green, K. and LeBihan, J. (1996) *Critical Theory and Practice: A Coursebook*. London: Routledge.

Griffiths, P. (1987) *Literary Theory and English Teaching*. Milton Keynes: Open University Press.

Hall, N. and Robinson, A. (1996) *Learning About Punctuation*. Clevedon: Multilingual Matters.

Hardy, T. (1891; edited by Skilton, D. 1985) *Tess of the D'Urbervilles*. London: Penguin.

Harland, R. (1987) *Superstructuralism*. London: Routledge.

Harrison, B. (1983) *Learning through Writing*. Slough: NFER–Nelson.

Harrison, B. (1994) *The Literate Imagination*. London: David Fulton Publishers.

Harrison, G. (1990) 'Three Glorious Summers', *Times Educational Supplement*, 24.8.90.

Hayhoe, M. and Parker, S. (1988) *Words Large as Apples; Teaching Poetry 11–18*. Cambridge: Cambridge University Press.

Hayhoe, M. and Parker, S. (eds) (1992) *Reassessing Language and Literature*. Milton Keynes: Open University Press.

Head, J. (1997) *Working With Adolescents: Constructing Identity*. London: Falmer Press.

HMSO (1921) *The Teaching of English in England* (The Newbolt Report). London: HMSO.

Holderness, G. (ed.) (1988) *The Shakespeare Myth*. Manchester: Manchester University Press.

Holderness, G. and Lalljee, B. (1997) *An Introduction to Oracy: Frameworks for Talk*. London: Cassell.

Holmes, E. (1911) *What Is and What Might Be*. London: Constable.

Hornbrook, D. (1989) *Education and Dramatic Art*. London: Blackwell Education.

Hourd, M. (1949) *The Education of the Poetic Spirit*. London: Heinemann.

Howker, J. (1986) *Badger on the Barge and Other Stories*. London: Lions.

Hoyles, M. (ed.) (1977) *The Politics of Literacy*. London: Writers and Readers Publishing Co-operative.

Hunt, P. (1991) *Critcism, Theory and Children's Literature*. Oxford: Blackwell.

Inglis, F. (1990) *Media Theory: An Introduction*. Oxford: Blackwell.

Iser, W. (1978) *The Act of Reading*. London: Routledge.

Jeffcoate, R. (1992) *Starting English Teaching*. London: Routledge.

Johnson, P. (1996) *Words and Images on the Page*. London: David Fulton Publishers.

Johnstone, B. (1987) *Assessing English: Helping Students to Reflect on Their Work*. Milton Keynes: Open University Press.

Jones, P. (1988) *Lipservice: The Story of Talk in Schools*. Milton Keynes: Open University Press.

Kempe. A. (1990) *The GCSE Drama Coursebook*. Oxford: Basil Blackwell.

Knight, R. (1996) *Valuing English: Reflections on the National Curriculum*. London: David Fulton Publishers.

Kress, G. (1995) *Writing the Future: English and the Making of a Culture of Innovation*. Sheffield: NATE.

Kyriacou, C. (1991) *Essential Teaching Skills*. Cheltenham: Stanley Thornes, first published by Basil

Blackwell.

Landsberg, M. (1988) *The World of Children's Books*. London: Simon and Shuster.

Lewis, M. M. (1946) 'Spoken English in the School', in De Sola Pinto, V. (ed.) *The Teaching of English in Schools*. London: Macmillan.

Lunzer, E. and Gardner, K. (1984) *Learning from the Written Word*. Edinburgh: Oliver and Boyd.

Lurillard, D. (1993) *Rethinking University Teaching*. London: Routledge.

Marsh, G. (1988) *Teaching Through Poetry*. London: Hodder and Stoughton.

Marson, P., Brockbank, K., McGuire, B. and Morton, S. (1990) *Drama 14–16*. Cheltenham: Stanley Thornes.

Masterman, L. (1992) *Teaching the Media*. London: Routledge.

Mathieson, M. (1975) *The Preachers of Culture*. London: Allen and Unwin.

McCourt, F. (1996) *Angela's Ashes*. London: HarperCollins.

McCulloch, R., Mathieson, M. and Powis, V. (1993) *English 16–19: Entitlement at A Level*. London: David Fulton Publishers.

McEwan, I. (1989) *A Move Abroad: Or Shall We Die? and The Ploughman's Lunch*. London: Pan Books/Picador.

McGuinn, N. (1995) 'What is Left of Drama and Media', in Protherough, R. and King, P. (eds) *The Challenge of English in the National Curriculum*. London: Routledge.

Medway, P. (1996) 'Representation and Making: Student Production in English', *Changing English*, **3** (2).

Michael, I. (1992) *The Teaching of English from the Sixteenth Century to 1870*. Cambridge: Cambridge University Press.

Michaels, A. (1997) *Fugitive Pieces*. London: Bloomsbury Publishing.

Midgley, M. (1979) *Beast and Man – the Roots of Human Nature*. Brighton: Harvester Press, reprinted in 1980 by Methuen.

Miller, A. (1987) *Timebends*. London: Methuen.

Mittins, W. (1988) *English: Not the Naming of Parts*. Sheffield: NATE.

Mittins, W. (1990) *Language Awareness for Teachers*. Milton Keynes: Open University Press.

Monaghan, J.E. and Saul, E.W. (1987) 'The Reader, the Scribe, the Thinker: A Critical Look at the History of American Reading and Writing Instruction', in Popkewitz, T.S. (ed.) *The Formation of the School Subjects: The Struggle for Creating an American Institution*. New York: The Falmer Press.

Montgomery, D. (1997) *Spelling*. London: Cassell.

Moon, B. (1996) *A Guide to the National Curriculum*, 3rd edition. Oxford: Oxford University Press.

Morgan, H. (1997) *Motivation of Sixth Form Students*. London: Teacher Training Agency.

Mudd, N. (1994) *Effective Spelling: a practical guide for teachers*. London: Hodder and Stoughton.

Neelands, J. (1990) *Structuring Drama Work*. Cambridge: Cambridge University Press.

Neelands, J. (1992) *Learning Through Imagined Experience*. London: Hodder and Stoughton.

Norris, C. (1991) *Deconstruction Theory and Practice*. London: Routledge.

O'Neill, C. (1995) *Drama Worlds*. Portsmouth, New Hampshire: Heinemann.

O'Toole, J. (1992) *The Process of Drama (Negotiating Art and Meaning)*. London: Routledge.

Peach, L. and Burton, A. (1995) *English as a Creative Art*. London: David Fulton Publishers.

Peim, N. (1993) *Critical Theory and the English Teacher*. London: Routledge.

Perera, K. (1987) *Understanding Language*. London: National Association of Advisers in English.

Peters, M. (1985) *Spelling: Caught or Taught?* London: Routledge.

Pinker, S. (1994) *The Language Instinct: The New Science of Language and Mind*. London: Penguin.

Pirrie, J. (1987) *On Common Ground*. London: Hodder and Stoughton.

Potter, F. (ed.) (1990) *Reading, Learning and Media Education*. Oxford: Blackwell.

Protherough, R. and King, P. (eds) (1995) *The Challenge of English in the National Curriculum*. London: Routledge.

Quirk, R. and Stein, G. (1990) *English in Use*. Harlow: Longman.

Reynolds, P. (1991) *Practical Approaches to Teaching Shakespeare*. Oxford: Oxford University Press.

Rifaterre, M. (1978) *Semiotics of Poetry*. London: Methuen.

Ross, M. (ed.) (1985) *The Aesthetic in Education*. Oxford: Pergamon.

Sampson, G. (1921) *English for the English*. Cambridge: Cambridge University Press.

Sawyer, W., Watson, K. and Adams, A. (eds) (1989) *English Teaching from A to Z*. Milton Keynes: Open University Press.

Scott, P. (1989) *Restructuring A Level English*. Milton Keynes: Open University Press.

Shayer, D. (1972) *The Teaching of English in Schools 1900–1970*. London: Routledge.

Shelley, M. (edited by Stevens, D. 1997) *Frankenstein*. Cambridge: Cambridge University Press.

Shreeve, A. (ed.) (1997) *IT in English: Resources for Learning*. Coventry: NCET and Sheffield: NATE.

Smith, A.E. (1954) *English in the Modern School*. London: Methuen.

Smith, F. (1988) *Joining the Literacy Club*. London: Heinemann.

Sockett, H. (1976) *Designing the Curriculum* London: Open Books.

Soloman, N. (1990) *Help Your Child to Read*. Cambridge: Cambridge University Press.

Staples, A. (1992) *An Approach to English*. London: Cassell.

States, B. (1994) *The Pleasures of the Play*. New York: Cornell University Press.

Stead, C.K. (1964) *The New Poetic: Yeats to Eliot*. London: Hutchinson.

Steiner, G. (1978) *On Difficulty and Other Essays*. Oxford: Oxford University Press.

Stenhouse, L. (1975) *An Introduction to Curriculum Research and Development*. London: Heinemann.

Stevens, D. (1998) 'Finding the Perfect Balance', *English in Education* **32** (1), 38–44.

Stibbs, A. (1991) *Reading Narrative as Literature: Signs of Life*. Milton Keynes: Open University Press.

Stobart, G. and Gibbs, C. (1997) *Assessment: A Teacher's Guide to the Issues*, third edition. London: Hodder and Stoughton.

Styles, M. (ed.) (1989) *Collaboration and Writing*. Milton Keynes: Open University Press.

Styles, M. and Triggs, P. (1988) *Poetry 0–16*. London: Books for Keeps.

Styles, M., Bearne, E. and Watson, V. (eds) (1992) *After Alice: Exploring Children's Literature*. London: Cassell.

Styles, M., Bearne, E. and Watson, V. (eds) (1994) *The Prose and The Passion: Children and their Reading*. London: Cassell.

Styles, M., Bearne, E. and Watson, V. (eds) (1996) *Voices Off*. London: Cassell.

Sweetman, J. (1998) *Curriculum Confidential*. Suffolk: Courseware Publications, updated annually.

Swift, G. (1995) (edited by Hoyes, R.) *Learning to Swim*. Cambridge: Cambridge University Press.

Tarleton, R. (1988) *Learning and Talking*. London: Routledge.

Taylor, K. (ed.) (1991) *Drama Strategies*. London: Heinemann.

Thomas, P. (1997) 'Doom to yhe Red-eyed Nyungghns from the Planet Glarg: Boys as Writers of Narrative', *English in Education* **31** (3) 23–31.

Thompson, L. (ed.) (1996) *The Teaching of Poetry*. London: Cassell.

Tomkinson, W.S. (1921) *The Teaching of English: A New Approach*. Oxford: Oxford University Press.

Tomlinson, S. (ed.) (1997) *Education 14–19: Critical Perspectives*. London: The Athlone Press.

Traherne, T. (c. 1665, edited by Margoliouth 1960) *Centuries of Meditations*. Oxford: Clarendon Press.

Tunnicliffe, S. (1984) *Poetry Experience*. London: Methuen.

Tweddle, S. *et al.* (1997) *English for Tomorrow*. Milton Keynes: Open University Press.

Watson, K. (1981) *English Teaching in Perspective*. Epping, Australia: St Clair Press, republished in 1987, Milton Keynes: Open University Press.

Waugh, P. (1992) *Practising Postmodernism, Reading Postmodernism*. London: Edward Arnold.

Way, B. (1967) *Development Through Drama*. London: Longman.

Wilkinson, A., Davies, A. and Berrill, D. (1990) *Spoken English Illuminated*. Milton Keynes: Open University Press.

Wilkinson, E. (1966) 'At First Hand', *Trends in Education* **1**, January.

Wilkinson, J. (1995) *Introducing Standard English*. Harmondsworth: Penguin.

Williams, T. (1947) *A Streetcar Named Desire* in *A Streetcar Named Desire and Other Plays*, edited by Browne, E.M. 1962. London: Penguin.

Wittgenstein, L. (1953) translated by Anscombe, G. *Philosophical Investigations*. Oxford: Basil Blackwell.

Woods, E. (1995) *Introducing Grammar*. Harmondsworth: Penguin.

Woods, P. (ed.) (1996) *Contemporary Issues in Teaching and Learning*. London: Routledge.

Wray, D. and Medwell, J. (1994) *Teaching Primary English*. London: Routledge.

Index